Denys Kaz

Maryna Vorotyntseva

HOW UKRAINE LOST DONBAS

2024

Denys Kazanskyi, Maryna Vorotyntseva

How Ukraine Lost Donbas.

"How Ukraine Lost Donbas" delves into the circumstances surrounding Russia's military intervention in Ukraine, particularly the events leading up to and following the annexation of Crimea and the occupation of parts of eastern Ukraine, specifically Luhansk and Donetsk in 2014. It highlights Russia's use of propaganda, corruption, and covert operations to instigate separatist sentiments and orchestrate conflicts within Ukraine. The book provides detailed accounts of Russia's aggression and its impact on Ukraine, serving as a valuable resource for understanding the geopolitical dynamics of the region. It also acknowledges the mistakes made by Ukrainian politicians, including their role in exacerbating the situation in Donbas in 2014 and earlier.

Second edition, revised and expanded.

Ukrainian Edition published in 2020. All rights reserved by Chorna Hora Publishing House LLC, Ukraine.

English Edition published in 2024. All rights reserved by Maryna Vorotyntseva and Denys Kazanskyi.

FOREWORD
for English edition

"How Ukraine Lost Donbas" chronicles the onset of Russia's military intervention into Ukrainian territory in 2014. Following the seizure and annexation of Crimea, Russia expanded its control to include portions of eastern Ukraine, notably Luhansk and Donetsk, collectively referred to as Donbas.

The military escalation in 2014 unfolded within a specific context and set of conditions. Russia had long been engaged in informational warfare, economic infiltration, and the establishment of illicit paramilitary groups within Ukraine. Propaganda and corruption emerged as pivotal tools, employed to stoke separatist sentiments and fabricate unrest, painting a picture of "civil protests" and a "civil war" within Ukraine.

The groundwork for these operations was laid as early as 2003. Despite a decade of effort, Russia struggled to establish robust military-political structures under the guise of "separatists." Recognizing the limitations of this approach, Russia escalated its aggression, deploying regular army units and covert operatives to Ukraine. They seized control of administrative buildings, perpetrated violence against civilians, and orchestrated the occupation while maintaining the facade of "separatist" movements. Ultimately, Russia's tactics resulted in the annexation of Crimea and the occupation of southern Luhansk and Donetsk oblasts from 2014 to 2022, achieved through coercion, political manipulation, and conflicts both within Ukraine and across

Europe. Only in 2022 did Russia formally declare the "integration" of Donbas into its territory, acknowledging Ukraine's refusal to tolerate proxy entities within its borders.

The events of 2014 transformed Donbas into a theater of conflict and suffering for millions. While Russia initially isolated Donbas politically and economically, by 2024, it had inflicted physical devastation upon the region. Many of the cities ravaged by war are industrial centers within Donbas.

This book contains vital details, names, and dates and serves as a comprehensive documentation of Russia's military aggression and information warfare against Ukraine. It offers valuable insights for experts in information security, disinformation countermeasures, and information-psychological operations, as well as policymakers and English-speaking historians specializing in Ukraine, Eastern Europe, and Russia.

For readers new to the topic, it's advisable to supplement this book with knowledge of fundamental Ukrainian history and geography. Familiarity with terms like "Novorossiya" and "Malorossiya," understanding the Ukrainian Insurgent Army (UPA), and acquainting oneself with key figures such as Ivan Mazepa, Stepan Bandera, and Roman Shukhevych is recommended. Additionally, understanding contemporary Ukrainian history, including the biographies and political agendas of presidents Leonid Kuchma, Viktor Yushchenko, and Viktor Yanukovych, is crucial for contextualizing the events described in the book.

The book does not endorse or justify the Ukrainian government. It critically examines the role of Ukrainian politicians, acknowledging instances of professional incompetence and corruption that facilitated Russia's aggressive actions. The mistakes made by Ukrainian politicians, including their interference in the judiciary, which contributed to the tragedy of Donbas in 2014, are thoroughly explored.

Initially published in Ukraine in 2020, "How Ukraine

Lost Donbas" remains highly relevant. Its analysis of Russia's propagandist tactics continues to shed light on the ongoing conflict, offering invaluable insights into the dynamics of the region's geopolitical landscape. This book was translated into English in 2024.

PROLOGUE

In this book, you will not find descriptions of maneuvers or battles. Let those who have been to the front lines and personally took part in the fighting write about them. Here, we will talk about events that preceded the armed conflict.

We've gotten used to learning a lot from the news about the course of military actions and receiving detailed information about casualties and destruction. Still, we know very little about how the mechanism that compels yesterday's neighbors to destroy each other with unprecedented zeal was set in motion.

In the summer of 2012, Donetsk hosted matches of the European Football Championship. At the time, it seemed that this city was the last place on earth where military action could take place. War? That's somewhere far away, on the outskirts, in backward, savage countries. Here, amid shining shop windows and blooming roses, there could never be a war. After all, this is almost Europe. Entertainment, football, restaurants, carefree youth, flashy cars. Who here could take up arms and kill?

And in just two years, this carefree, contented world disappeared and turned into a surreal horror. Shells began to explode on the streets, tanks rumbled down the roads, and the region with a population of several million was engulfed in anarchy. It all happened in a matter of months. And even after the first shots rang out on the streets, it was hard to believe that the war was already here. By the time it sank in, it was already challenging to figure out the point of no return: when it still could have been stopped and when it was too late.

To understand this, we undertook this book.

In it, we will pick apart, bit by bit, the long chain of events that led Donbas to the tragedy of 2014 and attempt to unriddle who and how pushed it into the war. A fair warning: the purpose of this work is not to provide simple answers like "Putin is to blame" or "the Kyiv junta is to blame." The conflict in the Donbas was instigated by the synergy of a whole number of external and internal factors. Each of them, on its own, would be unlikely to lead to such a catastrophic outcome, but together, they formed a deadly, explosive mix that undermined the region.

TURNING POINT

On March 1, 2014, a truly massive rally took place in the downtown of Donetsk. Approximately 15,000 to 20,000 people attended. For the capital of the Donbas, this was an extraordinary event, as Donetsk had never been politically active. Above the crowd, dressed in typical dark Donbas colors, flags fluttered, but there were no Ukrainian flags among them. Mostly Russian tricolor flags were waving, and Soviet symbols and flags of the "Russian Bloc" party. Some held banners with slogans such as "In Russia, our brothers; in Europe, we are slaves" and "Donbas against the Banderites." The crowd was charged with aggression.

Donbas was never the "powder keg of Europe." It couldn't even be compared to a matchbox of Europe. Unlike the Balkans or the Caucasus, where a mere spark was enough to set off a flare-up, the Donbas was inert and far from warlike sentiments. In this young region, which began to be actively populated only in the mid-19th century, there were no relict layers of centuries-old interethnic hostility and hatred that typically exist in all hotspots. Considerable effort was required to ignite the Donbas, to kindle an uncontrolled outbreak of violence.

The rallies on March 1 that took place in various cities in the south and east of Ukraine are considered the beginning of the "Russian spring." This is how the Russian media referred to the anti-Ukrainian uprising that began after the overthrow of Viktor Yanukovych and later escalated into military actions in the east of the country. It took a while to brew up the war. To make it possible, various political technologists and ideologists had to work hard to create the theoretical basis for future conflict. Of course, from the day it appeared on the world map, Ukraine had regional differences shaped by well-known historical events. Throughout the past, different parts of the country belonged to different states and developed independently of each other. However, this did not mean that Ukraine was doomed to conflict.

In the first twenty years of independence, regional differences did not lead to armed clashes. In the 1990s, historical, ideological, and linguistic discordances in Ukraine were not a top issue. At the time, both the residents of Donetsk and Lviv were primarily concerned about the economic situation in the country, and politics came second.

Certainly, some friction and conflicts arose periodically. In the early 1990s, there was a major threat of separatism in Crimea, but even there, the situation was resolved peacefully. In eastern Ukraine, although political passions sometimes flared, nobody anticipated anything like what was happening in Yugoslavia and some other former Soviet republics. In Ukraine, only fringe radicals were at war with each other, even that was mostly on the pages of leaflets and newspapers.

Ukrainians had been seeing the horrors of war only on television screens for a long time. Nearby, Transnistria was in upheaval. Reports on the siege of Sarajevo and battles on the streets of Sukhumi were shown in the evening news. However, the most powerful impression on Ukrainian citizens was made by the reports from Chechnia. In the early years of Ukraine's independence, Russian television was readily broadcast, so Ukrainians had the opportunity to witness the Chechen bloodbath in all its gory details and perceived it as their own war.

In the 1990s, against the backdrop of the problems of former socialist allies, Ukraine appeared as an island of serenity and stability. The Ukrainian government considered this state of affairs one of its main achievements. During the 1999 presidential campaign, in a campaign video for President Leonid Kuchma, who was running for a second term, the slogan "Our soldiers are coming home" was used. The sequence showed a happy soldier returning to his family after serving in the army. For people who were aware of the scale of the tragedy in Chechnia, such imagery looked convincing. Kuchma won the election by a landslide against the more pro-Russian opposition candidate, Petro Symonenko.

At the time, it seemed that our soldiers would always come home. However, just five years later, a completely different campaign video aired on all central television channels in Ukraine. This video was created by Viktor Yanukovych's PR team—he was the acting Prime Minister at the time and was considered Leonid Kuchma's successor. In this video, voiced by the Russian singer Iosif Kobzon, Yanukovych's team threatened peaceful Ukraine with civil war if it voted for the pro-Western "orange" candidate Viktor Yushchenko

What changed in the five years since the previous elections? Why did the motif of a future war appear in political advertising in 2004, and a decade later, this war became a reality? What sequence of events led to mass protests in the cities of the Donbas in the spring of 2014 and then to the appearance of Russian saboteurs in Slovyansk?

To answer these questions, it is necessary to rewind the tape to the beginning of the 1990s, recall the recent history of the region, and delve into the essence of political events that took place in it. The sinister processes that ultimately led Donbas to tragic events were set in motion in eastern Ukraine long before the war began. Examining their every detail, we can see that in the history of Ukraine and Donbas, there were several pivotal moments when the war could have been avoided. However, in each of these cases, the politicians chose the wrong path...

Donetsk separatism in Ukraine became more active in a certain cyclical pattern—once every ten years. At that, each subsequent activity significantly surpassed the previous one in scale. In 1993–1994, there were strikes and threats that ended with a meaningless pseudo-referendum —a "consultative poll of public opinion." In 2004, the Sievierodonetsk Congress took place, and the country was already on the brink of a real split. And in 2014, the situation escalated to large-scale military actions involving armed forces from a neighboring state.

The past cannot be changed, but lessons should be learned from it. Wars do not arise out of nowhere. There is always someone who first pulls the trigger and someone who suggests doing it. And sometimes, a lot of time passes between these two events—years and decades. They clamored for the war in the Donbas for a long time. Some deliberately hastened it, while others did not realize what they were doing. And until the last moment, no one believed that it would actually start. Even in the heat of May 2014, when apple blossoms fell from mine explosions, barricades rose on the roads, and entire cities came under the control of armed groups, it seemed that all of this was just a passing phase, that everyone would soon come to their senses and stop shooting.

So, what is this butterfly that, by flapping its wings in the past, caused this storm? We should look for it in the prenatal period of the development of the Ukrainian state. Donbas separatism always emerged simultaneously with the proclamation of an independent Ukraine as a reaction to that proclamation. The first time this happened was in 1918 when the Bolsheviks, contrary to the declared Ukrainian People's Republic (UPR), declared the Donetsk-Kryvyi Righ

Republic (DKR). It didn't last long, and no one even noticed its existence, but for future Donetsk separatists, **the DKR became** an important symbol.

The next time separatism reared its head in Donbas was simultaneously with the collapse of the Soviet Union. And once again, it was directed against the young Ukrainian state, which was about to emerge on the world map. A symbolic reference point for this new era can be traced back to the moment when the black-red-blue tricolor was conceived in Donetsk. Initially adopted as the flag of Donetsk separatists, in 2014, it became the flag of the unrecognized quasi-republic declared after the revolutionary events in Kyiv. It was then that Donbas separatism emerged in its modern form, and its early history vividly illustrates how insignificant this movement was when it lacked external support. Even during times of heightened politicization of society, with various parties, movements, and civic organizations emerging across the country, Donbas separatists struggled to find support and influence the course of events.

PART ONE

PIONEERS FROM THE '90S

Today, it's hard to believe that Donetsk was once at the forefront of democratic transformations. However, there was a brief period in the city's history that occurred from 1990-1991. However, at that time, independent Ukraine did not yet exist; there was the Ukrainian Soviet Social Republic, which was on the verge of leaving the flatlining USSR.

The Perestroika was in progress. March 1990 elections had an unexpected outcome: independent candidates secured the majority in the Donetsk City Council, while Communist Party representatives found themselves in the minority and lost power. The decaying apparatus government could no longer control the situation, so a different group of people took the initiative: strike organizers, professors, intellectuals, and cooperators.

The little-known head of the department at Donetsk Polytechnic Institute, Oleksandr Makhmudov, became the head of the city council (then called the mayor). Among all the mayors of Donetsk, he was probably the most unusual. The soft-spoken, intelligent Makhmudov clearly did not fit the image of the "typical Donetsk resident" that is deeply rooted in the public consciousness today. He also did not conform to the Soviet leader stereotype of a "strong entrepreneur," which people still appreciate. However, Makhmudov did not stay at the helm of the city for long. He lacked managerial experience, and his run as a mayor coincided with the most challenging times. The economy of the Soviet Union was collapsing, money was rapidly depreciating, and the city faced shortages of essential goods.

By 1991, Makhmudov was dismissed by the decision of the city council session, and he never did return to politics. In 2005, he died in a car accident.

For about a year, Donetsk experienced a power vacuum. The city witnessed the collapse of the Soviet Union practically without a leader. In November 1992, the "entrepreneurs" returned to power in the capital of the Donbas. The one who took the mayoral seat was later dubbed the "godfather of Donetsk" —an authoritarian leader of the Soviet type, the director of the Zasiadko coal mine, Yukhym Zvyahilsky. This marked the beginning of the rise to power of the criminal and political clans of the Donbas, which culminated in a bloody denouement in 2014.

However, the democratic Donetsk city council led by Makhmudov still managed to play a decisive role in the fate of the Donbas. During a short and extremely complicated transitional period, when the question of how to divide the "Soviet legacy" was being resolved, Communist and Komsomol officials in Donetsk (unlike neighboring Luhansk and many other regions of Ukraine) lost their initiative. They were forced to step back in the face of new realities. Power transitioned to the so-called "new Ukrainians": a class consisting of workshop managers, cooperators, and "red directors." *(Red director is a term that describes well-connected and skilled top managers and directors in post-Soviet countries who took leadership positions before the fall of the USSR and maintained them even as the countries transitioned to a market economy. —T. Ed).*

In this turbulent period, separatists attempted to take action, too. The first calls for the separation of the Donbas from Ukraine emerged as early as 1990-1991, on the eve of the Soviet Union's dissolution. In Donetsk, the organization "Interdvizheniie Donbassa" ("International movement of Donbas") was formed, and in Luhansk, there were "Narodnoie dvizheniie Luganshchiny" ("People`s movement of Luhansk") and "Demokraticheskii Donbass," ("Democratic Donbas") which opposed Ukraine's independence. While the Donetsk organization was spontaneously created by pro-Russian residents of the city, the Luhansk ones were established by the local party nomenklatura to blackmail Kyiv, threatening the separation of Donbas from the UkrSSR if its leadership did not sign a new union agreement. *(Nomenklatura refers to people in the Soviet Union who, being vetted by the Communist Party, held various key administrative positions. —T. Ed)*

> "Our movement advocates for autonomy within Ukraine, of course, as long as the republic signs a union agreement. If this does not happen, then we can only consider transitioning under the jurisdiction of the RSFSR, " said Valerii Cheker, the leader of the "People's Movement of Luhansk," who was a deputy of the Luhansk City Council from the Party of Regions until 2014. *(RSFSR - Russian Soviet Federative Socialist Republic, the largest and most populous constituent republic of the Soviet Union. —T. Ed)*

In September 1991, the "Democratic Donbas" movement, through the pages of the Luhansk newspaper "Molodohvardiiets," called on deputies of all levels in the region to hold a Donetsk assembly and adopt a decision to create the republic of Malorosiia (Little Russia) based on the Donbas. It was envisioned that Malorosiia should "conditionally secede from Ukraine," i.e., separate from Ukraine in the event Ukraine itself seceded from the USSR. If Ukraine agreed to remain part of the Union, "Democratic Donbas" proposed leaving Malorosiia as an autonomous entity to protect its interests in the Ukrainian parliament rather than "dancing to the tune of Kyiv-Galician pipes."

Calls for leaving Ukraine and joining the RSFSR

were also heard in Donetsk. On July 20, 1991, a month before the declaration of Ukraine's independence, an article titled "Donetsk Autonomous Republic: Is It a Way Out?" was published in the newspaper "Komsomolets Donbasu." It proposed resolving this issue through a referendum. However, at that time, in the early '90s, the discussion did not go further than newspaper pages. Apparently, the aspirations of Donetsk and Luhansk separatist-irredentists were not supported in Moscow. Gorbachev and Yeltsin were clearly not interested in them, and without a green light from Russia, no one in Donbas dared to embark on adventurous actions. The Union collapsed, and further confrontation between Donbas and Kyiv took place within the framework of the Ukrainian state.

The year 1993 can be considered the birth year of Donetsk separatism in the new realities of independent Ukraine. Realizing that the USSR had definitively collapsed and the Ukrainian republic was setting sail freely, local authorities persistently advocated for regional autonomy and called for the federalization of Ukraine to secure their territory within the framework of the new state.

Separatism in Donbas was driven by two components —ideological and economic. Economic separatism was fueled by representatives of local authorities primarily motivated by their own interests. They used separatist rhetoric as a bargaining tool with Kyiv to achieve their own political goals. The ideological camp consisted mostly of intellectuals: journalists, university professors, and supporters of various fringe political trends, who were, for the most part, not separatists but irredentists. In the early '90s, these "romantics" not so much campaigned for the independence of Donbas as, out of nostalgia for the USSR, dreamed of the revival of the Union in one form or another. To them, Donbas represented a kind of unifying link between Ukraine and Russia—a region with a special, unifying mission that stood against nationalist separatists from Galicia, preventing them from completely breaking Ukraine away from Moscow.

DONETSK TRICOLOR

The best-known pro-Russian forces in Donetsk in the early '90s were the "Civil Congress of Ukraine" (CCU) and the "Interrukh Donbasu" (IRD, "Intermovement of Donbas"). Even for their time, when wild political formations were emerging across the country, both were relatively marginal and had little influence. However, these movements, at the dawn of independence, laid the ideological foundation that Donetsk oligarchic clans later adopted when they emerged as a formidable force and aimed for power over the entire Ukraine. Then, the theoretical developments of the ideologues in their old stretched-out sweaters proved to be highly relevant.

The "Intermovement of Donbas" was founded in Donetsk even before the collapse of the USSR by Dmytro Kornilov, a school teacher, and his friends. The organization's birthday is considered to be November 18, 1990. One of the founders, Ihor Sychov, later wrote that about 100 people were present at the founding conference. At that point, the movement chose as their leaders three individuals who would later become well-known: Dmytro Kornilov himself, his younger brother Volodymyr (now a renowned political scientist, living in Russia since 2014), and future People's Deputy from the Party of Regions Vitalii Zablotskyi. The flag of "Intermovement" was a black-blue-red tricolor, which later became the official flag chosen by separatists in the "DPR" in 2014.

Later, in 2015, Volodymyr Kornilov, in an interview with the Russian website Ukraine.ru, explained how the flag of "Intermovement" was created:

"My brother and I came up with the flag. We quickly

agreed on it, considering the context of the all-Ukrainian ideological struggle. The thing is, during the period of independence, there were two contending concepts—either accepting the blue and yellow flag of the Petliurist-Skoropadskyi camp as the symbol of Ukraine or keeping the red and blue flag of the Ukrainian SSR (even sans the star and hammer and sickle). Obviously, we advocated for the second option—the red and blue. That's how the flag of Donbas appeared. We added a black stripe, symbolizing the coal of our region, to the red and blue. This became the flag of "Intermovement," flying over all our rallies."

As implied by the organization's name, its activists positioned themselves as a counter to Ukrainian nationalists and considered themselves internationalists. At the time, similar "internationalist" organizations were emerging in other Soviet republics in opposition to local national movements. Their goal was to prevent the dissolution of the USSR. But in fact, these activists did not adhere to internationalism; rather, under the banner of "friendship among nations," they advocated for the preservation of the empire with its center in Moscow.

"We created the Interfront-Intermovement not to secede from the Ukrainian SSR but to oppose the secession of the Ukrainian SSR from the USSR. [...] Already at that time, in 1989–1990, we called for a federative structure of Ukraine with broad autonomy for Donbas. I want to emphasize that we did this not to separate from anyone but to prevent the separation of Ukraine," explained Volodymyr Kornilov.

As is clear from these words, "Interfront of Donbas" was, in its rhetoric, actually a typical nationalist organization. However, it was not Ukrainian but Russian nationalist. The "internationalists" considered the

Ukrainian people's desire for independence as "fascism." "Intermovement" prioritized the interests of the pro-Russian population of Ukraine. Before the referendum on December 1, 1991, which determined the fate of the Ukrainian state, organization activists urged the population of the Donbas to vote nay on independence. The right of Ukrainians to self-determination was denied, and supporters of independence were blackmailed by the threat of civil war.

Leaflets distributed by the IRD activists before the referendum declared: "Donbas says NO to the ambitions of Kyiv officials and party bureaucrats, the collapse of the economy, civil war, hostility between peoples, the revival of Bandera ideology, and nationalism." The fact that, in the USSR, there was indeed a Ukrainian people with the same right to statehood as the Russian people was completely ignored by these "internationalists." In this aspect, the "Kornilovites" were no different from various Russian organizations of the "Black Hundreds" that did not recognize the existence of Ukraine and Ukrainians. Interestingly, in the same interview in 2015, Volodymyr Kornilov essentially accused the then Donetsk Regional Committee of the Communist Party of Ukraine (CPU) of assisting Ukrainian nationalists and providing insufficient support to "Intermovement":

> "We actively communicated with the local CPU leadership and the then ideologist of the regional committee, Petro Symonenko (who led the Communist Party of Ukraine until its ban in 2015. —A/N). They, at the very least, did not hinder us. Sometimes, they provided premises (for the People's Movement as well). But until June 1991, the CPU did not display any ideological struggle against separatism and nationalism."

The peak of the IRD activity occurred in the early 1990s. However, the actual core of this organization consisted of only a few individuals, and its public face was essentially just Dmytro Kornilov, who represented the "Intermovement" at various round tables and conferences. In the late 1990s, after Kornilov Sr. stepped back from active involvement and focused on opinion journalism, the IRD was pretty much never mentioned. After Dmytro Kornilov's death in 2002, "Intermovement of Donbas" completely ceased its activities, although it was never formally dissolved.

Volodymyr Kornilov claimed that the IRD was suppressed by the regional authorities in the mid-90s; however, these statements do not reflect reality. The peewee organization simply got drowned out in the powerful chorus of other, more popular and influential pro-Russian parties and movements. The entire pro-Russian electorate rallied around the Communist Party of Ukraine (CPU) and the Progressive Socialist Party of Natalia Vitrenko (PSPU), while speculations about federalism lost relevance after Leonid Kuchma came to power, as will be discussed below.

The "Civil Congress of Ukraine" (CCU) appeared on the scene slightly later than the IRD, but from the beginning, it was a far more impressive organization. The founding congress of the CCU took place in May 1992 in Donetsk. According to official information, it was attended by 200 delegates from 9 regions of Ukraine, and the chairman of the congress was the future Prime Minister of Ukraine, Mykola Azarov. Among the founders of the CCU was the same Dmytro Kornilov with his "Intermovement," and Oleksandr Bazyliuk, an associate professor of Donetsk State University, became the leader of the organization. Interestingly enough, as the flag of the CCU was chosen the raspberry Cossack flag from the time of the Khmelnytskyi era, and its emblem featured the silhouette of Khmelnytskyi pointing with a mace towards Moscow. Unlike the "Intermovement of Donbas," there was already a nationwide scope felt here. Bazyliuk dreamed not so much about federalization but about building a puppet, pro-Russian Ukraine that would be in vassal dependence on the former metropolis.

As soon as 1993, the "Civil Congress of Ukraine" became a political party. In 1993-1994, the CCU demanded regional autonomy for the Donbas, granting Russian the status of national language, close integration of Ukraine into the CIS *(The Commonwealth of Independent States— a regional intergovernmental organization in Eurasia, formed after the dissolution of the USSR in 1991. —T. Ed.)* and even the return of the country to the ruble zone. In the 1994 presidential elections, CCU supported Leonid Kuchma, who was considered a pro-Russian candidate at the time, while Leonid Kravchuk was seen as a Westerner and a nationalist. Donbas voted for Kuchma in those elections, and he emerged victorious. However, by early 1995, CCU was disappointed in its favorite and declared a shift to the opposition. According to Bazyliuk, Kuchma deceived his voters and turned out to be not enough of a pro-Russian president.

In 1998, the "Civil Congress of Ukraine" became" (CCU) participated in parliamentary elections as part of the "Labor Ukraine" bloc but did not make it into the parliament. At that time, a 4% electoral threshold needed to be overcome to enter the Rada, but "Labor Ukraine" only gained around 3%. The majority of these votes came from the Donbas region. In the Donetsk region, 14.8% of voters supported "Labor Ukraine," and in the Luhansk region, it was 5.5%.

After the elections, the CCU changed its name and became the Slavic Party, but this did not help either.

Soon, the Bazyliuk project was definitively marginalized and began to be used by the Donetsk elite to organize various provocations against political opponents. For example, in 2002, the Slavic Party joined the "For Yushchenko" bloc, which was created without Yushchenko's knowledge to divert votes from the "Our Ukraine" party during parliamentary races. And in 2003, Bazyliuk's party was the nominal organizer of Donetsk protest rallies against Yushchenko and lent its name to negative campaigning efforts as well.

The best reflection of the hopes of Donbas separatists in the early '90s is conveyed through newspaper publications of that time.

The mouthpiece of Donbas separatism in the early years of independence was considered to be the newspaper "Donetskyi Kriazh," which first came out in January 1993. In the newspaper, primarily two ideas were promoted—the federalization of Ukraine and closer collaboration with Russia, even to the extent of creating a confederation. Additionally, "Donetskyi Kriazh" was involved in popularizing pro-Russian parties and movements.

The founders of the newspaper were the Hlotov couple. They did not have a lot of money, so initially, they published "Donetskyi Kriazh," which had a relatively small circulation. Nevertheless, the newspaper gained its audience. An interview with the leader of the CCU, Oleksandr Bazyliuk, was published in the second issue, and later, articles by Dmytro Kornilov were regularly featured. By the way, neither one of them lived to see the beginning of the events in 2014 and witness the ultimate outcome of their years of labor.

The interview with Bazyliuk, which appeared in the second issue of the newspaper "Donetskyi Kriazh" under the title "We Will Save Ourselves," vividly illustrates the viewpoints held by Donbas separatists as they were at the dawn of Ukraine's independence. As such, it is worth quoting a few excerpts from it.

> "Among the sovereign republics, Ukraine is one of the most 'independent.' It, or more precisely, its political leadership, made the greatest contribution to the destruction of the Soviet Union and is now dismantling the CIS. Naturally, having exited the ruble zone and achieved success in the Cold War with Russia, it faces enormous difficulties. Today, prices for basic groceries and goods in Ukraine are 2-3 times higher than in Russia. Production is declining, businesses are shutting down, and looking at our disheveled finances, one is tempted to ask, what will happen sooner—the entire paper supply will turn into Ukrainian money, or conversely, our money will turn into plain paper," said Bazyliuk.

It is not difficult to see clear manipulations here. In this and other interviews, Bazyliuk portrayed Ukraine's economic problems as a consequence of "excessive sovereignty" and the exit from the USSR. Although it was evident that the root of the problems lay elsewhere—the entire post-Soviet space was undergoing a transitional period. The socialist planned economy had collapsed, and the market economy had not yet formed. Soviet enterprises were shutting down because they simply could not operate in a capitalist environment. This was happening, understandably, not only in Ukraine but also in Russia, where the same processes were taking place. Russian rubles in the early '90s were turning into paper just as rapidly as Ukrainian coupons. However, the objective economic reality contradicted the perspective held by Bazyliuk and his like-minded comrades, so they considered it better to ignore inconvenient facts.

The same interview makes clear who the Donetsk separatists considered their main adversaries and who they held responsible for all the country's troubles.

"The responsibility for the collapse of the economy lies with the nomenklatura leadership of the former Communist Party of Ukraine. But nationalist forces —Rukh, URP, and other similar organizations—should also bear this responsibility," asserted Bazyliuk. *(The People's Movement of Ukraine (Rukh) is a Ukrainian political party, instrumental in the holding of a referendum on independence in the Ukrainian SSR, which led to the establishment of Ukraine as an independent state. Ukrainian Radical Party (URP), established in 1890, was one of the founding members of the short-lived but independent polity West Ukrainian People's Republic. —T. Ed)*

In summary, he listed the key policy objectives of his own party, including the following points: the fight against the ideologies of nationalism and totalitarianism, a federal Ukrainian state, two national languages, support for integration processes in the CIS, and the return of Ukraine to the ruble zone.

All these points, except the last one, later formed the basis of the ideology of various pro-Russian forces in Ukraine and migrated from one election program to another over the next 20 years. The return to the ruble zone, which seemed feasible in 1993, soon became an impossible task, and this demand was later abandoned.

The early Donbas separatists did not go as far as outright denying Ukraine in their publications, although, really, they dreamed of merging Ukraine with the Russian Federation. Since they couldn't print explicit calls for the elimination of statehood, pro-Russian figures in the eastern regions began to push a concept of "Anti-Ukraine" in their articles. This "Anti-Ukraine" envisioned a Ukrainian state devoid of anything Ukrainian: a Ukraine without the Ukrainian language, Ukrainian national heroes, and Ukrainian history. Only those state figures oriented toward an alliance with Russia were deemed "proper" in this "Anti-Ukraine." All others were labeled as traitors, fascists, and hostile mercenaries.

STRIKE IN DONETSK AND THE 1994 REFERENDUM

In the early '90s, the Donetsk elite had not yet solidified into the formidable monolith it would become a decade later, but it was already not shy in declaring its ambitions.

The key position in Donetsk was taken by Yuhym Zviahilskyi, who epitomized the image of the "red director." His team, including many members such as Volodymyr Shcherban, Volodymyr Rybak, and Oleksandr Lukyanchenko, who later on became influential politicians, came aboard the city council as well. The formation of the "Donetsk clan" began.

The first serious outbreak of separatist sentiments in the Donbas occurred in 1993. Essentially, this was the starting year of real independence, when Ukraine had already become a fully-fledged, independent state. Throughout 1992, it still remained the Ukrainian SSR out of habit. Soviet rubles were still in circulation until November 1992, and in the same year, Ukrainian athletes participated in the Olympics as part of the CIS team. It seemed that until 1993, not everyone fully realized that this independence was for real. Many believed that the USSR would somehow be restored. Pro-Russian forces placed great hopes on the CIS, seeing it as a prototype of a future renewed Union. At that time, this union still seemed promising, and no one could know its ignominious fate in the near future.

The force of habit was also moving the socialist economy, even though the bureaucratic apparatus was no longer able to control it. Ukraine was grappling with a severe crisis, and the leadership at that time had very few ideas on how to navigate through it. Pro-Russian politicians eagerly took advantage of this situation, rushing to explain all the problems with the rupture of economic ties between the former Soviet republics. This explanation seemed plausible to millions of residents in the industrial regions of eastern Ukraine.

In 1993, when it became clear that Ukraine had indeed emerged as an independent state, the Donbas elite realized that it would have to find its place within the framework of the new governance system and made the first attempt to assert itself. Local authorities (major business entities did not exist at that time) actively began to promote the idea of regional autonomy.

In February 1993, the chairman of the Donetsk Regional Council, Vadym Chuprun, gave an interview to the newspaper "Donetskyi Kriazh," expressing support for the federalization of Ukraine. At that time, he articulated the position of virtually the entire regional elite, which was then composed mainly of the nomenklatura and "red directors."

> "Discussions about federalization have been ongoing for a long time. Unfortunately, we have not made much progress beyond words. Many civilized states, considering their particularities, have long gone down this path. We study the experiences of Germany, Switzerland, and the USA. We have taken everything we find acceptable for us. We have advised the introduction of an official article into the draft Constitution of the country. Regions should have internal and external autonomy. The autonomy of regions will strengthen the state," said Chuprun.

It's important to understand that in 1993, "regional autonomy" did not mean the same thing as it did in 2014.

At that time, all the major enterprises in the region were still owned by the state and operated by "red directors" appointed by Kyiv. Understandably, this did not sit well with the regional elite. The regional autonomy that the Donetsk faction wanted would allow them to establish factual and legal control over the industry in the Donbas.

In Kyiv, they were not thrilled about such an idea. No one wanted to give in to the pressure from regional leaders, so the Donbas elite decided to leverage the protest sentiments of the region's residents for their own benefit by blackmailing the central government. Throughout 1993, the economic situation in Ukraine deteriorated. Prices were rising rapidly, and the introduced coupons were depreciating just as swiftly. Disruptions in the operation of enterprises began, leading to delays in salary payments. It was clear that hundreds of thousands of people were destined to lose their jobs, as the plants that worked for the defense industry of the USSR had no chance of survival in the new market conditions. After the end of the "Cold War," they simply became unnecessary.

The coal industry, where problems had been accumulating for decades, was particularly hard-hit by the crisis. It's a well-known fact that mass strikes of miners in Donbas started in the Soviet years. Even back then, miners complained about unbearable working and living conditions. The Soviet myth of wealthy miners living in abundance during the USSR times has little to do with reality, although it still exists today.

In 1991, Soviet journalist Volodymyr Molchanov made a film called "Zabii" (Mine's Face), where he discussed the problems of Donbas miners. The Soviet miners portrayed in the film did not look happy at all; they complained about numerous issues. With the collapse of the Union, the situation in the coal industry continued to worsen. However, the majority of miners did not know or did not want to know the real reasons for the crisis. The populace, as a rule, is not inclined to analyze the situation when simple answers are offered.

There were many reasons for the economic crisis of the early '90s, but the populists of that period provided simple answers to all of society's questions—the blame for everything lies with the collapse of the USSR and the actions of the "enemies." The Donetsk elite understood just in time how to use the protest sentiments of hungry people for their own best interests. It blamed its opponents in Kyiv for the crisis. On top of that, the population was being convinced that regional autonomy was necessary for the Donbas, as all the money it earned was being "taken away."

In early June 1993, there was another surge in prices. This was the formal reason for the start of a miners' strike in the Donbas. On June 7, workers from the Zasiadko mine, which was unofficially controlled by the then Mayor of Donetsk, Yukhym Zvyahilsky, were the first to go on strike in front of the Donetsk Regional Council. Soon, miners from other mines joined them. The strike wave was growing. According to newspaper publications of that time, employees from 230 coal mining enterprises joined the strike.

The strike had an important feature—miners not only demanded a salary increase but also put forward political demands. They wanted a referendum on confidence in the President of Ukraine, regional autonomy for the Donbas, and the restoration of economic ties with Russia. The local authorities responded to the miners' demands quite promptly, which suggested that the political demands of the miners had been pre-coordinated with regional leaders. The very next day after the start of the strike, regional council deputies supported the miners' demands and, allegedly "fulfilling the will of the people," brought the issue of autonomy for the Donetsk region to the 15th session of the regional council.

The protests indeed turned out to be massive and threatened to completely paralyze the economy of the region, potentially escalating into widespread unrest. From the podium, quite radical statements were made, including calls for the separation of the Donbas from Ukraine. The central government was openly alarmed by the scale of the protest, so it immediately expressed readiness to make concessions. Within four days of the start of the mass demonstrations, Yukhym Zvyahilsky was appointed the first deputy prime minister in Leonid Kuchma's government. In a few more days, it was announced that the government would increase miners' salaries.

Such steps immediately cooled the fervor of the discontented miners. The majority of workers were only interested in the material side of the matter, and they were indifferent to politics. Therefore, the government's actions were seen as a victory, and soon the strike was called off. However, in the conditions of inflation in 1993, the increased salaries didn't last long. By the end of the year, the rising prices completely "ate up" all the pay rises. The only person who unequivocally benefited from the strike was Yukhym Zvyahilsky, who quickly moved towards higher positions and became one of the top officials in the country. After Kuchma resigned, Zvyahilsky took on the role of acting prime minister and basically led the Cabinet. The Zvyahilsky case defined the format of relations between the Donetsk faction and Kyiv for many years. In 1993, the regional elite of the Donbas became convinced that blackmailing the capital with separatism was an effective way to gain power. And it didn't come down to just one strike. Passions flared throughout 1993. The local elite continued to talk about federalization and did not cease attempts, in one form or another, to negotiate autonomy from Kyiv. In the fall of 1993, the abbreviation "RES," which stood for "regional economic self-government," began to appear in Donetsk media.

Journalist Oleksandr Piekhotin described these events in his 2005 article for the Donetsk website "Ostrov" as follows:

> "In early October 1993 [...] a decision was made that the miners would guarantee support to the regional council in implementing the main provisions of RES. In case of resistance to the Donetsk initiatives, the miners promised to resort to extreme measures, including the cessation of exporting products produced for state orders beyond the region, blocking bank accounts, and picketing transportation arteries. As the newspaper 'Horod' wrote, 'rejecting all suspicions of separatism, the miners do not hide that they see RES as the first step towards a federative-territorial structure for Ukraine.'"

Quite radical calls were voiced by some leaders of Donetsk enterprises. For example, Yurii Baranov, the director of the Donbas Mine Management, at a meeting of representatives of the coal industry, called for the creation of revolutionary headquarters and armed forces to defend the idea of regional autonomy. However, the chance was lost. After the end of the miners' strike, the threats emanating from Donetsk no longer seemed as dangerous. Moreover, elections were approaching, and the "Donetsk clan" had other concerns.

However, on March 27, 1994, the Donetsk and Luhansk elites still managed to hold the first separatist referendum, which was called the "advisory poll of public opinion" and ultimately had no impact. Local newspapers only published short announcements about it. The residents of the Donetsk region were asked whether they agreed to the federal restructuring of Ukraine, granting

Russian the status of a state language, and closer integration of Ukraine into the CIS. For all issues, the majority of voting participants voted yes.

"In the vote on the issue, "Do you agree that the Constitution of Ukraine should establish a federal structure for Ukraine?" 2,795,221 people participated. "Yes" answered 2,227,538, "No" — 419,794. Invalid ballots — 147,889.

For the issue "Do you agree that the Constitution of Ukraine should stipulate the functioning of the Russian language as a national language of Ukraine alongside the national Ukrainian language?" out of 2,788,802 voters, "Yes" said 2,430,821, and "No" — 238,017. Invalid ballots — 119,964.

In the vote on the issue "Do you agree that on the territory of Donetsk region, the Russian language should be the language of work, business, documentation, as well as education and science, alongside Ukrainian?" out of 2,793,806 citizens, "Yes" answered 2,455,949, and "No" — 191,791. Invalid ballots — 116,068.

In response to the issue "Are you in favor of signing the Statute of the CIS, full participation of Ukraine in the economic union, in the Interparliamentary Assembly of the CIS states?" out of 2,797,424 voters, "Yes" said 2,481,981 people, "No" — 190,907. Invalid ballots — 124,536," reported the newspaper "Vechernii Donetsk" on April 1, 1994.

A similar survey was conducted in Luhansk. According to official data, 1,558,173 people participated out of 2,085,764 registered voters, which constituted 74.7%. Unlike Donetsk, Luhansk did not have a ballot issue about the federal structure of the country. However, for each of the three other issues, about 90% of citizens who participated in the survey answered positively. How truthful were the results of these surveys? Did they reflect the true picture or were they manipulated? It's challenging to answer this question today. In any case, the referendums had no consequences. However, seven months later, on October 27, 1994, the Luhansk Regional Council did adopt a decision on regional bilingualism. Yet, this did not stop local politicians from more trading on the language issue.

NEW "LUHANSK CLAN"

In the early 1990s, an informal business group consisting of former Komsomol members and representatives of the Soviet bureaucracy was in power in the Luhansk region. However, like in the rest of the country, a new class of businessmen was emerging—without a communist past but with a semi-criminal reputation.

In 1990, the seat of the first secretary of the city Komsomol in Luhansk (effectively the mayor of the city) went to Viktor Tykhonov. One of the founders of the Luhansk Komsomol political clan, he played a significant role in the region's history. At that time, Tykhonov was around 40 years old and had experience working in the party committee (partkom) at Luhansk's largest enterprise, the Luhansk Locomotive Plant ("Luhanskteplovoz"). In the same year, Tykhonov was elected to the Supreme Council of the Ukrainian SSR, where he formed a friendship with Leonid Kuchma. This peculiar friendship became the foundation for the seemingly inexplicable stability of the "Luhansk Komsomol" until the beginning of the conflict in Donbas.

"We got introduced (to Kuchma. —Original Ed.) when I was the secretary of the party committee at the October Revolution Plant (the Soviet name for the Luhansk Locomotive Plant. —A/N), and he was at Pivdenmash. Later, we were both deputies in the Verkhovna Rada. [...] In parliament, he wasn't particularly sociable. But we truly got to know each other when, already being deputies, we went on a foreign business trip together— it was his first trip abroad after the collapse of the Soviet Union. Before that, working at Pivdenmash, he couldn't leave the country. The delegation was quite large, and he asked me to support him—he had never been abroad before and was afraid of getting into trouble. He said that if he did or said something wrong, I should kick him in the leg—we joked later, saying his entire leg would be covered in bruises..." Tykhonov recounted in an interview with the "Ostrov" publication in 2008.

Another titan of Luhansk politics, Oleksandr Yefremov, managed to build a rapid career in the Komsomol before the collapse of the USSR. After holding the position of the first secretary of the city Komsomol, he became the secretary of the party committee of the Luhansk Lenin Machine-Building Plant, and in 1989, at the age of 35, he was already a candidate for the People's Deputies of the USSR. After the dissolution of the Soviet Union, Yefremov entered the business world and worked primarily on his political connections.

Following the ban on the Communist Party at the dawn of independence, Volodymyr Pantiukhin became the mayor of Luhansk (later a long-time deputy of the Luhansk Regional Council from the Party of Regions and a business partner of Viktor Tykhonov). In fact, in the Luhansk region, "communism" did not end even after the collapse of the USSR, and the same old cadre remained in power after 1991.

But this lethargic slumber did not last long. In 1994, earthshaking shifts began. That year, the mayor of Luhansk became a young local businessman (31 years old at the time) without higher education but with good connections in criminal circles—Oleksiy Danilov (as of November 2019, he is the Secretary of the National Security and Defense Council of Ukraine). Danilov was associated with the most well-known criminal authority in Luhansk—Valerii Dobroslavskyi, also known by the nicknames "Dobryk" and "Dobroslav," whose reputation echoed throughout the region. Dobroslavskyi was from the new generation of criminals, made his money in the post-Soviet period, and understood that real power could only be obtained through political means. On local TV channels, "Dobryk" declared big ambitions and hinted unequivocally that he intended to participate in the parliamentary elections.

Oleksiy Danilov, who challenged the old communists, was an entirely new face in politics. Many still consider him the most successful mayor in the city's recent history. During Danilov's term in Luhansk, a viaduct near the railway station, a puppet theater, and a maternity hospital were built—all in the midst of a severe economic crisis. Danilov's supporters were primarily young voters who didn't yearn for the Soviet Union, desired freedom, and believed in the success of market reforms. For them, he embodied the image of a politician from a new era and stood out favorably against the backdrop of the gray mass of former Komsomol members and party bureaucrats.

However, there were plenty of scandals surrounding the young mayor as well. Danilov didn't really hide his contacts with Dobroslavskyi. On top of that, he was accused of illegal currency export and exchange. Nevertheless, in the realities of the '90s, neither of these allegations was considered horrendous, and it didn't significantly affect the mayor's rating. Danilov was not an idealist—he was an entrepreneur. Tellingly, he was initially a co-owner of "Ukrkomunbank" with Oleksandr Yefremov, which indicated that he had business contacts not only with criminals but also with "Komsomol members." Danilov had all the prerequisites to become one of the leading politicians not only in Luhansk but in the entire region and even the country. He had grand ambitions.

The mayoral elections in Luhansk, won by Danilov, took place in May 1994—a month before the presidential elections. Just before the presidential elections, everyone who would influence politics in the region for the next 20 years gathered in Kuchma's headquarters. In addition to Tykhonov, there were Hennadii Fomenko, Volodymyr Ivanov, Oleksandr Kyselov, and Oleksandr Yefremov, later known as the "master of Luhansk region." All of them had significant political experience during the Soviet era, having served as Komsomol leaders and party functionaries, as well as being candidates for and members of the Verkhovna Rada. In various capacities, all of them directed or influenced the decisions of the authorities in the Luhansk region until 2014. Viktor Tykhonov helmed the headquarters. It was believed that Tykhonov talked to Kuchma almost on equal terms and had a monopoly on this communication. Kuchma's victory was expected to significantly strengthen Tykhonov and his associates, helping them consolidate control over the region.

To understand the particularities of these individuals, it is important to know that Komsomol leaders and Party organizers of major industrial plants were significant figures in Soviet times. For example, Viktor Tykhonov was, as one would say today, one of the top managers of "Luhanskteplovoz," where over 35,000 people worked. He later headed a regional administrative center. The Luhansk Machine Tool Manufacturing Plant, where Oleksandr Yefremov worked as a partorg, produced strategic equipment—precision tools for defense and space industries—and also had a cartridge production line. The leaders of such enterprises had direct access and broad political and production contacts in Moscow ministries, considering Kyiv to be a secondary city in this environment. This circumstance, even in the early '90s, formed a somewhat condescending attitude of the "Luhansk Komsomol" towards the Ukrainian capital and Ukrainian politicians.

PART TWO

ALLIANCE OF KUCHMA WITH THE DONETSK FACTION

Leonid Kuchma won the 1994 presidential elections thanks to the support from the southern and eastern regions. The division in Ukrainian society during the 1994 elections was not as pronounced as in the 2004 elections, but even then, the western and eastern parts of the country voted for different candidates. In the second round, western regions predominantly supported Kravchuk, while eastern regions supported Kuchma. In the Donetsk region, he received 79% of votes, and in the Luhansk region, it was 88%.

The Donbas considered Kuchma its candidate. Being from the industrial Dnipropetrovsk, a Soviet manager who barely spoke Ukrainian, he was more in tune with the Donetsk electorate than Volyn-born Leonid Kravchuk. Kuchma promised to develop relations with Russia and integrate within the framework of the CIS, so Donbas perceived his victory in the elections as its own.

The victory of the "pro-Russian" candidate temporarily eased tensions over federalist sentiments in the Donbas. However, in practice, it quickly became apparent that Kuchma was an even more staunch opponent of any federalism than his predecessor. The new president swiftly strengthened the power vertical. At his initiative, gubernatorial elections in Ukraine were abolished, and since 1994, the heads of regions began to be appointed directly by the president. And the new Constitution, adopted in June 1996, definitively settled the disputes over Ukraine's political structure and enshrined the unitary model. The Donbas elites accepted this calmly. By then, they were not concerned with federalism; the country was in the midst of privatization, and they needed to maintain good relations with the authorities to secure their share of state property.

Today, no one disputes that during the mass privatization of state enterprises in Ukraine, they were sold at non-transparent auctions for undervalued prices. Enormous enterprises changed hands literally for pennies. Typically, everything was sold primarily to "their own" — those who were loyal to the president and had the trust of Kuchma and his circle.

Later, Kuchma admitted that he consciously set the goal of creating a national bourgeoisie from scratch. At the beginning of privatization, there was no large business in the post-Soviet state. Kuchma simply had to create it artificially because it had nothing to emerge from. He appointed oligarchs just as before he appointed officials and directors. Interestingly, one of such "appointees," as it later turned out, was his own son-in-law.

"Capitalism without capitalists, without a national bourgeoisie, especially a significant one, doesn't exist. But for all 15 years of our independence, we were pushed onto the path of creating capitalism for small traders, small businesses, capitalism without a large national bourgeoisie. Like in Poland. I spoke about it more than once. Such a model is deadly for Ukraine. It is deadly even from the perspective of the structure of the Ukrainian economy – its foundation consists of industrial giants..." explained Kuchma in his book "After the Maidan 2005–2006. President's Notes."

Today, when Poland, with its "small traders," has reached a level unattainable for Ukraine, these lines appear to be a mockery. However, there is no undoing history. The goal that Leonid Kuchma set for himself has been achieved. By the end of the '90s, a new class had emerged in Ukraine—the class of big capitalists, the oligarchy.

The Donetsk group also managed to get its share of state property. Kuchma did not try to fight the local clans in the Donbas. Their support was necessary for him to feel confident in his position and easily secure re-election for a second term. Therefore, the president allowed the regional elites of the Donbas to take control of the industrial giants that were operating in "their" territory. In this situation, there was no reason to blackmail Kuchma with another referendum or to mess with him about federalization in the Donetsk and Luhansk regions.

In 1995, a company with a rather flashy name, the "Industrial Union of Donbas," appeared in the Donetsk region. Its creator was Vitalii Haiduk, who, in 1994, took the position of deputy governor of the Donetsk region. At the initial stage, one of the co-owners of the Union was also Rinat Akhmetov, who eventually received the main assets of this company.

Initially, The Union emerged as a natural gas trader and had no assets at all. Similar intermediaries engaged in providing natural gas supplies from Russia to Ukrainian enterprises appeared in large numbers in the mid-90s. Besides the Union, the most well-known among them were United Energy Systems of Ukraine of Pavlo Lazarenko and Yulia Tymoshenko, "Respublika" of Ihor Bakai, and the "Fond," controlled by the "Luhansk clan," which will be discussed later.

Natural gas trading opened up significant prospects for gas traders. Ukrainian enterprises generally lacked money in the mid-90s. At the same time, they required a lot of fuel because, in the Soviet Union, they knew nothing about energy efficiency. Factories quickly accumulated debts and became dependent on natural gas suppliers, who, in turn, gained the ability to take over the production and assets of enterprises in debt resolutions and appoint their managers. Understandably, such companies couldn't operate without powerful connections. Only chosen businessmen close to the government had the right to import fuel into Ukraine and supply it to state-owned enterprises. Under such conditions, fair competition was impossible.

In the Donbas, the leadership of Donetsk and Luhansk regions began to profit from natural gas trading. In February 1996, the then governor of Donetsk region, Volodymyr Shcherban, signed decree №71, obliging all enterprises in Donetsk to buy natural gas only from the "Industrial Union of Donbas" and thereby making this company a regional monopolist. The Donetsk region was heavily industrialized and, at that time, accounted for about a quarter of Ukraine's GDP, so supplying high volumes of natural gas promised extraordinary profits to a trader. Intermediary transactions and favorable conditions created by the authorities helped gas traders accumulate significant capital funds with minimal investments. With this money, natural gas intermediaries began to buy up state-owned assets, usually at very discounted prices.

In 1996, Serhii Poliakov, a former mayor of Torez and ex-minister of the coal industry in Pavlo Lazarenko's government, became the head of the Donetsk Regional State Administration. Along with him came a person who was little known even in Donetsk at that time but would later play a menacing role in the history of Ukraine. It was Viktor Yanukovych, the CEO of the "Donetskavtotrans association". Initially appointed as Poliakov's deputy, he quickly rose to the position of the first deputy.

Already in 1997, Poliakov was dismissed. He couldn't stay in his position for long, as he was an underling of Lazarenko, who, to put it mildly, was not particularly respected in the Donbas. This circumstance defined the political future of the governor. Yanukovych took Poliakov's place. In the mid-90s, governors in the Donetsk region changed every year, so another reshuffle did not evoke special emotions. Yanukovych seemed to be as temporary and insignificant a figure as his predecessors.

Why did Kuchma choose him? Yulia Mostova, the editor-in-chief of the newspaper "Dzerkalo Tyzhnia," offered this answer in 2004.

> "In 1996-1997, Lazarenko led a tough and unsuccessful war for control over the Donbas and, ultimately, came to a conclusion: it is necessary to make agreements with the local landlords and, in alliance with them, try to control the industrial region. As agreed with Rinat Akhmetov, Pavlo Lazarenko removed a loyal but unwanted governor, Poliakov, and lobbied for the president to appoint Viktor Yanukovych to the vacant position. Thus, Viktor Fedorovych is drafted twice. However, he doesn't have time to return this favor to Pavlo Ivanovych: Lazarenko is sent into retirement for health reasons. But with Rinat Leonidovych, Yanukovych did settle his tab when he cleared the administrative and political field in the region for business and, above all, the privatization move of the true master of Donetsk," wrote Mostova in the summer of 2004 in the article "The Obscurity of Yanukovych."

In that same year, 1997, the infamous Party of Regional Revival of Ukraine—or the Party of Regions for short—was born. The founding congress of the party took place in October, and its founders were influential figures in Donetsk politics: Yukhym Zvyahilsky, Volodymyr Rybak, and Mykola Azarov. The Donbas elite, gaining strength, was filled with ambitions and understood that for the effective protection of its interests, it needed its own political party.

The 1999 presidential elections were approaching, and Leonid Kuchma planned to be re-elected for a second term. To achieve this, as in 1994, he needed to secure the votes of the Donbas voters. However, this time, the task was more complicated. Due to the economic crisis and a decrease in the standard of living, Kuchma's popularity was declining, and the trend of nostalgia for the USSR was increasing. Along with it, the support for left-wing populists was growing. The electorate of parties that combined left-wing rhetoric with pro-Russian slogans was concentrated mainly in the industrial centers of the southeast of the country. In 1994, voters in these regions supported Kuchma in the elections, but by the late '90s, many had become disillusioned with him. Kuchma could not halt the rapid decline of the Soviet industry and the fall in the standard of living.

In this situation, the president needed to secure the support of the regional elite in the Donbas. Such an alliance was formed. Kuchma needed loyalty and support from the Donetsk faction. In exchange, he guaranteed them full freedom of action in "their" territory.

> "Kuchma promised autonomy to the Donetsk region in exchange for falsifying election results in his favor. Donetsk residents could appoint their own prosecutors, judges, and manage the region at their discretion in exchange for loyalty to the central government and the necessary results," recounted journalist Volodymyr Boyko in the program "Historical Truth," discussing those times. Boyko began his professional career in the '90s in Donetsk and investigated the activities of the Donetsk mafia during

that period.

During his visit to Donetsk in the summer of 1998, President Kuchma openly stated that Viktor Yanukovych would remain in the governor's chair as long as Kuchma remained president. Kuchma eventually even overfulfilled this promise. Yanukovych remained governor until 2002, then he moved up and became the head of the government. In 1998, the fortunes of the unofficial master of the Donetsk region, Rinat Akhmetov, rose sharply. The company "Industrial Union of Donbas," of which he was a co-owner, quickly began acquiring assets and taking control of the largest enterprises in the region. This included the giant Ukrainian metallurgical plant, Mariupol Iron and Steel Works "Azovstal."

Akhmetov obtained ownership of this plant practically for free. As another co-owner of the "Industrial Union," Serhii Taruta, recalled in one of his interviews, they had to pay only about $35 million for a 44% stake in "Azovstal." With the money earned from gas sales, they also purchased other industrial enterprises, which later formed the foundation of the economic empire of the chief Donetsk oligarch. In 1999, the so-called "clarification of ownership" of the "Industrial Union" took place. Akhmetov and other owners of the company decided to divide the jointly acquired assets. Enterprises in the Donetsk region then came under the control of Rinat Akhmetov's new company, SCM, while the plants in the Dnipropetrovsk and Luhansk regions remained under Taruta and Haiduk, branded as the "Industrial Union of Donbas."

RENAISSANCE OF THE KOMSOMOL

After Leonid Kuchma's victory in the presidential elections, the leaders of his campaign headquarters in the Luhansk region, Hennadii Fomenko and Viktor Tykhonov, became the heads of the Luhansk Regional State Administration (RSA). In 1997, Oleksandr Yefremov became the deputy head of the RSA, and in 1998, Kuchma dismissed Fomenko and appointed Yefremov as the governor. Viktor Tykhonov, at that time, was already the head of the Luhansk Regional Council.

In the second half of the '90s, Tykhonov and Yefremov, within a few years, formed a monolithic "Komsomol team" in the region, characterized by clear subordination and succession. It was a revived Komsomol, where becoming the "first secretary of the regional committee" (obkom) was possible only after being the "first secretary of the city committee," having the "party tenure," the right origin, and references. Those who rose to power included the former second secretary of the Komsomol obkom, Oleksandr Kobitiev, the former first secretary of the Sievierodonetsk city department of the Communist Party, Valentyn Dzon, the former secretary of the Luhansk City Komsomol committee, Valeriy Holenko (who led the regional council after Tykhonov and fled to Russia after the events of 2014 to escape criminal prosecution), and another Komsomol leader, Volodymyr Prystiuk (Luhansk governor in 2012–2014, a protégé of Yefremov).

In the late '90s, Luhansk governor Oleksandr Yefremov (like the entire Luhansk "Komsomols" team) also received guarantees of immunity from Leonid Kuchma in exchange for loyalty. Serious accusations of corruption were voiced against Yefremov, but the president chose to ignore them. The Luhansk faction became as much a support for "Kuchmism" as the Donetsk one.

The first victim of the "Komsomols" in Luhansk was the young mayor Oleksii Danilov. In 1997, a coalition against him formed in the Luhansk City Council and, after a lengthy political process and a major scandal, forced Danilov to resign. Viktor Tykhonov unofficially controlled the case. Instead of Danilov, Anatolii Yahoferov, a godfather of Tykhonov's child and his close friend, became the mayor of the city. He was a former member of the Ukrainian Parliament and the head of the Parkhomenko machinery plant. However, he did not last long either: in 2001–2002, he, too, was dismissed from his position with a major scandal, and he and Tykhonov remained bitter enemies. Until 2014, Yahoferov supported the newspaper "Molodohvardeets," which weekly published critical and exposé articles against Tykhonov and Yefremov.

The formal reason for expressing distrust in Danilov was criminal cases investigated by the Security Service of Ukraine (SSU) and the tax authorities. These cases were related to the property of Danilov and his family. However, the real reason for Danilov's dismissal was, of course, not corruption but him being an outsider rather than part of the "Komsomols" team. Immediately after his dismissal, he tried to challenge the city council's decision in court but lost the case. Danilov planned to participate in the 1998 parliamentary elections. The former mayor ran in one of the majoritarian districts, but his candidacy was withdrawn shortly before the elections by a court decision (again, probably for political reasons). After that, he moved to Kyiv and returned to regional politics only in 2004 as the head of Viktor Yushchenko's campaign headquarters, following a court decision that recognized his former dismissal as unlawful.

In the summer of 1997, the convoy of the criminal authority Valerii Dobroslavskyi was fired upon with grenade launchers and automatic weapons. "Dobroslav" was killed on the spot, and over the next year, several more people from his inner circle were killed. In a short time, political control over Luhansk practically completely passed into the hands of the "Komsomols."

By 1997, Oleksandr Yefremov and his Komsomol comrade Oleksandr Kyselov had already built a powerful business empire. At the time of his appointment as the head of Luhansk Regional State Administration (RSA), Yefremov was the chairman of the board of "Ukrkommunbank" (the bank was liquidated in 2015 as insolvent), the owner of the insurance company "Oranta-Luhansk," and a co-founder of Closed joint-stock company (CJSC) "Fond." Kyselov was a partner in most of Yefremov's businesses. Like the "Industrial Union" of Taruta and UESU of Tymoshenko, "Fond" was a natural gas trader. The peak of the company's activity was during the period of 1997-2001, curiously coinciding with Yefremov's governorship.

"Fond" and its associated "Luhansk Energy Alliance" operated exclusively in the Luhansk region, supplying fuel to about 380 regional enterprises. Their annual supply volume exceeded 1 billion cubic meters (for comparison, in 2015, Ukraine's total usage was about 33 billion cubic meters of natural gas, including approximately 11 billion for the industry). "Fond" had a monopoly in the region, making its owners the wealthiest individuals in the area. They not only earned substantial profits but also acquired some assets in exchange for debts if consumers couldn't pay for the gas.

The operation scheme of "Fond" was straightforward: the regional authorities compelled the directors of industrial enterprises and coal associations to purchase gas exclusively from this company. Since all major enterprises in the region were still state-owned at the time, their management had to follow the directives of officials. Consequently, "Fond" quickly plunged several state-owned enterprises into debt and subsequently pushed them into bankruptcy. The fate of these enterprises was predictable: their assets were either sold or disassembled for scrap metal.

This fate befell several large enterprises, including the Stakhanov Coke Chemical Plant, Almaznianskyi Metallurgical Plant, a rubber products plant in Lysychansk, and other sizable enterprises. According to the former director of the Stakhanov Coke Chemical Plant (SCCP), Serhii Tytov, after Yefremov took over the leadership of the Luhansk region, the heads of industrial enterprises in the region were summoned to the Luhansk Regional State Administration. There, Yefremov or his deputies coerced them into signing contracts to purchase gas from the "Fond" company.

> "They summoned us to the regional state administration, and there was this guy, Dzon (Yefremov's deputy —A/N). They sent us from one office to another—either to Yefremov or to Dzon. Under the same pretext—to buy gas only from the 'Fond' company for $85. Thus, with this gas, they got the entire region cornered. The same was happening everywhere, even in the mines. Then, they cut the enterprises into scrap metal to cover the debts as best they could," said Serhii Tytov.

In 1998, after the SCCP accumulated debts, the "Fond" ceased to supply natural gas to the enterprise, causing the plant to shut down. The "Fond" then imposed a condition on the plant's management: natural gas would only be supplied to the SCCP if the plant processed raw materials owned by the "Fond." If the SCCP tried to collaborate with other commercial entities, natural gas would not be provided to the plant. This placed the Stakhanov Coke and Chemical Plant in a form of indentured servitude. After this, it operated for a short time. In the fall of 1999, the most profitable resin processing unit of the plant was auctioned off to cover debts. Only two structures close to Yefremov participated in the auction—the "Fond" and the "Luhansk Energy Alliance." The "Fond," represented by Yefremov's partner, Yevhen Slapak, who would become the future head of the machinery department in the industrial management of the Luhansk Regional Administration, won the auction.

In 2000, the SCCP was declared bankrupt. Within a few years, only ruins remained of the enterprise—the equipment was sold for scrap metal, and the workshops were dismantled for construction materials. Several other plants in the Luhansk region shared the SCCP's fate. Despite all this, the Yefremov clan could not gain ownership, even partially, of the main industrial giants of Luhansk —the Alchevsk Metallurgical Plant and the Lysychansk Oil Refinery. This happened for political reasons. The metallurgical plant was given to the more powerful and influential Donetsk group from the Industrial Union of Donbas, while the oil refinery was sold to the Russian company TNK-BP. According to Luhansk insiders, the son-in-law of President Kuchma, Viktor Pinchuk, who had a stake in the profits of the "Fond" company, oversaw its operations. However, former co-owner of the "Fond," Oleksandr Kyselov, refuses to discuss this matter to this day.

The financial infrastructure of Yefremov's business was managed by his partner, Eduard Lozovskyi (the head of "Ukrcomunbank" and the first vice-governor of the Luhansk region from 2010–2014). The industrial group of companies was registered under Yefremov's son, Ihor, and other family members, as well as a Bulgarian citizen, Hristo Kolev. Numerous companies belonging to Yefremov were involved in the supply and repair of mining equipment through state tenders and had a turnover of billions of hryvnias (*Hryvnia (UAH, ₴) is the national currency of Ukraine. —T. Ed.*) In 2004, the business group moved a significant portion of its assets offshore.

Less is known about the business of another influential figure from the Luhansk faction—Viktor Tykhonov. The only time he directly "exposed" his business interests was during the sale of the Luhansk sewing factory "Styl" to the Russian company "Gloria Jeans." In the early 1990s, Tykhonov worked as the director of this factory for several years, which he later privatized. However, he either could not or did not want to develop the business independently and decided to sell the enterprise. The press reported that the company was sold for $60 million, while Tykhonov claimed it was only six million.

If in Donetsk Kuchma managed to grow real oligarchs, in Luhansk, this plan failed. Tykhonov and Yefremov simply weren't suited for such a role. The businessmen of Donetsk in the '90s were significantly different in their psychological makeup from the Luhansk "Komsomol members," who proved incapable of building large holdings and effectively managing them. Additionally, the structure of the economy itself played a crucial role—the complex production schemes required involving dozens of enterprises, most of which were already controlled by the Donetsk faction. The Luhansk faction did not invest in such infrastructure. Gradually, Yefremov's group began to lose ground in the region, and Yuriy Boyko's clan eventually rivaled it in the extent of influence.

Interestingly, Yuriy Boyko owed his rapid rise to Yefremov's business partner, Oleksandr Kyselov. In 1999, with Kyselov's support, Boyko, who was then the director of the "Zoria" chemical plant in Rubizhne, was appointed the CEO of the Lysychansk Oil Refinery, which was in a critical financial condition at that time. He managed it until the plant was sold to the Russians. After that, his career went up, and by the early 2000s, Boyko headed the company "Naftohaz" and later moved to work in Yanukovych's government.

His rapprochement with the oligarch Dmytro Firtash played a crucial role in his further rise. Over time, a political clan around Yuriy Boyko gradually formed in the Luhansk region. Its key interests lay in the so-called "chemical triangle"—the cities of Rubizhne, Lysychansk, and Sievierodonetsk, where the chemical industry of the region was clustered. On the eve of the war, not only Yefremov but also Boyko were considered the most influential politicians in Luhansk.

TWILIGHT ZONE OF THE ECONOMIC CRISIS

The explosion of the wealth of a small group of individuals who claimed in the '90s the right to be called the "regional elite of the Donbas" unfolded against the backdrop of a severe economic crisis and a rapid decline in the standard of living of the region's residents. Privatization, contrary to officials' promises, did not make people richer. The so-called "common people" didn't even have time to understand what had happened. Privatization certificates, distributed to all Ukrainian citizens, allowed everyone to claim their share of state property. However, many people left them lying in closets and attics. The populace didn't understand how to handle these vouchers, where, and how to invest them. However, the country's leadership was not particularly concerned about this. After all, Leonid Kuchma was not interested in "small traders." He was creating a big bourgeoisie.

By 2000, Ukraine's economy was only declining. During the period from 1990 to 1999, the Ukrainian GDP shrank by 59.2%. For a country in peacetime, this was a terrible performance. In the mid-90s, the country was chronically paralyzed by coal miner strikes; enterprises didn't unload coal for weeks, and a critical situation arose due to a lack of fuel at thermal power plants and coking plants. Power outages began. Industrial workers went for months without receiving wages, demanding payment of debts. However, the budget didn't have the resources to settle with everyone.

A premonition of collapse and chaos hung over the country. And the place with the highest concentration of this anxiety became the Donbas—a region overloaded with

Soviet industry, where the process of the industry's decline was hurting the most. Since the early '90s, a stereotypical belief had been ingrained in the minds of the Donbas residents for many years that the sharp deterioration in their standard of living was a consequence of the declaration of independent Ukraine.

In the mid-90s, one by one, production facilities geared towards the Soviet defense industry and unprofitable enterprises, which existed only through state support during the Soviet era, began to shut down in the Donbas. Often, these were plants with workforces in the tens of thousands that had previously seemed invincible. Even more promising companies, which had every chance of fitting into the market, were affected. Some of them fell into the hands of criminal groups and corrupt officials. They coerced into using their intermediaries or deliberately drove to bankruptcy in order to take over the business.

Blatant embezzlement of assets reached horrifying proportions. Both the management and ordinary workers were involved in theft. State-owned enterprises were considered as if they were "ownerless." If salaries were delayed at such enterprises, their employees would start taking home anything they could, considering it a kind of "compensation."

The most challenging situation arose in the coal industry, where unprofitable mines were numbering in dozens. A decisive solution to all the problems in this sector came down to a simple and cheap way—to eliminate all struggling enterprises without much ado. This process was termed "restructuring of the coal industry."

Restructuring became one of the most dramatic events in the history of the Donbas. The senseless destruction of mines undoubtedly had a significant impact on the subsequent course of history and played a crucial role in the events of 2014. In terms of its destructive impact on citizens' lives, the consequences of this move could very well be compared to a war. Long before the beginning of armed conflicts, some mining towns in Donetsk and Luhansk regions looked as if battles had already taken place there.

The collapse of the coal industry left its mark not only on the economic situation but also on the mentality of the residents of mining territories. Over the years of living in an atmosphere of decline and decay, millions of Donbas' citizens became embittered and disillusioned with the life that unfolded after the collapse of the Soviet Union. The restructuring of mines shattered the backbone of the miners' movement, transforming miners from the formidable force they were in the early 1990s into disenfranchised, intimidated, and hungry laborers. It is understandable that in these circumstances, people couldn't help but feel nostalgia for the times when coal mining was considered an honorable profession.

The coal industry in Donbas had been degrading since the 1980s, and by the mid-90s, it had reached an economic dead end. Coal production volumes were declining every year. Salary arrears were increasing. In 1995, coal production in Ukraine decreased by 10.8 million tons compared to 1994. As of January 1, 1996, the accounts payable of coal enterprises amounted to 252.2 trillion karbovanets, exceeding accounts receivable by 134.2 trillion. The total of payroll owed reached 31 trillion karbovanets. *(Karbovanets here refers to Ukraine's national currency in 1992–1996 before the introduction of the hryvnia. —T. Ed.)*

In such a situation, the government urgently needed to make changes. The document that marked the beginning of the mine restructuring program was the Decree of the

President of Ukraine, "On the Structural Reorganization of the Coal Industry," dated February 7, 1996. Initially, there seemed to be nothing ominous in this document. It proposed the complete elimination of only certain especially unprofitable mines and open-pit mines, the list of which was to be compiled within three months by the Ministry of Coal Industry and the governors of coal-producing regions. It was decided to privatize or lease unprofitable mines. The soft infrastructure assets of such mines were to be transferred to municipal ownership or sold to private investors.

However, in practice, Kuchma's decree turned out to be a "green light" for numerous officials and bureaucrats who decided to eliminate as many coal enterprises as possible without much hassle. Moreover, destroying "unnecessary" manufacturing companies could bring substantial profits. Valuable equipment and thousands of tons of ferrous and non-ferrous metals were located underground. All this inventory was written off after the mine was destroyed.

Many of the mines destroyed at that time could have been saved. In the early 2000s, the price of energy carriers increased, and coal mining became profitable again. Private investors managed to buy and revitalize some previously closed enterprises. However, in the mid-90s, the "restructurers" were convinced that there was no future in the coal industry, and they ruthlessly dealt with the mines. Enterprises were hastily closed and looted, leaving millions of tons of unmined coal underground. The infrastructure also suffered, and those crumbling ruins would serve as grim monuments to wastefulness for a long time to come. Even with a cursory study of the history of this destructive campaign, it's clear that the restructuring of mines became a massive economic crime against Ukraine's economy, and those responsible deserve befitting punishment.

In 1996, out of the planned 130 million hryvnias for the closure of mines, only 69 million were allocated from the budget. Underfunding on such a scale was bound to have catastrophic consequences. Cost-cutting was a must, so the mines were closed hastily and recklessly. The stopes were being flooded without regret. In Stakhanov, located in the Luhansk region, all mines were closed on the quickest schedule possible, and the city, named after the most famous Soviet miner, was left stripped of its entire coal production. The "Stakhanovvuhillia" association was completely liquidated. According to experts' estimates, the four closed mines of this association had reserves of 82 million tons of coking coal, which remained underground.

The process of liquidating mines in Stakhanov was described in an interview by the former mayor of the city, Serhii Levachkov:

"When they started closing the mines, I was the mayor of Stakhanov. There were no projects. No one managed to even notify the local authorities. I, as the mayor, found out about the closure of the 'Central-Irmino' mine by accident. The head of the department responsible for extinguishing spoil tips fires called me and informed me that the sealing of the shaft had begun. The minister signed the order to close the mine; the general director confirmed it and immediately gave the order to fill the shaft. Even more so, they filled it completely with everything that was in there. All the machinery, all the equipment, they left it all there."

The consequences of such an approach left the city in shock. Before the start of restructuring, 18% of the city's residents worked in Stakhanov's coal mining, and its share in the city's economy was 28%. In just a few years, this share fell to 1.5%. Compensating for this decrease in such a short period was impossible. After the mine closure, 17,000 people lost their jobs, mostly men who had to support their families.

Stakhanov began to lose its population rapidly, and the average life expectancy of people decreased by ten years. The city couldn't recover from such a blow. Even in 2012, 40% of its budget were government subsidies, essential for Stakhanov's very existence. The culmination of the destructive processes was the events of the spring of 2014, which in many ways resembled a delayed social explosion. The disenfranchised population of mining towns readily joined the so-called "people's militia" to seek revenge on Ukraine "for everything."

In neighboring Brianka, things were no better. The former chief mechanic of the "Annenska" mine, Yurii Khokhlov, described the closure of this mine as follows:

> "The mine was closed on September 1. And the liquidation started somewhere in mid-October. And all this time, there was chaos. The whole town rushed in, looting everything that was left—after all, it belonged to no one. My parents told me there was a time like this in 1941, when ours had already retreated but the Germans hadn't yet entered the city. And during that time, the populace took everything in sight—looting stores, houses. Complete anarchy. That's exactly what I saw at my mine. It was scary to watch."

In 2014, Khokhlov, who was a deputy of the Luhansk Regional Council from the Communist Party at that time, actively participated in anti-Ukrainian rallies in Luhansk from the first days of March. With the onset of hostilities, he sided with the armed formations of the so-called "'Luhansk People's Republic" ("LPR").

The social situation in mining towns at that time is well reflected in the article "We Want to Eat" in the "Horniak" newspaper (city of Torez) dated February 10, 1999. It describes the so-called women's revolt at the "3-bis" mine—a protest rally of miners' wives.

"On February 5, the '3-bis' mine stopped working, and the wives of miners picketed the lamp room and shafts. "We are afraid, but we want to eat," said one of them. Lack of money is the biggest hot-button issue. "My husband drinks a glass of water—that was his lunch, off to work," says one of the picketers. Several people mention that they feed the children with animal feed—"it's the cheapest." Potatoes helped for some time—they distributed them in August and September as payment for [salary owed] debts. Ten months—the average delay in salary payments at the mine. Nothing in their pockets, tears in their eyes. Even metal has its limits of tensile strength, and people couldn't bear it anymore."

The main problem was not that the old Soviet enterprises were disappearing. Worse was that new producing companies were not emerging to take their place. Investors were not coming to the Donbas, especially to the Luhansk region. Investing money in the region was seen as either suicidal or a venture for a well-connected businessman. The few daring adventurers willing to take risks and invest in troubled enterprises faced conflicts with local political elites, which often resulted in the collapse of their businesses. For example, in one of his interviews, entrepreneur Kostiantyn Ilchenko from the city of Sverdlovsk talked about such confrontation. In 1997, he leased mine №68 and attempted to get coal mining up and running there.

"Within four months, I restored the mine, investing significant funds. It became effectively the only coal enterprise in the city at that time that paid its employees in real money, not in potatoes or bacon. However, we were able to work for only three months. Then came a real clash between me and the team of Oleksandr Yefremov, who was the first deputy governor of the Luhansk region at the time," Ilchenko recounted in an interview with the "Ostrov" website in 2012.

According to him, under Yefremov's order, the electricity to the mine was cut off, then pit water flooded stopes, and the enterprise came to a halt. It all ended with the complete destruction of mine №68 with coal reserves enough for several decades.

"All sorts of supervisory bodies, from the technical inspection to the local authorities and the prosecutor's office, basically arm-twisted the leased enterprise. Once, the police guys called me and warned me not to go to the mine tomorrow because a squad would arrive, and they would simply 'lock me up,' send me to jail without any explanations. On that day, I was standing not far from the mine and observing what was happening there. In fact, they were 'killing' the mine. Indeed, a police squad arrived with automatic weapons, a representative of the city prosecutor's office, and the justice department (we had already filed a lawsuit against the lessor for illegal actions). Threatening with handcuffs, they took all the people out of the mine, closed the administrative facilities, secured the shafts, and posted guards. And within a month and a half, the mine was completely razed: nothing was left of the above-ground facilities, all the equipment was hauled away to an unknown destination," Ilchenko recounted.

With the closure of mines, the coal industry in the Donbas region regressed to 19th-century technologies. Small makeshift mines, where miners extracted coal through primitive manual labor, quickly proliferated on the sites of demolished and closed enterprises. Unemployed miners had no other option but to enter these "holes." So-called "pickers" or "baggers" emerged—people who started collecting coal from coal refuse piles. Along with rocks, some coal always ended up in the spoil tips, so impoverished residents of depressed towns gathered it for sale or heating their own homes. The business of "pickers" was perilous, as occasional landslides led to tragic, deadly accidents.

People also turned to the remains of dead Soviet plants as a source of income. Residents of depressed cities dismantled abandoned workshops for bricks, extracted rebars from reinforced concrete slabs, and dug up cables. In Horlivka, they disassembled a large mercury plant, which went bankrupt in the mid-1990s. In Kostiantynivka, it was the "Special Glass" plant, and in Stakhanov, the coking plant. What did the residents of the Donbas, once glorified by Soviet propaganda as hardworking laborers, feel as they witnessed the collapse of their familiar world? Disorientation, disillusionment, despair... Few residents of industrial towns were capable of objectively assessing what was happening and impartially analyzing the causes of the economic crisis. Most stuck to simple answers provided by populist politicians from pro-Russian parties and movements.

Unemployed miners were not willing to delve into why their mines were closed. For them, the simple fact that "everything worked under the Soviet Union, and now it has fallen apart" was sufficient. As is often the case in such situations, people saw the roots of all problems in some conspiratorial plot, which was easier to believe than in objective economic factors.

A stereotype still persists in the Donbas: officials from Kyiv and western Ukraine are to blame for the destruction of mines. According to one version, they supposedly knew nothing about the industry and decided to bury the coal sector. According to another version, they intentionally destroyed the mines because they hated the Donbas or were "following the orders of Western masters." But the truth is, the fate of the mines was sealed chiefly by the Donbas' own.

The first to implement the presidential decree on the restructuring of mines was Minister Yurii Poliakov (the same person who preceded Yanukovych as the governor of the Donetsk region). He led the Ministry of Coal Industry from 1995–1996 and was one of the developers of the restructuring project. In 1996, Yurii Rusantsov, a native of Yenakiyeve, took over from him. Before joining the Cabinet, Rusantsov headed the "Artemvuhillia" association. The following year, the ministry was headed by Stanislav Yanko from Selydove, Donetsk region. A year later, perhaps the best-known of the "coal undertakers," Serhii Tulub from Khartsyzk, who led the Ministry in 1998–2000, was appointed as a minister. It was during this period that the epidemic of mine closures reached its peak.

The professionalism of these managers is vividly illustrated by the results of their activities. It is enough to note that in 1996, experts from the Ministry of Coal Industry predicted that restructuring would increase coal production in Ukraine from 80 million tons to 110-120 million tons per year by 2005. In reality, coal production in 2005 amounted to only 60 million tons. Small mining towns and settlements were unable to recover from the harsh crisis of the '90s and turned into preserves of poverty and ruins. In 2000, the Luhansk region was recognized as the poorest region in Ukraine, with a poverty rate of 44.8%. For comparison, in the neighboring Kharkiv region, this indicator was only 19.6% that same year.

In these mining ghettos, by 2014, an entire generation had grown up who had never seen anything around them except for drinking, hostility, and devastation and who had become accustomed to living in degrading poverty.

Devastated by crisis and corruption, the Donbas region became an ideal Petri dish for crime and anti-government sentiments, with its disenfranchised residents becoming fuel for the armed conflict. Notably, soon after the start of the war, leaders of pro-Russian armed groups, such as Olexander Khodakovsky and Igor Strelkov, confessed in their interviews that joining the "militias" was quite attractive for antisocial characters with criminal backgrounds, drug addicts, and outcasts. Khodakovsky, for instance, mentioned in his interviews that in some units of the "DPR" 20-30% of personnel had a criminal record. If you add other disadvantaged individuals without education and steady employment to these percentages, it turns out to be more than half. For these people, a gun became an unexpected social elevator they no longer waited for. The answer to how this happened can be found precisely in the turmoil of the 1990s.

LUHANSK MAIDAN

One of the most dramatic episodes of the '90s crisis in the Donbas region was the infamous "Luhansk carnage"—the beating of striking miners by Berkut special militsiya unit in downtown Luhansk on August 24, 1998. The fact that the incident occurred on Ukraine's Independence Day added a gloomy symbolism to it.

The late '90s became the darkest period for the Ukrainian coal industry. It was paralyzed by perpetual non-payments and endless strikes. In 1998, miners' pickets in Luhansk lasted almost half a year, from July 15 to December 17. Miners from the city of Krasnodon (employees of the Barakov, Sukhodolska-Skhidna, and Duvanna mines) picketed the Luhansk regional administration.

The leader of the protest was Dmytro Kalitventsev, the head of the Independent Miners' Union of the Barakov Mine. According to him, the salary arrears and delay in workers' comp at some mines in Krasnodon and Pervomaisk reached 14 months in 1998. The situation was dreadful: mine directors, at their whim, picked who gets the pay and who doesn't. Sometimes, miners could receive a portion of their salaries only after paying a kickback to the management. There were cases when salaries were paid in expired groceries, flour, or cereal groats.

In the summer of 1998, miners' patience ran out again, and they camped in the square in front of the Luhansk Regional Administration. The authorities took an openly hostile attitude toward the miners. The website of the Barakov mine's charter of the Independent Labor Union of Miners reported that officials from the very beginning tried to hinder the picket in every way possible.

"Miners noted the contemptuous attitude towards them from the authorities, constant insults and threats from the militsiya, petty provocations, and administrative pressure. For example, initially, they tried to corral the miners in a pen near the building, like cattle, and forbade them to talk to passersby. The officers wouldn't even allow them to put up plastic sheets for rain cover, let alone set up tents. Day and night, people were exposed to the elements. An active information war was waged against them; local TV stories referred to them as alcoholics and renegades." *(Militsiya was a national law enforcement agency in Ukraine from 1919 to 2015, when it was reformed to become the National Police of Ukraine. —T. Ed)*

Every morning and evening, when officials from the regional administration arrived to work and went home, miners staged a "plastic rock" for them—hitting plastic bottles on the asphalt. However, this did not help them receive their due salaries. Communication with officials also yielded no results. Throughout the picket, the then Prime Minister Valeriy Pustovoitenko visited the Luhansk region twice, and President Kuchma visited once. However, none of them talked directly with the protesters, either in person or through their representatives.

On August 16, 1998, an explosion occurred at the 19th Partyzanska coal mine in the town of Bile (known also as Sutohan, after the local mine built before the Russian revolution of 1917) in Lutuhyno district, resulting in the death of 24 people. This tragedy further fueled the miners' protests. The picketers decided to participate in the funerals. They collected money and rented buses, but half an hour before departure, traffic police officers stopped the convoy and, threatening to confiscate the vehicles, prohibited the miners from leaving Luhansk. At that point,

250 people walked to Bile, located 30 kilometers from the regional center. While the column was passing through the city, several protocols were drawn up against the miners for obstructing traffic.

In Bile, militsiya special forces units met the convoy and did not allow the miners to approach the cemetery, where Prime Minister Valeriy Pustovoitenko was participating in the ceremony. While some miners were buried with media coverage and official condolences, others were ignored. Miners were only allowed to the graves of their colleagues after the departure of the prime minister.

On August 24, 1998, Independence Day, the strikers planned to organize a torchlight procession in Luhansk and symbolically burn an effigy of a "parasite." However, a few hours before the start of the action, they were surrounded by militsiya and special unit Berkut in full gear. As it got dark and the protesters began to distribute torch kerosene, militsiya chiefs approached the leadership group and claimed that there was an explosive device in the effigy. They tried to take the effigy from the miners, a dispute arose, and at that moment, Berkut attacked the miners. The beating lasted for 15 minutes, and as a result, 22 people were hospitalized; the rest, with minor injuries, remained in the square and lit their torches. In the evening, this incident was featured in the news on the "1+1" channel (prior to this, main channels had not covered the protest at all), and the scandal moved to the political domain. However, the issue of paying off salary arrears and worker's compensation was not resolved even after this. The authorities tried to present the incident as an attempt to restrain drunken hooligans, claiming that the protesters themselves were armed with clubs and rebars. The officials behaved in the same way as they did later in 2013 when they portrayed beatings of peaceful protesters in Kyiv as neutralization of dangerous militants.

In September, information about Berkut's attack on the peaceful protest was discussed in the parliament, and people's deputies began to visit the protesters, but nothing yielded results. The picket continued, and salary arrears were increasing. By the end of November, Dmytro Kalitventsev received from miners eight statements of intent to commit self-immolation. Hunger, hopelessness, and endless humiliation were pushing people to such desperate measures.

On December 3, 1998, the parliament adopted a resolution stating that all debts to miners should be repaid, and this information had to be reported to the Verkhovna Rada by December 15. The Cabinet was tasked with this, but the government was not in a hurry to execute it. The delay had tragic consequences. On the night of December 14, when everyone in the camp was already asleep, Krasnodon miner Oleksandr Mikhalevych doused himself with gasoline and set himself on fire. Militsiya officers on duty near the administration building saw the burning man running through the park. They rushed to extinguish the fire and called an ambulance, but severely burned Mikhalevych was at death's door.

On the evening of December 16, enraged miners, reeling from the tragedy, spontaneously stormed the Luhansk Regional Administration. Kalitventsev managed to stop the miners already inside the building, on the ground floor. Two hours later, they were introduced to the new CEO of "Krasnodonvuhillia," Semen Kerkez, and by 6 a.m., salary arrears and workers' compensation were settled. Oleksandr Mikhalevych passed away in intensive care on December 28.

The Luhansk "Maidan," unlike the events in Kyiv, did not demand the resignation of officials and was satisfied immediately after the authorities agreed to settle the debts owed to miners. The events in Luhansk did not even lead to a change in the governor, although miners experienced enough humiliation from officials. In the following year, 1999, strikes continued, but now the authorities did not escalate the situation to riots and bloody clashes. Krasnodon miners started two more marches to Kyiv. During the first one, about a thousand workers from the Talivska mine managed to reach the Donetsk region before the government could settle the debts. Then, miners from the Liutikov mine also embarked on a similar march, and their issues were resolved halfway through, after one and a half months.

In the late '90s, the Donbas region was on the verge of rebellion. The streets of mining towns were haunted by the ghost of hungry riots, but all the pent-up steam went up in smoke. People finally expressed their dissatisfaction only in the elections. The impoverished and devastated population of the Luhansk region in the 1998 parliamentary elections voted en masse for the Communist Party of Ukraine (CPU), which had no intention of engaging in opposition activities at all. Later, in the presidential elections, they voted for the leader of the Communists, Petro Symonenko, who also had no intention of actively pursuing the presidency. Of course, such voting did not bring about any improvements.

For some time, the names of the real destroyers of factories and mines were on everyone's lips. People cursed, hated, demanded trials and imprisonment for them. "Not even the plague could do what Kuchma has achieved," wrote supporters of Communist Petro Symonenko on their leaflets in 1999. But soon enough, just a few years later, the Donbas had new enemies—the "orange" politicians *(named so after their campaign color scheme. —T. Ed.)* And the old wrongdoers quickly became allies in the fight against the new, now "orange," plague. In 2004, the Communists supported Viktor Yanukovych, former governor of the

Donetsk region, in the presidential elections and, together with the Luhansk and Donetsk factions, stood united against opposition leader Viktor Yushchenko.

Strange, but true. Instead of demanding punishment for the real culprits behind the closure and looting of enterprises, the populace of the region, which had suffered a terrible decline, suddenly directed its anger at completely innocent people who had nothing to do with it. Moreover, it was based on completely absurd claims like "American wife" or an imaginary division of the country into classes. Meanwhile, the real architects of the prolonged depression, whose actions led miners to set themselves on fire and entire cities be turned into ruins, were considered "patriots of the Donbas" and honorary citizens of mining towns. It's as if there had never been factories dismantled for scrap, flooded workings, and bleak years of destitution.

PART THREE

"RISE UP, UKRAINE"

In March 2002, Ukraine held parliamentary elections. President Leonid Kuchma once again, as in 1999, received strong support in the Donetsk region. The bloc of parties "For United Ukraine," aligned with him, received 36.8% of the votes there. This was their best result over the rest of the country, making the Donetsk region the only region where the "For United Ukraine" bloc won the elections. In the Luhansk region, "For United Ukraine" garnered only 14.4%, trailing far behind the Communists, who received almost 40%. Additionally, candidates nominated by the administration won in the majority of single-mandate districts in Donbas. However, nationwide, the pro-government party received only 11.8%, a result significantly lower than what Kuchma had hoped for.

Initially, deputies from the "For United Ukraine" coalition formed a single faction in the parliament, but in June 2002, it split into several smaller groups. Deputies from the Donetsk region then created the "Regions of Ukraine" faction, which later became the basis for the Party of Regions faction, while those from Luhansk formed their own parliament group called "People's Choice." Mykola Hapochka, former deputy head of Yefremov in the regional administration, became the head of the Luhansk faction.

In the regional Luhansk press from that period, publications may be found where Yefremov unabashedly praised himself for such a wise tactic—the creation of his own group in the Verkhovna Rada. The regional elites had high hopes for it, hopes that, however, did not come to fruition.

"At some point, Yefremov, as known, decided to become an independent entity. From Kyiv, he was politically and geographically separated from two powerful regional formations—the Kharkiv and Donetsk 'clans.' In doing so, Oleksandr Serhiiovych continued to play his political role, subtle but significant. He belonged to the regional leaders who were considered favorites of the president. And the social hierarchy standing below his neighbor Viktor Yanukovych was not something he desired. Therefore, at the first opportunity, Yefremov decided to create his own faction in parliament," wrote the newspaper "Dzerkalo Tyzhnia" in the summer of 2002.

For some time, Yefremov aspired to be an independent player but could not compete with the Donetsk clan for long. Unlike his neighbors, Yefremov's clan lacked sufficient resources. On top of that, a new "orange" threat pushed them towards joining forces. The "Our Ukraine" bloc led by Viktor Yushchenko won the parliamentary elections in 2002, and it was in opposition to Kuchma. Yushchenko received 23.5%, surpassing even the Communists, who had 20%. Another 7.2% went to Yulia Tymoshenko's bloc allied with Yushchenko. After the threat of the "red revenge," so feared in the late '90s, the unexpected result of the national democrats inspired optimism among supporters of the European vector. It became clear that Ukraine was gradually parting ways with its Soviet past.

The result for Yushchenko confirmed his potential as the main opposition candidate in the upcoming presidential elections in 2004. However, it remained unclear who his opponent, the candidate of the current government, would be. Ukraine was undergoing significant changes, with Kuchma's second term coming to an end, and he was not eligible to run for a third, according to the Constitution.

The president needed an "heir apparent," but no one was, well, apparent. Meanwhile, the government's popularity was dropping, as clearly evidenced by the results of the parliamentary elections.

Empowered by their success, the "orange" forces decided to advance further. In April, Yulia Tymoshenko demanded the early resignation of the president and the government. The Socialists immediately joined her demands, and a little later, deputies from "Our Ukraine" did the same. The opposition announced its intention to organize a massive rally and civil disobedience campaign in the fall, dubbed "Rise up, Ukraine!" The beginning of the campaign was set for September 16, on the grim anniversary of the disappearance of journalist Georgiy Gongadze. Politicians also alleged that President Kuchma had ordered his murder.

The protest turned out to be truly massive, uniting both pro-Russian and pro-Western opposition against the current government. In addition to the Socialist Party, the Yulia Tymoshenko Bloc (BYuT), and "Our Ukraine," the Communists also participated in the demonstration. On September 16, 20,000 people gathered on European Square, demanding Kuchma's resignation. After the rally, participants marched towards the Presidential Administration building to deliver the resolution of the rally to him. However, as they approached the Presidential Administration, the opposition was met by a cordon of law enforcement officers that prevented people from entering the building. Protesters began to set up tents in the government district, but the authorities decided to take harsh actions. On the night of September 16-17, the tent camp was dispersed by militsiya forces.

The protests resumed in a week—on September 24. On this day, clashes between demonstrators and law enforcement occurred again near the Presidential Administration building. Later, the events of the fall of 2002 were referred to in the press as a "rehearsal for the Maidan." The "Rise up, Ukraine!" protests indeed made the authorities extremely nervous. Almost all Ukrainian television channels were controlled by the Presidential Administration at that time, providing highly biased coverage of the protest actions. Protesters were portrayed as extremists and radicals. Government representatives accused the opposition of attempting a state coup.

The heads of regional administrations, mostly from the southern and eastern regions and appointed by Kuchma, also made statements in support of the president. The most strongly worded statement came from the head of the Donetsk Regional State Administration, Viktor Yanukovych.

"I would like to say something else about our position regarding the preparation, I'm not afraid to use this word here, for a creeping state coup, political losers being its driving force. Such a position leads not to the politics of creation but to the politics of destruction, with the entire nation becoming a hostage. I think it's time to ask a simple question: who gave them the right to blackmail the whole country? And I think patience can run out very soon," said the governor of the Donetsk region.

Ukrainian TV channels featured Yanukovych's statement in the news. Criticism and threats against the opposition also came from deputies of the Donetsk and Luhansk regional councils. In particular, Luhansk deputies published an appeal promising to obstruct opposition rallies and called on President Kuchma and leaders of all branches of power to "decisively stop the unlawful actions of the organizers of the protest."

We, the deputies of the Luhansk Regional Council, warn the leaders of the 'Rise up, Ukraine!' action that we will do everything to legally counter your actions. Do not try to speak on behalf of the people. They will determine their position on their own," the statement said.

However, another, more interesting, fragment of this document revealed a poorly concealed threat.

"If it comes to the implementation of your declared demands—the complete severance of all relations with Russia—political forces capable of framing the issue differently, regarding Ukraine's accession to the union of Russia and Belarus, will undoubtedly emerge, and the matter will be resolved through a referendum," warned the Luhansk Regional Council.

The specific "political forces" mentioned became clear two years later at the congress in Sievierodonetsk, where the Luhansk Regional Council openly supported separatist calls for the division of Ukraine.

PRIME MINISTER FROM THE PENITENTIARY

In the early 2000s, Leonid Kuchma became involved in a series of unpleasant stories that destroyed his reputation in the West. The murder of journalist Georgiy Gongadze, scandalous recordings by Major Melnychenko, information about the alleged sale of "Kolchuha" radar systems to Iraq in violation of sanctions—all this made the Ukrainian president toxic to leaders of first-world countries and put an end to the so-called "multivector" policy. If, by 2002, Ukraine managed to maintain good relations with both Russia and the West and even planned to apply for NATO membership, the incident with the "Kolchuha" forced the country to abandon those plans.

Given the situation, Kuchma predictably turned towards rapprochement with Russia. The large-scale rallies of opposition only spurred this trend. The national democrats demanded Kuchma's resignation, which increased pressure and forced the president to seek allies in a different camp. These allies he found were oligarchic groups from the eastern part of the country. Those who, thanks to Kuchma, managed to privatize and divvy up key assets in their regions. The Donetsk and Luhansk factions, unlike the "orange" national democrats, leaned towards Russia, and the course towards the East aligned with their financial interests. Thus, the parliamentary elections of 2002 and the protests that followed mapped up that future interregional contention.

Politics here was closely intertwined with the economy. The industry of the Donbas region was primarily oriented toward the Russian market, which determined the pro-

Russian position of the owners of local enterprises. Finding new markets for the "red directors," who were accustomed to working their entire lives under Moscow's directives, was a challenging task. Outdated manufacturing facilities needed modernization, and they had difficulty competing with Western industries. So, the industrialists from the eastern part of Ukraine saw further economic integration with Russia as the optimal solution. For them, it was the easiest way that did not require extra effort, expenses, and creativity.

In these circumstances, Leonid Kuchma's alignment with the political elites of the Donbas region seemed like a logical step. The Donetsk leaders were hardwired to be opponents of the pro-Western national-democratic parties and could help the president rein in the unruly opposition. Thus, Kuchma made his choice—on November 21, 2002, Viktor Yanukovych, the governor of Donetsk, was appointed as the Prime Minister of Ukraine.

With two years remaining until the presidential elections, it meant that if Yanukovych could hold on to his position, he would likely become Kuchma's successor and the ruling party's candidate in 2004. Assessing the balance of power, political groups began quietly coalescing around the main figures of the future presidential campaign—Yanukovych and Yushchenko.

The candidate from the Donetsk faction looked like a poor choice from the get-go. Yanukovych's biography made him an easy target for criticism. Information about the Donetsk governor's criminal record had leaked to the press in the late '90s when he headed the Donetsk Regional State Administration. While in the Donetsk region, this was treated as just another chapter in the book, in other regions of Ukraine, Yanukovych's criminal past was met with disapproval. The new Prime Minister immediately became the subject of numerous jokes and ridicule. His peculiar communication style didn't help his popularity, either. It'd have been hard to nominate a more controversial character for the presidency, but the Donetsk faction had no other candidate.

In Luhansk, the new appointment was met unfavorably—the rise of the Donetsk faction was not good news for the local "Komsomol" faction. With Yanukovych's growing influence, economic pressure from neighbors increased, and the Luhansk faction simply lacked the strength and resources to resist him. Moreover, another factor was Yefremov's personal dislike of Yanukovych, as he sincerely considered himself a more intellectual and presentable figure than Yanukovych, counting on Kuchma's favor.

A few people from the "Komsomol" circles claimed that Yefremov, during those times, viewed Yanukovych with disdain and openly referred to him as a "blockhead." Therefore, when a direct instruction came from Kuchma to Luhansk to start preparing for the presidential elections and ensure the outcome for Yanukovych, Yefremov either refused or took a time out (here versions are different in details but are not contradictory in substance). After a conversation with the governor of Luhansk, Kuchma called his old friend Viktor Tykhonov and threatened him with trouble if the Luhansk faction did not support Yanukovych in the elections.

While Yefremov was negotiating, two of his deputies —Valentyn Dzon and Oleksandr Kobitiev, who had strong business contacts with the Donetsk business group of Yuriy Ivanyushchenko and Ivan Avramov—decided to play their own game. Learning about the conflict, they went to see the president and informed him that they were ready to lead the headquarters and **ensure victory for the Donetsk candidate.**

After talking to them, Kuchma called Tykhonov again and asked what was happening in Luhansk and how he should understand all of this. The reaction did not take long. While Dzon was returning to Luhansk, his things were already packed and taken out of his office.

The conversation with Yefremov, as they say, was "stormy" and almost escalated into a brawl. Dzon was transferred to the position of director of the "Blahovist" fund, through which the election campaign of the "For United Ukraine" party was financed in 2002, and Kobitiev was fired shortly after. There was no public scandal. Moreover, the "farewell" ceremony with Dzon took place in the column hall of the regional administration, and Yefremov even presented him with flowers. However, they remained bitter enemies forever. For many years, Yefremov administratively blocked any attempts by Valentyn Dzon and Oleksandr Kobitiev to return to politics.

Only after this unsuccessful coup within the "Komsomol" ranks did Yefremov agree to ensure Yanukovych's victory in Luhansk. Volodymyr Ivanov, a professional technocrat and political technologist who had been involved in elections in the Luhansk region since 1994, was appointed as Yefremov's first deputy. He became the de facto head of Viktor Yanukovych's campaign headquarters in the region.

The Donetsk elite perceived Yanukovych's appointment as prime minister as their triumph. They had the recent example of Vladimir Putin's rise to power in Russia, who also moved into the presidential chair after working as prime minister. Those who acted with an eye on their eastern neighbor had no doubts that a similar scenario could be brought about in Ukraine. Having advanced their protégé into power and taken over the reins of the country, the Donetsk faction had no plans to relinquish them.

However, President Leonid Kuchma insisted that "Ukraine is not Russia" for a reason (his book with this title was published in 2003, a year before the elections). In Ukraine, it was not enough to simply appoint a government candidate as the "successor" and wait for the populace to approve this decision. Citizens had their own opinions, and for Yanukovych to lead the country, he still had to win the elections.

In the fall of 2003, when it became definitively clear that the incumbent president had chosen Yanukovych as his successor, the entire power system started to conform to him. The remnants of the parliamentary faction "For United Ukraine" once again came together into a single powerful faction aligned with the prime minister. This time, consolidation occurred around the "Regions of Ukraine" faction, mainly composed of individuals from the Donbas region. While this faction had previously been just one of many similar groups in the diverse parliament, by November 2003, the "Regions of Ukraine" became the second-largest faction in the Rada, trailing only behind "Our Ukraine" in terms of the number of deputies. This laid the groundwork for the future Party of Regions, which would become the most powerful Ukrainian party over the next decade and upon which Viktor Yanukovych would rely until his escape from the country.

COLD SHOWER FOR YUSHCHENKO

In the fall of 2003, Viktor Yushchenko had the highest rating among Ukrainian politicians, while the level of trust in the government, on the contrary, was steadily decreasing. The situation was not in favor of the Bankova (Office of the President of Ukraine is situated at Bankova street in Kyiv – T.Ed.) and something needed to be done urgently. Since there was apparently no real dirt on Yushchenko, it was decided to demonize the opponent using a simple technique. Pro-government media increasingly began to compare national democrats with fascists and xenophobes and to portray Yushchenko himself as a puppet of the USA.

A year before the presidential elections, Viktor Yushchenko decided to visit the Donbas. Initially, he planned to speak in Luhansk and then hold a congress of the "Our Ukraine" party in Donetsk. However, in both Yefremov's homeland and Yanukovych's stronghold, he was prevented from doing anything.

On October 20, 2003, the "Forum of Democratic Forces" was scheduled to take place in Luhansk, where the leader of "Our Ukraine" was expected to visit. About two thousand delegates from various parties and civic organizations arrived at the forum, but the Lenin Cultural Center, rented in advance for this event, was suddenly closed "due to the unsafe state of the premises." Moreover, the local administration completely blocked Yushchenko's access to TV channels. IRTA, owned by Volodymyr Landyk (at that time, the head of the Luhansk regional organization of the Party of Regions), simply ceased broadcasting 10 minutes before the scheduled broadcast. The state-owned LOT referred to a lack of available time slots, and the general director of LKT (then owned by the regional council) directly offered to Yushchenko's team to "ask Viktor Tykhonov for airtime." Yushchenko, together with those present, marched from the cultural center to the regional administration, held a rally there, and then left.

The main event of the Donbas tour was supposed to take place on October 31 in Donetsk. The plan was for the congress of "Our Ukraine" to serve as the informal start of Yushchenko's election campaign. Naturally, Donetsk was not an unintentional choice of the venue. The "orange" team wanted to show that Yushchenko was a politician of a national scale, not just a candidate from western regions, as political analysts and journalists loyal to the government called him. However, this idea did not sit well with Yanukovych's team for obvious reasons. In the capital of Donbas, such a move by the chief rival was seen as an encroachment on their territory. Since local politicians were molded by the harsh realities of the '90s, they decided to respond to the challenge even more harshly than in Luhansk and not let the opponent into "their city."

The congress of "Our Ukraine" was supposed to take place in the Youth Palace "Yunist," but the day before, it became clear that holding the event would be an uphill battle. On October 30, a delegation of deputies from "Our Ukraine" arrived in Donetsk, but they were not allowed into "Yunist." At the entrance, the deputies were met by sturdy young men who identified themselves as security. They resorted to force to prevent the deputies from entering.

The "orange" deputy, Yevhen Chervonenko, had to appeal to the secretary of the Donetsk Regional Council, Borys Kolesnikov, to resolve the conflict. Kolesnikov promised that on the morning of October 31, deputies would be able to enter "Yunist" and hold their congress. However, by then, it was already clear that officials wanted to disrupt the event.

They decided to have outside help do the dirty work. While the mayor, governor, and head of the regional council assured that they would not create any obstacles for Yushchenko, officials hastily prepared a massive anti-Yushchenko campaign. They planned to bring workers from Donetsk markets, public sector employees, and students from technical colleges to the "Yunist" building. Meanwhile, the local authorities denied any involvement in this protest. The marginal Slavic Party of Oleksandr Bazyliuk, which had been on the fringes of political life since the mid-90s, came in handy for the officials. It became the formal organizer of the protest against "Our Ukraine."

"We believe that the arrival of a large number of people, hostile to the Russian-speaking population, known for their nationalist radical antics, and, moreover, the holding on our land a congress of sworn enemies of the language of their ancestors is a direct challenge to all of us," said a statement released on behalf of the Slavic Party on the eve of Yushchenko's visit to Donetsk.

In the early morning of October 31, it became clear that the congress would not be held. The Palace of Youth "Yunist" turned out to be occupied by a crowd hostile to Yushchenko. In addition, overnight, advertising boards depicting the leader of "Our Ukraine" in a Nazi uniform appeared throughout Donetsk. The Slavic Party was also involved as the sponsor of those mudslinging ads.

Officials managed to gather a few thousand people under the walls of "Yunist," they distributed offensive anti-Yushchenko posters and Russian flags. Since Yushchenko himself was running late, and the crowd had to be kept in check, people were entertained with alcohol and sweets from the "Konti" factory owned by Borys Kolesnikov. In the olden days, when a video capture gadget wasn't yet in every teenager's pocket, and the internet was available to very few people, there was no need to worry about maintaining decorum. So, the organizers of the rally openly handed out bottles of alcohol and cookies from boxes. But the "feast" still was caught on camera, and Donetsk appeared in an unflattering light in those images.

The appearance and behavior of the people gathered at the rally were, to put it mildly, off-putting. Some of the protesters quickly got drunk, shouted insults, made indecent gestures in front of journalists, burned newspapers, and tore apart the party symbols of "Our Ukraine." Clearly, this whole "show" did not help promote either the Donetsk faction or Donetsk itself. The organizers of the rally only reinforced negative stereotypes about the Donbas and made the region look like a citadel of ignorance and intolerance. The crowd's behavior and primitive anti-Yushchenko caricatures on billboards inadvertently made people in other regions sympathize with Yushchenko. However, Yanukovych's team considered the task accomplished. They managed to create an impression of aggressive rejection of Yushchenko in Donetsk and confirm the words of pro-government experts who claimed that Yushchenko was popular only in the western regions of Ukraine.

Yushchenko arrived in Donetsk by plane, but he also was met with a "warm" reception at the airport. On the instructions of local authorities, a few hundred people were brought there, attempting to block the leader of "Our Ukraine" and prevent him from entering the city. When Yushchenko finally managed to break through the crowd with the help of Alpha special forces, he first went to the offices of the Donetsk Regional State Administration to have a word (or a few choice words) with representatives of local authorities.

The head of the Donetsk Regional State Administration, Anatolii Blyznyuk, awkwardly denied the involvement of Donetsk authorities in the scandalous events, but, as usual, no one believed his justification.

"You made an agreement with the management of the 'Yunist' Palace of Youth. What complaints do you have against me? I was in that venue, asking people why they came. They said they came to see Yushchenko and talk to him. I understood that it was impossible to throw them out," lied Blyznyuk in response to accusations of organizing the disruption of the "Our Ukraine" congress.

In turn, Viktor Yushchenko was outraged by the billboards that portrayed him as a Nazi. "My father spent four years in Auschwitz. For you, flunkies!" the leader of the "orange" party emotionally rebuked Blyznyuk and Kolesnikov. This phrase became a gift for Yanukovych's political consultants. Local media gleefully took it out of context and presented it as if Yushchenko was not addressing the representatives of the local authorities but was insulting all residents of Donetsk by calling them "flunkies." Later, this quote was regularly used in Yanukovych's propaganda as evidence of Yushchenko's anti-Donbas sentiments.

"Donbas residents! Have you forgotten how Yushchenko, visiting Donetsk a year ago, called us 'flunkies'? Don't you understand that if he wins, in his disdain, he will "tear apart" our region?" wrote the newspaper "Holos Donbassa," which was published by Yanukovych's team during the election campaign (Issue №7 dated November 12, 2004).

The events of October 31, 2003, were not just

another political scandal. That day in Donetsk set alarm bells ringing for Ukraine. After a long break, just as it did in the early 1990s, the Donetsk political elite once again utilized pro-Russian fringe organizations and their slogans to blackmail political opponents. It became clear that, for the sake of victory in the elections, Yanukovych's team was willing to resort to drastic measures, including playing the separatist card.

These alarming trends did not escape the attention of journalists. "Today, in Donetsk, there was a rehearsal for a civil war! If a drunken crowd simply shouted 'Yushchenko, go away!' it would be a political confrontation. However, when anti-Yushchenko sentiments are fueled by interethnic and interregional symbols and calls, it is the fanning of interethnic hostility," wrote the well-known Donetsk journalist Serhii Harmash the day after the events.

"The most interesting and important is the substantive analysis of slogans used in Donetsk. The conclusions are not comforting. Blinded by fear of Yushchenko and hatred for him, the authorities bring volatile issues such as language issues, interethnic relations, relations between the West and East of Ukraine, and its geopolitical orientation to the forefront of the election campaign. Without a doubt, the slogans for Donetsk "protesters" were not devised in student dormitories but in government offices. It was there that they decided what equipment to arm the demonstrators with, and the Russian tricolors in the hands of drunken students did not appear by chance," wrote journalists from "Ukrainska Pravda" in the article "The Split of Ukraine as the Main Election Strategy of Incumbent Authorities" on November 3, 2003.

Anatolii Blyznyuk and Borys Kolesnikov, who were the real organizers of the mass action against Yushchenko, did manage to set in motion the wheel of interregional hostility, which unfolded throughout the entire pre-election campaign. The repugnant behavior of the drunken crowd in Donetsk triggered a completely predictable reaction among Yushchenko's supporters in other regions. "Ukrainska Pravda" and other opposition media wrote about the "Neanderthal political culture of the Sarmatian region." In Donetsk, in turn, they eagerly seized any negativity coming from the opponents' camp and presented it as evidence of the "orange" party's biased attitude towards the Donbas. After October 31, this momentum was beyond stopping.

Certain tensions that existed between the western and eastern regions of Ukraine escalated to the breaking point. And this happened not only because of Yanukovych and his team but also because of President Leonid Kuchma, who in good time could have reined in the Donetsk faction and prohibited them from fanning the flames of enmity but chose not to do so. The second president of Ukraine, whom many still consider a wise and competent leader, merely silently observed how the Prime Minister fueled tension and pitted citizens against each other.

Journalists' concerns were confirmed in 2004 when Yanukovych's political technologists divided Ukrainian citizens into classes, and a song about civil war with a poorly concealed threat played on television. The main pre-election strategy of Yanukovych and Kuchma became enmity and division. However, a year before the elections, no one could have imagined how far politicians would be willing to go.

THE BURNING YEAR 2004

To this day, the standoff between Yanukovych and Yushchenko remains the dirtiest and most scandalous election campaign in the country's history. At the end of 2004, Ukraine found itself on the brink of real territorial division. Having suffered defeat, Yanukovych's team at some point tried to claim a "consolation prize": the southeastern regions of Ukraine, where Yanukovych received significantly more votes than Viktor Yushchenko. Fortunately, they decided to abandon this plan at the last moment.

The actual voting took place after months of escalating tensions and demonizing political opponents. In the Donbas, the election campaign at times resembled wartime propaganda. Yanukovych's political strategists sought to convince the population of the eastern regions that the "orange" faction hated the Donbas and wanted to destroy it. They claimed that if Yushchenko were to win, he would punish the region for their defiance. This way, the Party of Regions tried to rally the electorate in the region; it was crucial for Yanukovych to ensure a high turnout of potential supporters.

Residents of Donetsk were led to believe that the leader of "Our Ukraine" would ban the Russian language, exploit the Donbas to feed impoverished western Ukraine, reduce pensions and salaries for Donbas residents, and even bury nuclear waste from Europe and the USA in closed mines. The last scare tactic has become what we would now call a viral meme. Perhaps Viktor Yushchenko and his team did not genuinely harbor great affection for Donbas, but they clearly had no intention of doing any of the things their opponents alleged.

The spread of the smearing campaign reached unprecedented levels. Leaflets depicting Yushchenko as Hitler were placed into the mailboxes of residents in the Donetsk and Luhansk regions, along with newspapers from the Slavic Party accusing Yushchenko of Russophobia and fascism. The agitational newspaper "Holos Donbassa" occasionally ran compilations of alleged Internet quotes from Yushchenko supporters that insulted Donbas and its residents. One such collection, under the telling headline "We are not considered humans," was published in № 7 on November 12. In Luhansk, the newspaper "Izvestiya Luganshchiny" of the Luhansk Regional Council was used for such purposes. Also, at the taxpayers' expense, the regional council placed finished, already typeset pages with anti-Yushchenko materials in other newspapers.

In the fall of 2004, a rather malicious advertisement gained widespread popularity—a commercial in which the map of Ukraine was divided into three parts. Western regions were labeled as first-class, central ones as second-class, and southern and eastern ones were called third-class. The caption to the map asserted: "This is how their Ukraine looks." Unlike other cases of mudslinging, this commercial did not just discredit the "orange" faction. It incited discord in the society. Later, it turned out that the idea of three classes of Ukrainians was born in Yanukovych's shadow headquarters led by Andriy Klyuyev. The concept belonged to political consultant Volodymyr Hranovskyi, and the formal sponsor of this advertisement was the already mentioned Oleksandr Bazylyiuk from the Slavic Party. However, it should be noted that President Kuchma's entourage also actively contributed to their efforts to splinter Ukraine. The scandalous advertisement was aired heavily on the "Inter" TV channel, controlled at that time by People's Deputy Ihor Pluzhnykov from the SDPU(o) faction led by Viktor Medvedchuk.

With even greater zeal, local television engaged in propaganda. On the Luhansk State Television (LOT) channel, they incessantly aired clips where an audio recording of Yushchenko's speech was superimposed on a psychedelic video sequence with marching Nazis, rotting oranges, and animals fighting each other. They appealed not to reason but to emotions. And such a spectacle left viewers feeling uneasy, even those with nerves of steel and critical thinking.

Despite the overt simplicity of the anti-Yushchenko materials, they were mostly uncritically accepted in the Donbas region. Many people genuinely believed these scare tactics and were seriously afraid of the "orange plague." Over time, residents of the eastern regions began to regard the mild-mannered and intellectual Yushchenko as virtually the embodiment of evil. However, in other regions, things were going quite differently. Overall, throughout the country, Yushchenko's rating in September 2004, despite all the government's efforts, exceeded Yanukovych's rating by 7–9%. Surveys indicated that in the second round, the opposition candidate would win. For example, according to the SOCIS Center, in the second round of the presidential elections, 40.9% of voters were ready to vote for Yushchenko, while 31.8% were for Yanukovych.

Yanukovych often caused his troubles all by himself. Time and again, he found himself in awkward situations that only confirmed the widespread belief that his intelligence level wasn't particularly high. First, there was the widely popular story of filling out a questionnaire in which Yanukovych made numerous mistakes, including misspelling his own academic title. The prime minister wrote the word "professor" with two "f"s, and instantly created a new meme: "proffessor." People started laughing at Yanukovych. Yushchenko's headquarters quickly put together a humorous video titled "Operation 'Proffessor'" and distributed it on CDs and the internet.

A curious incident in Ivano-Frankivsk gained even more notoriety. During Yanukovych's visit to the city, a student named Dmytro Romaniuk threw a raw chicken egg at the prime minister. This minor episode might not have attracted much attention if Yanukovych himself had not acted strangely. For some reason, the prime minister pretended to faint and dramatically fell into the arms of his security guards in front of a crowd of students and journalists. The Yanukovych team tried to portray the "egg" incident as an attempted assassination, but this only added to the damage. The oppositional "5 Kanal" (The Fifth Channel) aired footage of the incident, clearly showing that Yanukovych was hit by a raw egg, not a "heavy blunt object" as claimed by the prime minister's press secretary, Hanna Herman. Of course, this incident did not boost the popularity of the government candidate.

To achieve victory in such circumstances, the prime minister needed the highest possible voter turnout in the Donbas. To accomplish this, Yanukovych's team had to invent more and more horrors. People were frightened by the prospect of a civil war that supposedly would start if Viktor Yushchenko won. There were reports claiming that Yushchenko was allegedly preparing armed militants in western Ukraine to seize power and "pacify" the Donbas.

The pro-government press designated the pro-Yushchenko organization "Pora" as the main "orange" bogeyman, depicting its members as bloodthirsty nationalists and hardcore radicals. "Pora" was accused of preparing an armed coup and being financed by the United States.

Before the first round of the presidential elections, flyers appeared on the streets of the Donbas cities. They featured Viktor Yushchenko in the likeness of Uncle Sam, asking, "Are you ready for civil war?" Russian singer Iosif Kobzon, who supported Yanukovych, persistently sang about the war. The music video for his song "If there is no civil war" was constantly played on TV ahead of the vote. All these gloomy prophecies resembled blackmail more than warnings. The message from Yanukovych's team was easily read between the lines: "If we lose, there will be a civil war."

Despite all the efforts of Yanukovych's staff, the Donetsk region did not show a high voter turnout in the first round of the presidential elections. In terms of this indicator, it ranked only sixth among Ukrainian regions. In contrast, voters in the western regions, where Yushchenko had support, turned out to be more conscientious. Yanukovych's campaign again tried to use this situation to incite interregional discord and pit the East against the West. "We cannot allow Western Ukraine to decide the fate of Donbas; we need to show them the 'Donetsk character'"—this was roughly the running theme of the Donetsk and Luhansk press in those days.

A vivid example of such incitement was an article titled "We Won't Surrender Donbas," published in the newspaper "Donetskyi Kriazh" (№42, November 19–25, 2004).

> "The election results directly concern each of us. Let's recall the recent history—the beginning and the middle of the nineties. When the Donbas worked tirelessly, and all the profit went to Kyiv, and then, like a Popandopulo from a Soviet movie, it distributed the earned income among the regions: this for you, Donbas, this for me, this again for me, me, me. Such a policy only stopped after a powerful economic and political elite was formed in the Donbas, which managed to establish itself so well that it now realistically lays claim to nationwide leadership and has the support of half the country. And now, in

such a situation where every vote counts, a quarter of our compatriots stayed at home. The Donetsk region in Ukraine ranks only sixth in terms of voter turnout. Ternopil, Volyn, Rivne, Lviv, and Sumy regions turned out to be more conscientious than we were. Do you see a pattern here? Four of these regions are located in Western Ukraine. While some of our compatriots are leisurely relaxing, decisions about our future are being made for us there," – asserted the article.

Here, in this single paragraph, you can see several manipulative claims actively used by Yanukovych's team. The first is the worn-out assertion that "Donbas worked, and Kyiv took the profits," which was used by Donbas separatist-federalists as early as the early 1990s. The second is the legend of the "strong entrepreneur" – the economic and political elite of the Donbas, which allegedly "managed to establish itself well." And the third is an attempt to exploit the wounded spirit of local patriotism: "Westerners are deciding for us."

In reality, it was, of course, a bit different. Kyiv, as an abstract entity, did not take away the Donbas's profits. The decisions were made by very real people with very real names. Incidentally, residents of the Donbas elected these people to office. As we already know, back in 1993, the government was effectively led by a Donetsk native, Yukhym Zvyahilsky, who was propelled to such heights with the support of miners' strikes. In 1994, Leonid Kuchma won the presidential elections—the Donbas considered him their candidate and voted for him. The region's residents had only themselves to blame for any unfair distribution of budget funds if indeed it had occurred. However, Yanukovych's PR teams ignored this fact and tried to convince the population of Donbas that in Kyiv, some foreign and hostile power had been sitting for all those previous years.

The painstaking attempts to portray the Donetsk faction as talented managers couldn't hold up to scrutiny, either. The Donetsk regional elite, which had emerged from the criminal murk of the 1990s, could not explain the origin of their fortunes for obvious reasons. Among them were no geniuses who had created new enterprises from scratch. Donetsk oligarchs were only able to rise to the economic and political elite because, due to political circumstances, they received state-owned plants and factories. They didn't buy them at a fair price but rather received them as a reward for their loyalty to Kuchma. Their business was not above board and often involved various corruption schemes and illegal dealings.

The "Komsomol" faction from Luhansk also did not fit the role of the country's saviors. Desolation was rife in the Luhansk region. Some cities, like Brianka and Zorynsk, were literally moribund. Empty Khrushchiovka-style apartments had broken windows and no roofs. The people who still lived in them heated their apartments with wood-burning stoves and fetched water from wells to the upper floors. In 2003, an outbreak of hepatitis A occurred in Sukhodolsk, just 40 kilometers from Luhansk, due to deteriorating water pipes. The threat of such epidemics persisted in other cities—water was supplied for a few scheduled hours a week in the southern part of the region. The largest industrial enterprises in the Luhansk region, such as Lysychansk Oil Refinery or "Luhanskteplovoz," essentially did not operate. Other plants were gradually dismantled by unemployed people for building materials and scrap metal.

The political propaganda of the Party of Regions ignored these facts. Obviously, Yanukovych's team was not interested in having the residents of the Donbas objectively assess what was happening. The goal of this team was the opposite—to play on fear and emotions and to evoke in people a misguided sense of threat and hatred towards the supporters of Viktor Yushchenko. That's why the residents of the Donbas were mainly threatened with concentration camps and war—there was simply no other way to scare people who had trouble meeting their basic needs for food, water, and shelter.

> "The Donetsk registration or origin can lower shut you out of admission to prestigious universities or advancement in your career on a nationwide scale. Our opponents have duly appreciated the Donetsk character, assertiveness, and professionalism. They don't want to deal with such competitors anymore. And that's why they won't let us raise our heads," stated the aforementioned article "We won't surrender the Donbas," published in the newspaper "Donetskyi Kriazh."

The claim about "freeloaders from Western Ukraine" was constantly reiterated, suggesting that the industrial East was forced to support them. The Donbas media regularly emphasized that western regions produce less than the eastern ones, never mentioning the significant volumes of subsidies directed to the Luhansk and Donetsk regions to support the unprofitable coal industry. There was no practical sense in such calculations since, by law, all Ukrainian voters are equal, and the weight of a citizen's vote does not depend on their income level. A scholar, a retiree, a student, and an entrepreneur in all regions of Ukraine have the right to cast only one ballot. Measuring the level of income or GDP per capita in different regions could be done endlessly, but the value of voters' voices in poor regions was not diminished by this. However, the Yanukovych team persisted in doing so. The goal of such publications was clear —to incite hatred in residents of the eastern regions toward those in the western regions and thereby motivate them to participate in the elections and vote for Yanukovych.

"According to official data from the Ministry of Finance, the Ivano-Frankivsk region currently spends 43.6% more than it earns, the Ternopil region—41.1% more, the Chernivtsi region—26.7% more, and the Zakarpattia region—11.3% more. The donor regions, which contribute to the maintenance of other regions, include Donetsk, Dnipropetrovsk, Zaporizhzhia, Kharkiv, and Odesa. That is, Eastern residents divert significant funds to support pensioners and teachers in the western regions governed by 'nationalists'. Local propagandists direct these funds to organize expensive provocations.

Here arises the question: are the subsidies deducted through Kyiv from the budgets of the Eastern regions of Ukraine too substantial? Perhaps it would be fairer to keep more of the earned funds locally. Could these finances be used to increase the salaries of the working population? In the Donetsk region, for instance, metallurgists and miners work in challenging and hazardous conditions, contributing to the country's economy, yet the average salary in September of this year was only 771 hryvnias. For comparison, in Kyiv, the average salary is 997 hryvnias and 34 kopecks. It's worth noting that Kyiv residents don't go into mines or stand near furnaces but prosper, like the residents of the western regions, thanks to the mooching of funds from other regions. Perhaps it makes sense to redistribute hard-earned money differently? Then the salary of a Donetsk miner would be much higher than that of a Kyiv official or a Galician loafer," stated the article "Left Bank, Right Bank" in the newspaper "Donetskyi Kriazh" (№41, November 12–18, 2004).

A lot has been written on how to manipulate using statistics. Given enough imagination, anyone can be labeled as a freeloader, as the situation dictates.

Even in a single region, there is always a way to draw an arbitrary line between poor and affluent areas. Even in the case of the Donbas region, the industry is notoriously unevenly distributed. Some areas in the Donetsk and Luhansk regions lack large cities and heavy industry manufacturing, while others have a very high concentration of industrial manufacturing. Moreover, the state of this industry was often dismal. In the early 2000s, some mining towns, having undergone destructive restructuring, were zones of social disaster. Many mines were closed, and the population left for work, abandoning homes and buildings. The budgets of these mining towns were hopelessly in the red and required substantial subsidies, but Yanukovych's propaganda conveniently never mentioned these "freeloaders." The aim was to generate hatred only towards those "dependents" who lived in the western regions of Ukraine and spoke Ukrainian.

The newspaper calls to keep more earnings at home and "increase the salaries of the working population using these funds" were outright nonsense. In 2004, the largest industrial enterprises in the Donbas region were already in private hands, and the salary levels were determined not by the government but by individuals like Rinat Akhmetov, Valentyn Landyk, Yukhym Zvyahilsky, the Klyuyev brothers, and other newly minted oligarchs. They indeed paid low salaries to their employees while rapidly accumulating wealth themselves. However, the residents of the Donbas were fed the narrative that some "Galician loafers" were responsible for their low salaries. And people believed these insinuations because it was psychologically easier to believe in the deceitful actions of a distant and wicked enemy than to search for the reasons for their failures within themselves.

The Party of Regions did not come up with anything new. Throughout history, the image of an external enemy has been used by politicians to mobilize society. With the help of this simple technique, rulers and leaders have succeeded in rallying and directing the masses against certain states or social groups for centuries. For the Donbas region, this external enemy was the residents of the western regions of Ukraine who had long been deliberately dehumanized in the media controlled by the local elites.

But despite all these efforts, Viktor Yanukovych still failed to win. The opposition candidate won the first round by a small margin, and the fate of the presidency was to be decided in the second round. There, the candidate from the ruling party faced a disappointing result. On the evening of November 21, after the voting ended, the results of the National Exit Poll were released. According to these data, Viktor Yushchenko defeated Viktor Yanukovych by a margin of 11%. 54% of voters cast their votes for the opposition candidate and 43% for the prime minister. However, the official vote count showed the opposite results—Yanukovych was ahead of Yushchenko by a few percentage points. Moreover, in the second round, there was a sudden abnormal increase in voter turnout in the Donbas. Yushchenko's team asserted that the voting results were falsified, and opposition supporters took to the streets. The Orange Revolution had begun.

On November 22, the session of the Lviv City Council recognized Viktor Yushchenko as the elected President of Ukraine. Deputies stated that they would execute his acts and orders. Following suit, a number of other regions of Ukraine, where Yushchenko won by a significant margin, refused to recognize the official election results. People with orange symbols began to take to the streets in Kyiv.

Yanukovych's team was not prepared for that. The Party of Regions did not anticipate that, despite ensuring

Yanukovych's campaign with manipulation, a majority in the commissions, high voter turnout, protocols with stamps, and the **Central Election Commission of Ukraine** (CEC) decision recognizing him as the winner, they could face public resistance. Even more surprising for them was that Leonid Kuchma, at the crucial moment, refused to act forcefully and prevent the outbreak of protests. Yanukovych's team realized that the situation was not turning in their favor, and the power was slipping through their fingers. This was reflected in the tone of TV reports and newspaper publications in media outlets under their control. The protests in the capital were labeled "orange psychosis," "orange coven," and "orange plague." Open threats and calls for the division of Ukraine began to emerge.

In all major cities of the Donbas, rallies in support of Yanukovych were organized by local authorities. At a rally in Slovyansk, local politician and businessman Valentyn Rybachuk stated that if supporters of Yushchenko did not recognize Yanukovych as president, the Donetsk region would secede from Ukraine and join the Russian Federation.

> "If our guarantor of the Constitution, Leonid Danylovych Kuchma, cannot defend the Constitution, and the lawlessness that Yushchenko and his team committed today continues, if the incitement to a civil war in Ukraine continues, then the Donetsk region in the Southeastern part of Ukraine, is going to set up a referendum. If you do not meet our demands, if you do not recognize Viktor Fedorovych Yanukovych as the president, who was backed by 15 million people and rightfully won in the elections on November 21, we, the Donetsk region, will join the Russian Federation as an autonomous republic," threatened Rybachuk.

Later, in 2006, he won the mayoral elections in

Slovyansk and, until 2010, led the city that would later become infamous for ensuing tragic events.

The demonization of opponents also gained momentum. For instance, a widely circulated story about Yulia Tymoshenko allegedly proposing from the Maidan podium in Kyiv to "fence off Donbas with barbed wire." Supporters of Yanukovych failed to find any documented evidence of this incident, but the tale stuck with people. Propaganda-fueled masses didn't require proof, and to this day, there are people who claim to have seen a video recording of Tymoshenko's speech with their own eyes, although no such video ever existed.On November 24, 2004, the Luhansk Regional Council held an emergency session. The deputies decided to ban the broadcast of opposition media—5 Kanal and TRC Era—on the territory of the Luhansk region. Additionally, they appealed to deputies of local councils at all levels with a proposal to hold an All-Ukrainian Congress of Local Council Deputies in Kharkiv and demanded that the Central Election Commission immediately announce the official results of the presidential elections.

On November 26, Viktor Tykhonov and Oleksandr Yefremov took it a step further. During the next session, the deputies decided to create an executive committee of the regional council and revoke the powers of the regional administration. Essentially, this meant establishing a prototype of a regional government not prescribed by the Constitution. Oleksandr Yefremov was elected as the head of the executive committee. Additionally, during the session, deputies also voted to create a "working group for the formation of the tax, payment, banking, and financial systems of the Southern-Eastern territories."

Within two days, on November 28, a similar decision was adopted by the Donetsk Regional Council. Deputies nominated Anatoliy Blyznyuk, the governor of Donetsk region, to lead the executive committee. In addition, the deputies decided to create their own armed formations—a "local militia"—and conduct a regional referendum "on the federal structure of Ukraine and granting Donetsk region the status of an autonomous republic within the federation."

Later, politicians of Luhansk and Donetsk explained their actions in 2004 by a desire to respond to the unwillingness of western regions to recognize Viktor Yanukovych's victory. However, this was sheer deception, as the regional councils of Volyn and Galicia only spoke about non-recognition of the CEC data and disagreement with them. No one in Lviv or Lutsk declared the creation of "independent republics" or the formation of a "financial system of western territories."

Media outlets under the control of the Party of Regions continued to fuel frenzy. In issue №43 of the "Donetskyi Kriazh" newspaper (November 26 - December 2), an interview with Russian State Duma deputy Oleksandr Krutov was published, in which he referred to the western regions of Ukraine as the "Galician tail that wants to wag the whole of Ukraine."

> "The current situation has highlighted not only a geographical and territorial but also an ideological split. So, if the 'Galician tail' wants to wag the whole of Ukraine, I am confident that all of Ukraine will not want this. The tail does not wag the dog, and if the westerners do not want to live in one state, the residents of the East have every right to express their opinion on this," stated Krutov.

This statement was overtly manipulative because not just Galicia voted for Yushchenko. He won in the majority of the regions in Ukraine, including those on the left bank of the Dnipro—in Sumy, Chernihiv, Poltava, and also in Kyiv. Moreover, the leaders of the Orange Revolution were not originally from western Ukraine. Viktor Yushchenko was born in the Sumy region, not far from the border with Russia, and his main associates—Yulia Tymoshenko, Petro Poroshenko, Yevhen Chervonenko, Davyd Zhvania, in general, were from the southeastern regions or other countries. However, in the Donbas media, enemies had already been designated. And these enemies were not just opposition politicians but also fellow citizens living on the opposite political pole of the country.

In the next issue of the same newspaper, an interview with one of the Cossack leaders of the Luhansk region, Ivan Sotnykov, was published, in which he openly threatened violence against representatives of the "Galician political elite." In response to the journalist's question about whether the division of Ukraine scares the Cossack leader, Sotnykov replied directly:

> "I personally foresaw such a course of events long ago. The Galician political elite, throughout all the years of 'independence,' forcefully imposed its vision of the future of the country, disregarding the Russian-speaking regions, consistently ignoring their rights. They were deaf to our protests and expressions of dissent. They labeled referendums in our regions on language and economic issues as unlawful. By closing the border with Russia, they cut off our factories from sales markets, condemning industrial regions to hunger and poverty. But everything comes to an end. We have chosen our president, and there is no other way. If I have to lay down my life for the right cause, so be it. Cossacks were never and will never be slaves, and they will never allow anyone to despise them."

Cossack Sotnykov did not mention any specific names

of representatives of the "Galician political elite." Who he was referring to remains a mystery. Because in the history of independent Ukraine until 2004, there was no president or prime minister from Galicia. However, there were many figures from the southern and eastern regions who held high positions. The most significant figures of the '90s political scene—Yukhym Zvyahilsky, Leonid Kuchma, Pavlo Lazarenko, Valeriy Pustovoitenko—were prominent representatives of those regions that were supposedly "oppressed" in Ukraine. Moreover, a Donetsk region native took the post of prime minister in the early 2000s.

By the way, Ataman Ivan Sotnykov did carry out his threats. He took up arms in 2014, ten years after the Orange Revolution. With the beginning of the so-called "Russian Spring," Sotnykov joined one of the Cossack formations and sided with the "LPR," fighting against the armed forces of Ukraine.

SIEVIERODONETSK CRISIS

On November 28, 2004, at the initiative of the elites working for Yanukovych, an All-Ukrainian Congress of People's Deputies and Deputies of Local Councils of all levels (later known as the Sievierodonetsk congress) took place in Sievierodonetsk, in the Luhansk region. Despite the name, the congress was not national: formally, representatives from most regions of the country were present, but the leaders of the southern and eastern regions played the leading role. In terms of scale, this event was unprecedented in Ukrainian history. For the first time, the country found itself on the brink of division and civil conflict. Direct threats of dividing Ukraine into several parts were heard from the podium, and these were not issued by fringe characters from red-brown organizations but by national-level politicians.

Sievierodonetsk was chosen as the venue for the congress, apparently for political reasons, to avoid gathering in Kharkiv, Luhansk, or Donetsk, thereby not indicating the priority of any regional group. In addition, Sievierodonetsk had a suitable venue for the congress—the Ice Palace, which could accommodate several thousand delegates. The moderator of the congress was Viktor Tykhonov, the chairman of the Luhansk Regional Council and one of the leaders of the Luhansk political clan.

After the second round of the presidential elections, it became evident that for the regional elites of the eastern regions securing their own political influence was a matter of life and death. One of the leaders of the Donetsk clan, Borys Kolesnikov, spoke directly and unequivocally about this. The full text of his speech is available in the transcript of the Sievierodonetsk Congress.

"Now we consider it vitally necessary for all regional councils to conduct referendums in their territories. The first issue to be put to a referendum is a vote of no confidence in all higher state authorities that have violated the law. The second is the creation of a new Ukrainian Southeastern state, a federative republic, where the interests and rights of citizens and regions will be actually protected, not just declared. We assure the world community that the new state entity will have the most democratic constitution in the world," Kolesnikov stated in his speech. He proposed making Kharkiv the capital of the new Southeastern state. The audience in the hall repeatedly punctuated his speech with applause.

Raisa Bohatyriova, who served as the Minister of Health in Mykola Azarov's government until 2014, also spoke no less radically at the congress:

"On the day when someone suddenly decides to conduct a repeat vote (the second round of presidential elections —A/N), we won't participate in it. Instead, we will hold a referendum on the creation of the Southeastern state!" she declared.

Other deputies expressed similar sentiments.

"We gathered here, first of all, to show the entire Ukrainian people that the East exists, that we have made our choice. And I support the idea of truly dividing and living independently. We will find a way to live, we will be able to provide for ourselves," said People's Deputy from Luhansk region, Liudmyla Kyrychenko.

"We are firmly convinced that negotiations with us are possible; the only thing that cannot be done is putting pressure on us. They pressured us and triggered today's union of the South and the East; continued pressure pushes us towards federation. My dear ones, from this podium, I want to say—do not push us so much that we'd seek sovereignty!" threatened another People's Deputy from the Luhansk region, Vasyl Nadraha (later he served as the Minister of Social Policy in Azarov's government).

"Yushchenko, look at me! Do you think I can be afraid of you? It's better to die standing than to live on my knees under your governance!" played up the situation then Luhansk Governor Oleksandr Yefremov. But it seemed that he himself believed in the phantoms created by the anti-Yushchenko propaganda.

The appearance of Russian politicians at the congress, historically perceived by the Donbas regional elites as senior comrades, added to the symbolism of these events. The main guest at Sievierodonetsk was the then-mayor of Moscow, Yury Luzhkov, who, at the very beginning of his speech, reminded those present that Vladimir Putin was the first to congratulate Yanukovych on his victory. The Party of Regions apparently hoped to intimidate their opponents and give significance to their initiative with Luzhkov's presence. However, the attendance of the Moscow mayor at the congress did not help Yanukovych.

Openly separatist statements and this readiness of the Donbas elite to tear the country apart for the sake of gaining power left a terrible impression on Ukrainian society. While the population in the Donbas and Crimea may have been predominantly pro-Russian, in other regions, the blackmail of the regional leaders and calls for secession were perceived negatively. Even Ukrainians who did not support the Orange Revolution were not inclined toward chaos and armed confrontation. Most importantly, the then-President Leonid Kuchma vehemently disagreed with such a scenario.

No matter how much the "orange hand-fed coven" (as Yury Luzhkov called the Orange Revolution in his speech) was blasted from the stands in Sievierodonetsk, the Regional Party's gathering was essentially another way to slam Kuchma. Some speakers directly blamed the acting president for not cracking down on participants of opposition rallies and not suppressing the protests. Kuchma's response did not take long.

The next day, on November 29, the Prosecutor General's Office and the Security Service of Ukraine (SBU) initiated criminal cases regarding the encroachment on the territorial integrity of Ukraine and intentional actions aimed at violently changing and overthrowing the constitutional order. These cases were initiated not at the request of Viktor Yushchenko, who at that time had no authority to give directives to government agencies. The legitimate incumbent president, Kuchma, intended to prosecute the organizers of the Sievierodonetsk Congress.

The Party of Regions clearly understood this message. The Donetsk Regional Council hastily reviewed its decision to hold a referendum, and the decision of the Luhansk Regional Council was challenged by the prosecutor's office. On December 3, the Supreme Court of Ukraine declared the results of the second round of the presidential elections invalid and ordered a rerun. After the Central Election Commission (CEC) scheduled the date for the repeat second round of elections, Donetsk and Luhansk realized that they had lost. The referendum on creating the "Southeastern state" never took place.

Borys Kolesnikov, who just called emphatically for the division of Ukraine and the creation of a new state with its capital in Kharkiv, quickly changed his plans. On December 10 in Donetsk, he informed journalists that they had decided to scrap the idea of holding a referendum in

January 2005.

"We have decided not to hold referendums in any of the regions until constitutional amendments on federal reform are in line with the legal framework. Let the experts analyze the situation, and then we will draw up a conclusive decision. And then it makes sense to hold a nationwide referendum," announced Kolesnikov. In fact, this meant acknowledging their defeat by the Donetsk side. However, it was not a war that was lost, but only in a battle.

In late December, a rerun of the second round of the presidential elections took place, in which Yushchenko won with a nearly 10% advantage. After this, Yanukovych's team had only two options—either to escalate tensions and incite uprisings among their supporters in eastern Ukraine or to accept defeat and move into opposition. In 2004, common sense prevailed. There was no one willing to escalate the situation and take up arms.

Throughout the whole campaign, only a few incidents of physical confrontation were recorded. One of the most serious incidents was an attack by young men armed with hammers and iron bars on a rally of "Our Ukraine" supporters in Luhansk, which occurred on November 29, in the hottest days of the political crisis. Initially, the local police stated that Yushchenko's supporters attacked Yanukovych's supporters and beat them. However, a few days later, the police finally admitted that it was representatives of the "orange" camp who were beaten.

Another incident occurred in the Donetsk region. An attack took place on a convoy of members of the organization "Pora," which arrived in Donetsk on December 21, 2004, shortly before the final and decisive vote. Yanukovych's supporters were waiting on the bypass road in Donetsk for the so-called "train of friendship." When the "orange" convoy approached, about 50 cars blocked its path, and burly, fit men threw stones and bottles at opponents, as well as punctured the tires of several cars. Representatives of "Pora" were unable to enter Donetsk on that occasion.

Betting on Yanukovych and the Donetsk faction, which had an all too obvious criminal background, was a major mistake of President Kuchma. And this mistake was not only in the fact that Yanukovych ultimately failed due to his high disapproval ratings. His candidacy had other consequences. It led to an increase in interregional tension, divided society, and sowed the seeds of future conflicts.

Yanukovych's persona elicited a completely understandable disgust among millions of Ukrainians. However, his political strategists worked diligently to ensure that all the negative things said about the Prime Minister, his Donetsk supporters perceived as aimed at them.

"They mock Yanukovych because they dislike the Donbas. They insult him, calling him a 'con,' because they believe that thugs and criminals inhabit the Donbas. For them, we are third-rate people," such were the messages that Yanukovych's team imposed on its electorate throughout the entire campaign.

"Commentators speak cheerfully about the backward agrarian Galicia, portraying the residents of the industrial and advanced East as gloomy, dull creatures, calling them 'bandits,' 'fascists,' 'occupiers,' and no one holds back in their word choices. American puppets pay no attention to the opinions of the 15 million people who voted for Yanukovych. They ruthlessly beat up on the industrial East, which has been supporting Western Ukraine for many years," wrote the newspaper "Donetskyi Kriazh" in December 2004 (Issue №43).

The plan was simple. Without a clear election program and real achievements to boast about, Yanukovych's team relied on the irrational—on emotions. Political strategists appealed to long-standing fears and stereotypes deeply rooted in the hearts of Donbas residents since Soviet times, and this plan turned out to be correct. Yanukovych himself had little chance of becoming a people's favorite. He was not a charismatic speaker or at least a talented demagogue, traits that people have always liked. He couldn't boast of success in business, wasn't known for a brilliant mind, and didn't deliver fiery speeches exposing the flaws of the system. A clumsy bureaucrat who writes his academic title with a mistake and has been convicted twice is definitely not the candidate that normal people would want to see as the president of their country. But it was enough to transform the political confrontation into the "us against the fascists" narrative, and the tables were turned.

The 2004 elections turned into a standoff of myths rather than a competition of programs. Voters were not interested in what specific proposals a candidate had, what reforms he planned to implement, or what path he envisioned for overcoming the prolonged economic crisis of the '90s. People went to vote "for their own" and "against the orange plague." From an awkward blockhead, Yanukovych transformed into "their guy," who stood up against the "American lackey" Yushchenko.

However, the supporters of Yanukovych didn't mourn for long after the defeat. The "Orange Fuhrer" turned out to be not as frightening as portrayed, and the Donbas clans quickly managed to reach a full understanding with him. A few years after the Maidan, the "proffessor" resurfaced from obscurity, took on the position of prime minister, and triumphantly returned to power. Nevertheless, despite this, the events of November–December 2004 left a painful scar in the hearts of Donetsk residents. Yanukovych's team began convincing the people in the eastern regions that "victory was stolen from the Donbas." Despite the obvious rigging, the Party of Regions insisted that Yanukovych actually won the election, but they simply didn't want to consider the opinion of the Donbas. And Yanukovych's electorate believed it. The defeat was **insulting not because their candidate didn't become president but because the "Banderites"**—political opponents demonized to the utmost by propaganda—won. The triumph of a fundamental adversary frustrated them more than their own failure. Donetsk politicians did everything to make Donbas perceive the victory of the "orange" camp as a slap in the face and humiliation. Their efforts were not in vain. In the future, such accumulated grievances would become a catalyst for tragic events that would result in tens of thousands of lives lost, millions of crippled destinies, and enormous financial losses.

PART FOUR

YUSHCHENKO'S LOST CHANCE

After winning the elections, Viktor Yushchenko decided to deviate from his program's slogans and negotiate with political opponents. The promise to send criminals to prison remained mere words. Yushchenko did not start dismantling the demoralized Donetsk clan and allowed it not only to survive but also to take revenge in the following year, 2006.

To avoid alienating the Party of Regions, the new president chose to appoint a weak and compromising figure to the position of Donetsk governor, someone who would accommodate the Donetsk elite. This turned out to be Vadym Chuprun, the same person who had previously led the Donetsk region in the early '90s and blackmailed Kyiv with federalization. Donetsk supporters of Yushchenko were shocked when they learned about this appointment. After the Sievierodonetsk congress, such an appointment seemed like mockery

Former mayor of Mariupol, Mykhailo Pozhyvanov, one of the few politicians in the Donetsk region who supported the "orange" team in the 2004 elections, himself aspired to the position of head of the Donetsk Regional Administration after Yushchenko's victory. However, at the last moment, the president chose Chuprun for the position. Pozhyvanov himself explained how and why this happened:

> "On Epiphany Day, January 19, 2005, Yushchenko asked if I was ready to work as the governor of the Donetsk region. I answered affirmatively. He asked if I had a team. I replied that I did. He said he was going

on a business trip to Europe, then returning for the inauguration, and after that, he would wait for me at his place for this matter. When he returned, his mother had passed away. We went to Khoruzhivka for the funeral. Naturally, I didn't start reminding him of our conversation there. He also remained silent, and he never brought up the topic again. Later, I found out that instead of me, they appointed Vadym Chuprun, who had always advocated for federalization. It turned out that Plyushch and Zvyahilsky came to Yushchenko and persuaded him not to appoint Pozhyvanov. They said that this appointment would provoke resistance from the managerial corps. Zvyahilsky swore that if Chuprun were appointed, there would be peace and grace, and the Donbas would love Yushchenko. And Yushchenko agreed to it."

In Luhansk, initially, everything looked more hopeful. In February 2005, Oleksiy Danilov, the former mayor of Luhansk who had been unlawfully removed from office in the mid-90s, was appointed as the head of the Luhansk Regional State Administration. Danilov seemed to have a personal score to settle with Tykhonov and Yefremov, and everyone expected him to make them pay. Before the first session with deputies of the regional council, who just a few months ago overwhelmingly supported Yanukovych, Danilov formed his own group and started gathering votes for the resignation of the head of the regional council, Viktor Tykhonov. These votes were secured a day before the session, but at the crucial moment, Danilov's plan failed.

"As there are rumors circulating about my dismissal from my position, I will respond: I have never served some clans or rulers; I have served only the homeland and the people," said Tykhonov, opening the first session of the regional council after the transfer of power in

Ukraine.

After that, he calmly suggested to the deputies to decide his fate "by a show of hands," that is, through a public, open vote, although usually, according to the regulations, the head of the regional council was elected by secret ballot. And here, the deputies got scared—only one person dared to face the giant in an open vote. Viktor Tykhonov triumphed.

"I propose to impose a moratorium on considering issues of personnel reshuffles in the leadership of the regional council and regional administration until the end of this term," Tykhonov said with a meaningful inflection.

Thus, the non-aggression pact in Luhansk between the new authorities and the "Komsomol members" was struck as early as March 2005: Danilov ceased attacks on Tykhonov, and the latter did not push the issue of a no-confidence motion against the governor, which could have been a reason for his dismissal. By summer, all those who had left for Russia under the threat of arrest after the "third round" of elections returned to Luhansk. Among them was Oleksandr Yefremov. And in November 2005, Danilov was dismissed following the resignation of Yulia Tymoshenko's cabinet.

Thunderous promises to punish separatists for calling for territorial division made at the Sievierodonetsk congress also turned out to be mere words. On April 6, 2005, the Prosecutor General's Office of Ukraine detained Borys Kolesnikov, but this arrest was not related to the Sievierodonetsk case. Kolesnikov was accused of extortion. Former director of the Donetsk shopping center "Bily lebid" Borys Penchuk claimed that Kolesnikov, threatening him with murder, forced him to sell his shares of "Bily lebid" at a low price. Kolesnikov denied these accusations.

According to him, he paid Penchuk $500,000 for the shares. The controversial Donetsk member of the Party of Regions spent several months in pre-trial detention but was released in August. The criminal case against him quickly fell apart and was closed. Kolesnikov was not charged with offenses related to political clauses. However, a few years later, Penchuk himself ended up in prison for giving false testimony—Borys Kolesnikov turned out to be quite vindictive.

In June 2005, the Prosecutor General's Office attempted to detain Viktor Tykhonov, the moderator of the Sievierodonetsk congress and the head of the Luhansk Regional Council, in a criminal case related to encroachment on territorial integrity. However, he managed to avoid arrest thanks to the guarantee provided by his old associate—then People's Deputy from SDPU(o) parliamentary group and former business partner of Yefremov—Oleksandr Kyselov. While Tykhonov was summoned for questioning in the separatism case, storm clouds were also gathering over Yefremov—the police investigators of the of the organized crime fighting department were collecting information regarding the commercial activities of businesses owned by him or his associates.

This pertained to the case of the unlawful transfer of a large property in the center of Luhansk on Volodymyr Shevchenko Street from communal ownership to Yefremov's "Ukrkomunbank." The investigation also covered the case of the company "Luhansklehinvest," which was supposed to create jobs for unemployed miners but, instead, somehow renovated sewing factories. However, by the end of 2005, these investigations were suspended, and no cases were brought to court.

The Prosecutor General's Office requested the

Luhansk Regional Council's consent to prosecute Viktor Tykhonov in the case of encroachment on Ukraine's territorial integrity only in February 2006—about a year and a half after the Sievierodonetsk congress. During the regional council session, Party of Regions members openly mocked the prosecutor presenting the submission, and since the prosecutor happened to be Tykhonov's neighbor, he wasn't really trying hard to fulfill his duty. As a result, the deputies predictably refused to pursue Tykhonov. The case ended without any charges, but it provided an excellent foundation for constructing a new ideological model—now, the "hot topic" for the Party of Regions became complaints about "political repression" and "harassment." Viktor Tykhonov even published a book titled "How We Were Tried," despite there being no trial. In the end, the politicians from the eastern regions faced no punishment for their actions against the state and its territorial integrity. As subsequent events revealed, such leniency came at a high cost for Ukraine. The main figures of the Sievierodonetsk events did not change their views and consistently fueled tensions in society, ultimately leading to a severe political crisis and bloodshed. Today, we cannot know how the course of history would have changed if the organizers of the Sievierodonetsk congress had been held accountable for their attempt to undermine territorial integrity after Yushchenko's final victory. However, it can be assumed that there would have been far fewer enthusiasts for engaging in separatism in such a scenario. Understanding the inevitability of punishment for such actions would undoubtedly have made the idea of secession of certain regions and the threat of creating various "republics" a highly toxic topic that politicians would prefer to avoid. Impunity, on the other hand, convinced the political elite that anything goes. The country would put up with anything. Society would gloss over everything. Law enforcement would let any case slide.

BLACKMAIL WITH FEDERALIZATION

After losing the presidential elections, the Donbas elites returned to the idea of federalizing Ukraine. While the new government almost always came to an understanding with regional leaders behind closed doors, they played the role of irreconcilable opponents in public. Backroom compromises were concealed from Donbas residents, keeping them tense and conveying the message that the new government was hostile and biased toward the people of the Donbas. During Yushchenko's presidency, this topic was regularly brought up by the Party of Regions at various forums, congresses, and in the media.

The controversial elections of 2004 and the Sievierodonetsk congress revived the rhetoric of the early '90s and made old slogans relevant again. Until 2010, the idea of federalizing Ukraine was one of the key policy objectives of the Party of Regions, contrasting with the "orange" faction's support of a unitary country. Supporters of a federal structure turned the concept of "federalization" upside down from the very beginning. The term "federation" translates as "union." Therefore, it implies the process of uniting certain disparate territorial entities into one state. Ukrainian "federalists," however, proposed the opposite process—splitting up existing unitary state.

So, it is not surprising that such proposals were consistently being frowned upon by a large portion of the Ukrainian population. It was obvious that the topic of federalization was being regularly hyped up to serve the political ambitions of certain individuals rather than because it actually brought any benefits to society.

Moreover, some supporters of federalization openly held Ukrainophobic views and did not hesitate to declare them. For this reason, opponents contemptuously referred to federalization supporters as "federasts."

The boldest radical calls for the autonomy of regions most often came from Donbas, where such ideas overlapped with existing stereotypes about the "distinctive Donbas character" and the region being a "breadwinner." In other regions (except for Crimea), where powerful and influential regional clans were not as dominant, calls for separation were mostly received with indifference. It was evident that the game of federalization was primarily necessary for the Donetsk faction to defend its own interests. For Kherson, Mykolaiv, or Zaporizhzhia, secondary roles were preemptively assigned in this game, and in the event of the formation of the "Southeastern Republic," they would once again have to settle for a peripheral position. Only now, it would be not within Ukraine but within the derogatorily nicknamed "PISUAR," the autonomy proposed by the regionalists in Sievierodonetsk (an acronym of "Southeastern Ukrainian Autonomous Republic" in Ukrainian is a homonym of a "urinal"). Such a prospect was unlikely to tempt anyone.

However, the topic of federalization became one of the key points of Donbas politicians for a long time. After the second round of the 2004 presidential elections and the refusal of the Party of Regions to hold a separatist referendum, a cross-regional public research center called "Constitutional Reform in Ukraine" was established under the Donetsk Regional Council. According to the organizers' plan, the center was supposed to develop a transition plan from a unitary to a federal system. Some unnamed experts in constitutional law and state-building were supposed to work on this plan. According to Borys Kolesnikov, the first results of the center's work were expected in the spring of

2005. "The task force will work for 90 days, and then we will make a decision," he promised. However, no further information about the activities of said group has appeared in the press.

The head of the Luhansk Regional Council and the moderator of the Sievierodonetsk Congress, Viktor Tykhonov, was one of the main speakers on the topic of the federalization of Ukraine. And he seemed to genuinely believe in this idea. As early as 2004, Tykhonov wrote a book titled "Manifest of Federalism, or the Path to a Democratic State." It was a 62-page brochure printed on cheap paper, resembling more of a political proclamation.

"A new stage of Ukraine's development requires a different structure of public authorities, characterized by decentralization and disaggregation, based on the respective internal territorial organization of the state. [...] While they are scaring the people with the division of the country and separatist sentiments allegedly present in the Southeast, they are the ones actually afraid of decentralization of state power and the loss of a significant part of their authority," wrote Tykhonov in 2004.

After the events in Sievierodonetsk, Borys Kolesnikov took up the topic of federalization in Donetsk. In an interview with "Hlavred" on January 20, 2005, he emphasized:

"There is the idea of federalization. And this is the goal. My opinion on the need for a federal system in Ukraine will not change."

Consistently advancing the federalization theme was the Donetsk website "KYD," controlled by Kolesnikov. In March 2005, Viktor Yanukovych himself spoke about the need for federalization in an interview with the well-known

Donetsk online publication "Ostrov."

"There are many countries where two or three languages are official, and it only removes the contradictions that exist in society. And it is the federalization of Ukraine will solve all these problems, and we will not have them," he emphasized.

In Yanukovych's article "Three Postulates of the Opposition. What the Party of Regions Aspires to Accomplish," published in the "2000" newspaper in October 2005 (№43), the author also wrote about the necessity of federalization. Moreover, judging by the title of the article, the change in the form of government was incorporated into the policy objectives of the Party of Regions.

"Today, the country's leadership attempts to fill in the trenches of mutual distrust between the East and the West of Ukraine, but doing so after everything that has happened is not that simple. We believe, and we have repeatedly stated, that internal political stability can be ensured through the federalization of the state. Merely calling for unity has not yielded the expected effect and is unlikely to do so in the near future. In the context of the cultural and historical development, Ukraine's regions are different, and this factor will always influence the internal political situation in the country," wrote Yanukovych (or whoever actually drafted the article). He wisely avoided mentioning who and how actually divided Ukrainian citizens, and memories of his political advertisement, where Ukrainians were sorted into classes, were still fresh.

In March of 2006, the Party of Regions achieved an absolute victory in local elections in the Donetsk and Luhansk regions, securing a majority in all city, district, township, and even village councils. The defeat in 2004 consolidated the political clans in the Donbas and strengthened their positions in the industrial region. The Party of Regions received at their disposal unlimited resources, allowing them to appoint anyone as the mayor or deputy in the Donbas, regardless of their talent and abilities. This is how Oleksandr Yefremov first gained control over the regional center, where he had never been able to install his "own" mayor before. In the 2006 elections in Luhansk, the winner was Serhii Kravchenko, a former military officer and head of the council of the remote and neglected Kamyanobridsk district. A man who always unquestionably and obediently fulfilled the will of his benefactor.

Thanks to the total dominance in the densely populated Donbas, the Party of Regions managed to win the parliamentary elections in 2006. Based on the the results, the Party of Regions secured the votes of 8.2 million voters (about a third of them in the Donbas) and formed in the Verkhovna Rada the largest parliamentary group of 186 deputies.

After this victory and due to the discord in the "orange" camp, Yanukovych managed to make an impressive comeback and once again lead the Cabinet of Ministers. There, he initially seemed to start implementing the ideas of expanding regional autonomy. In September 2006, Yanukovych announced that as a result of the local self-government reform in Ukraine from 2007, regional and district state administrations would be abolished. This meant the elimination of the executive branch hierarchy subordinated to the president.

> "If we consider this draft law during the fall session, then, starting in the new year, there will be different relations in the regions. There will be no regional state administrations; there will be regional executive committees and district executive committees. You will be the ones electing leaders. And the leaders will be

accountable to their constituents. We will build the structure of executive power, and our relations with the regions will be partnership-based," explained Viktor Yanukovych. "Now you will receive a law on local self-government that will enable you to shape regional policy. To adopt legislative acts here in the region, regional laws, the laws by which the regions will live."

However, Yanukovych and his team failed to carry out this plan. The year 2007 turned out to be a disappointing year for the Donetsk faction. In the spring, President Viktor Yushchenko dissolved the parliament, and in the fall, Yulia Tymoshenko's party showed unexpectedly strong results in the snap elections. As a result, Yanukovych lost his post as prime minister, and Tymoshenko became the head of the Cabinet.

The transition of the Party of Regions into the opposition once again intensified federalist rhetoric. Calls to change the country's structure and repeal the current unitary system were voiced by all the main speakers of the Party of Regions, as well as numerous puppet NGOs bankrolled by the Party of Regions.

"At one time, we said that our state consists of different territories, different regions—different in ideology, history, economic potential, and contribution to the country's economy. And this is good, but it should be taken into account. In this situation, a federal system is the most optimal option for Ukraine. I would say it's the only correct one. All the clamors for a united and indivisible Ukraine only conceal the desire to rule single-handedly and impose their own ideas of what is right and best on everyone," said the First Deputy Head of the Party of Regions faction, Oleksandr Yefremov, in an interview with the "KYD" website in July 2008.

In 2008, the Party of Regions decided to hold the

second Sievierodonetsk Congress. Unlike the previous event at the Ice Palace, the new congress was not so much a show of strength as it was a PR campaign and trolling of opponents. Victor Yushchenko was no longer a source of fear. The presidential elections were approaching, and the main task of Yanukovych's team was to mobilize its electoral base as much as possible by the beginning of 2010.

The second congress was just a poor replica of the first one. The were no more open calls for separatism. The most prominent speakers, notable for their radical statements in 2004, did not appear on the floor. Borys Kolesnikov silently sat in the assembly hall, and Rayisa Bohatyriova did not even come. This time, Russia was represented by State Duma deputy Konstantin Zatulin, who stated that he considered Luhansk and Sievierodonetsk part of his homeland. The main theme of the congress was no longer federalization but the "oppression of the Russian language" and "forced Ukrainianization."

> "Throughout the perimeter of the Ice Palace, a double police cordon has been set up, the building has been checked twice for explosive devices, law enforcement agencies are on high alert. Sievierodonetsk-2 is taking place under unprecedented security measures; almost four thousand deputies from all over Ukraine have gathered here to participate in the congress... One of the main issues is the state of the Russian language in Ukraine," - this is how the report on the Second Sievierodonetsk Congress began on the First Channel of the Russian Federation.

Next, for two minutes, Russian journalists conveyed the main messages of the Party of Regions representatives of that time.

> "Valeriy Holenko, head of the Luhansk Regional Council: 'Today we have oppression of the Russian-

speaking population, today we have problems in the humanitarian field, and I hope that the decisions of the Sievierodonetsk congress will help Ukraine become a homeland for representatives of all nationalities, regardless of religion, political beliefs, place of residence, and language of communication.

In five regions of Ukraine, there is no longer any Russian-speaking school, and in 19 regions, there is no higher educational institution where students could receive education in the Russian language. Deputies are sounding the alarm, concerned that if this continues, soon children in Ukraine will not only be unable to write and speak in Russian but even any of the other languages. Speakers reminded that such a situation violates several provisions of the European Charter for Regional Languages.

Olena Lukash, Member of Parliament, Party of Regions: "In our schools, the Ministry of Education of Ukraine introduces requirements to take the university entrance exam in Ukrainian. We know that our children study not only in Russian but also in Romanian, Polish; we are a multi-national state, and our Minister of Education cynically suggests that these children buy a dictionary for word translation. We are against this and want people to use the language they want. After all, it's about the constitutional rights of citizens."

Petro Symonenko, People's Deputy, Communist Party of Ukraine: "We need to face this issue head-on—granting Russian the status of the second national language and recognizing the Russian language and Russian culture as part of our common cultural heritage." About violations of local self-government rights, falsification of Ukraine's historical past, and yet again, about politics, about stance on NATO, spoke the leader of the

Party of Regions, Viktor Yanukovych: We believed and still believe that, taking into account the geopolitical situation in Eastern Europe, decisions on this issue should be made exclusively based on the results of a nationwide referendum. The latest public opinion poll showed that the majority of our citizens do not support joining NATO."

The delegates delivered demands of the second All-Ukrainian Congress not only to their respective regions, but also sent the adopted resolution to President Viktor Yushchenko and the Verkhovna Rada."

However, despite the loud statements and emotional speeches, the second Sievierodonetsk congress did not cause much of a stir. In 2008, just like in 2004, its organizers were preparing for elections and hoped to gain control over the entire Ukraine. The topics of federalization and the national language were brought up to mobilize their electorate once again.

The ideological task of the Party of Regions at that time was to retain the support of voters and prevent the rise of popularity of any other political force in their "home" regions. They aimed to maintain a relatively high level of political tension, creating the impression that people in Donbas lived under constant threat.

During this time, the Luhansk Regional Council, fully controlled by Viktor Tykhonov and Oleksandr Yefremov, conducted extensive propaganda aimed at promoting a "Little Russian" approach to the development of Ukraine. Everything was presented in the format of seemingly benign conferences such as "Pereiaslav Council: Historical Aspects and Modernity," "Federalism as a Prospective Path for Civil Society Consolidation," "Language Tolerance as the Guarantee of Stability and Prosperity of Ukraine's Regions," "Racism, Xenophobia, and Neo-Nazism in the

Modern World," "Anti-Fascist Forum of Ukraine," and so on. It's not difficult to guess who they were labeling as fascists. Speaking at these pseudo-scientific marathons were so-called "scholars" like People's Deputies from the Party of Regions Vadym Kolesnichenko and Oleg Tsaryov, Communist Spiridon Kilinkarov (since 2014, all of them have been living in Russia or annexed Crimea), as well as members of the State Duma of the Russian Federation such as Sergey Markov, Konstantin Zatulin, Vice-Speaker of the State Duma of the III–IV convocations Sergey Baburin (all active participants in the events of 2014 in Crimea and Donbas on the side of Russia), President of the "Historical Memory" Foundation Oleksandr Diukov, Oles Buzyna (assassinated in Kyiv in 2014), Vladimir Kornilov, and others. Often, political theses from speakers of the Ukrainian Orthodox Church of the Moscow Patriarchate (UOC-MP) and pro-Russian Cossack organizations were also part of these events. It's worth noting the consistent presence of speakers from Viktor Medvedchuk's ideological pool, such as Petro Tolochko and Heorhii Kriuchkov.

All these propagandists received extensive media support in Luhansk – local TV channels, regional and local newspapers, radio, in other words, access practically to every home and every set of ears.

Openly anti-Ukrainian statements were rare there; more often were heard imperialistic overtones regarding everything Ukrainian, with a clear identification of the people of Luhansk as "genuinely Russian," who ended up in "independent Ukraine" by chance and misunderstanding.

For example, Konstantin Zatulin, a State Duma deputy of the Russian Federation who was one of the coordinators of the annexation of Crimea in 2014 before being banned from entering the territory of Ukraine, engaged in such blatant manipulations in Luhansk:

"The idea of federalization of Ukraine is not someone's whim, conspiracy, or invention. Ukraine, more than any other country, including the Russian Federation, needs such a territorial form of democracy. And to avoid being hypocritical and accused of any conspiracy against the foundations of the Ukrainian state, I want to quote a person whose name and works are often used by the most ardent supporters of Ukraine's independence, sovereignty, and unity. I mean Mykhailo Hrushevsky. Here is what he wrote in 1907: 'Whether the Ukrainian Republic will formally be called federal or not, in fact, it must be organized as a federation of its republic-communities. Any imposition of mechanistic unity and forced connections on communities will be a big mistake, which will only provoke resistance, backlash pushback away from the center, or give grounds for new internal conflicts."

"The country and its population are heterogeneous. It's time to acknowledge that there are two different Ukrainian nations living in Ukraine. There are many disparities between us that need to be smoothed out. The first step in this direction was taken at the Sievierodonetsk congress in 2004; this congress rejected the division of Ukrainians by colors and classes," declared Valeriy Holenko, the head of the Luhansk Regional Council, at one of the pseudoscientific conferences. "The government of Ukraine equates the word 'federalism' with the word 'separatism.' However, we understand it as the decentralization of power. Ukraine needs a well-thought-out democratic decentralization. It is not an end goal in and of itself but a necessity for the country's development."

However, as the presidential elections approached, the Party of Regions mentioned federalization less frequently. Like before, this issue was not so relevant outside of the Donbas. Moreover, the political situation in the country was gradually changing.

Since the early '90s, federalization was viewed by the "Donbas clans" as a consolation prize. The idea was that if controlling the entire Ukraine was not possible, they should at least secure "their" regions in the south and east, attain autonomy for them, and impose total hegemony. However, by 2009, the prospect of gaining control over the entire Ukraine became a real possibility again. Ongoing conflicts within the "orange" camp and the weakness of Viktor Yushchenko made the chances of the Donetsk faction's comeback very significant. For this reason, Yanukovych ran for president without federalist slogans that could alienate voters. In his election program, titled "Ukraine for the People!", the words "federation" or "federalization" were not used at all.

One of the main speakers of the Party of Regions on the issue of federalization, Borys Kolesnikov, also essentially abandoned his views by the start of elections. On November 29, 2009, during a broadcast on the TBi channel, he expressed the opinion that Ukraine was not yet "mature" for a federative system.

> "Federation is impossible. A lot needs to be done in terms of legislative changes. A budgetary federation might be attempted already," he stated.

However, when Yanukovych finally won the presidential elections in 2010, his rhetoric did a complete 180, and he went from being a supporter of federalization to its opponent.

> "Ukraine is a unitary state. Period. Unitary and democratic," he declared in the summer of 2010 in an interview with the newspaper "2000."

After consolidating power in the hands of the Donetsk group, federalization was no longer needed. Along with Yanukovych, his party members suddenly changed their views as well. Artem Shcherban, a Member of Parliament from the Party of Regions, stated in June 2010 in an interview with the newspaper "Kyiv Telegraph" that "federalization is a distant prospect."

> "At this stage of political development, it is not acceptable. Paradoxically, in my view, federalism is only possible in a stable, economically strong state. Federated states must still be maintained so that we don't have some of them run to Russia and others to the European Union," Shcherban told journalists.

This abrupt metamorphosis suggested that Donbas politicians never truly believed in the positive impact of federalization for Ukraine. They promoted this topic only for their own selfish interests—to negotiate additional preferences for themselves. However, when the Donetsk faction came to power, there was no sense in weakening the central government anymore. The federalization issue gradually slid from the front pages of newspapers to the periphery of fringe forums and leaflets.

BORN BY THE MAIDAN.

SEPARATIST MOVEMENTS IN THE DONBAS IN THE MID-2000s

The victory of the Maidan-2004 and the associated myths of American interference with Ukrainian elections gave rise to a new wave of separatist movements in the Donbas. These predominantly fringe and puppet movements were controlled by politicians from the Party of Regions. However, not all of them openly proclaimed separatist slogans and adopted anti-Ukrainian rhetoric. Most of them masked their Ukrainophobia with an "anti-orange" political stance. Viktor Yushchenko embodied everything they feared and hated—the USA, NATO, the West, and Ukrainian nationalism.

After 2004, veterans of Donetsk separatism from the '90s took a back seat and almost disappeared. However, new entities with new, previously unknown leaders began to emerge. In Donetsk in early 2005, Andrei Purgin made his first appearance, leading a tiny organization, "Union of Those Born by the Revolution." In February 2005, this organization, created with the support of local authorities, set up a small tent camp in the downtown of Donetsk, which looked like a lousy parody of the Maidan in Kyiv. The camp was an outright fake; no one lived in it, and the tents were mostly empty. The participants of the action put forward 12 demands to the new Ukrainian authorities, including federalization and granting Russian the status of the second national language. However, the tents did not last long, and almost no one paid attention to the action.

In the interview that Andrii Purgin gave to the

"Novosti Donbassa" publication in March 2005 and that still can be found on the Internet, he talked about the plans of his organization. At that time, the main bogeyman for the residents of Donbas was the organization "Pora," which supported Viktor Yushchenko in the 2004 elections. In the interview, Purgin claimed that activists of this organization were terrorizing Donetsk, and at night, they were attacking girls on the streets. However, he provided no evidence for these accusations.

> "We are trying to find people who have suffered and who are still suffering at night in Donetsk. One girl has been unconscious for a day and a half, and another one in Krasnohorivka is in the hospital with knocked-out teeth and a broken jaw. We will still raise the issue that 'Pora' is a terrorist organization that terrorizes our city. And if the authorities cannot handle this, then we will handle it ourselves," Purgin explained.

In March 2005, the "Union of Those Born by the Revolution" held a protest against "Pora" near the walls of the Donetsk Regional State Administration. The activists of the "Union," led by Andrei Purgin and his deputy Serhii Rybalko, held banners with slogans: "Perfect time to punish 'Pora,'" "'Pora' —get out of Donetsk." In April, they protested against the visit of the "Okean Elzy" band to Donetsk, which supported the "orange" forces in the elections. It was then that another future well-known Donetsk separatist, the head of the Donetsk Regional Association of Small and Medium Business Entrepreneurs, **Oleksandr** Khryakov, took action. He founded the movement "For Ukraine without Yushchenko" in Donetsk, which regularly participated in various street activism in 2005–2006. However, like most fringe Donetsk organizations of this kind, it consisted essentially of a few people.

Khryakov and Purgin advocated quite radical slogans,

including calls for violence and the division of the state. Officially, the Party of Regions had no connection to these a figures, but unofficially, the regional leaders clearly supported them, as the radicals could freely voice what was unacceptable for top politicians and official representatives. The Party of Regions didn't particularly try to hide the connection to separatists. **Oleksandr** Khryakov, for instance, was an assistant to People's Deputy Andriy Klyuyev, who led the shadow election headquarters of Viktor Yanukovych in the 2004 elections.

In December 2005, Purgin, together with Oleksandr Tsurkan, founded another organization in Donetsk that was destined to gain much more popularity than the "Union of those born by the revolution." This new organization was named the "Donetsk Republic." At that time, few in the Donbas paid attention to this event. Hardly anyone could believe that this idea could turn into something serious in the future.

As the flag for their organization, Purgin and Tsurkan chose the banner of the "Intermovement of Donbas," which at that time had not been active. Starting in 2006, the "Donetsk Republic" occasionally held its rallies in the city. Although these rallies were always small in scale, and their participants looked like town lunatics, the speeches of the "Donetsk Republic" always attracted attention. For Donetsk, such a separatist organization looked exotic at that time.

In 2020, Oleksandr Khryakov admitted that Donetsk separatism did not arise spontaneously but under the patronage of politicians from the Party of Regions who deliberately created pro-Russian movements to counter the "orange" forces in Kyiv.

"In the presence of the Party of Regions representatives Yevhen Heller, Oleksandr Kasianiuk, Ihor Chychasov, Anatoliy Blyznyuk, and Ihor Shkiria, a decision was made that the Party of Regions, having had such a negative experience (referring to the arrest of Borys Kolesnikov in 2005), ought to facilitate the creation of public movements with the ideology of the Donbas orientation. It was also decided to facilitate the creation of the Russian-oriented theme based on the remnants of the 'Slavic Party,' the positions of the 'Russian Bloc,' and Oleksandr Tsurkan's 'Vigilant Movement.' This was the chosen vector within the framework of the Donetsk Republic, based on the Donetsk-Kryvyi Rih Republic, which was later transformed into the 'Donetsk People's Republic,'" wrote Khryakov in his article on the komitet.net.ua website in September 2020.

On June 22, 2006, representatives of the "Donetsk Republic" participated in a rally organized by the local branch of the Communist Party of Ukraine (CPU). During this rally, separatists, for the first time, called for the creation of the so-called "people's militia." However, at that time, no one took these calls seriously.

"Our movement calls for the formation of the people's militia. We are not saying that if it's a people's militia, it must necessarily run around wielding sticks. No. As long as there is an opportunity, as long as democratic transformations are declared, we will act within the law and protest without violating the law. But we will always keep in mind that we can lead actions of civil disobedience." – stated Oleksandr Tsurkan from the stage.

In his speech, the leader of the "Donetsk Republic" traditionally warned the residents of Donetsk about the invasion of the "orange parasites" and accused the ruling coalition of seeking to "destroy the Donbas."

"Today is a very tragic day for our people—the

beginning of the Great Patriotic War *(Russian version of WW II – T. Ed.)* Moreover, it happened that on this day, an anti-people coalition, the 'orange' one, was formed in the Verkhovna Rada, which pretty much united to completely destroy our Donbas. This is my deep conviction, so we cannot stay at home and wait until the 'orange parasites' come to us and devour what we still have left. We have already lost everything. We have nothing more to lose, and we will not stop", thundered Tsurkan.

However, in 2006, the mobilization effect from such scare tactics was nowhere near what it was in 2004. Donbas people still disliked Yushchenko, but they were no longer afraid of him. Two years after the Maidan, the horror stories no longer seemed plausible.

In November of that year, activists of the "Donetsk Republic" set up agitation tents in the very center of Donetsk, on Lenin Square, openly collecting signatures for a referendum on the creation of an "independent Donetsk Federative Republic" and distributing blatantly fascist brochures. The tents used by Tsurkan and Purgin belonged to the Communist Party of Ukraine (CPU). Separatists merely replaced the symbols of the Communists with the flags of their organization. Donetsk journalists noted that such an action could hardly have taken place without the tacit encouragement of the city authorities.

Even for the meekness of the age of Yushchenko's presidency, such audacity was a bit over the top. Representatives of national democratic political forces in Donetsk were outraged both by the action itself and by the "criminal inaction" of the city authorities and law enforcement. Complaints were filed against the separatists with the prosecutor's office and the Security Service of Ukraine (SSU). After lengthy deliberations, in 2007, the "Donetsk Republic" organization was eventually banned by the court in response to a lawsuit from the Donetsk Regional Department of Justice, and became illegal. In addition, the SSU initiated criminal cases against the leaders of the "Donetsk Republic" for encroachment on the territorial integrity of the state.

But actually, these activists were not persecuted, and they continued to operate openly in Donetsk. The investigation and court proceedings dragged on until 2013 and ultimately went nowhere. During Yanukovych's presidency, the case predictably fell apart.

The rhetoric of the "Donetsk Republic" activists resembled trolling. In his interviews, Oleksandr Tsurkan suggested renaming Ukraine to "Banderina," and the organization itself occasionally published absolutely bizarre statements that were hard to take seriously. For example, in 2008, a resolution was circulated on behalf of the "Donetsk Republic," among other things, proposing to "consider the artificially created entity known as the 'Ukrainian nation' a humanitarian crime against the Rus ethnic group."

Tsurkan also promised to create the "Rescue Army of the Donbas" to resist the "Ukrainian occupation," but his cohorts had to implement these plans without him. In 2009, Tsurkan passed away, and Andrei Purgin took over as the new leader of the "Donetsk Republic."

Judging from the photos that activists of the "Donetsk Republic" posted on social media in 2008-2009, separatists occasionally organized something resembling military camps in the Donetsk region. They would go to wild steppes, live in tents, practice shooting firearms and throwing bottles with incendiary mixtures. In the photos taken during such gatherings in 2009, "Donetsk Republic" activists posed with Kalashnikov assault rifles and sniper rifles, firing live rounds at portraits of Ukrainian nationalists. In addition to such outings, leaders of the

"Donetsk Republic" also closely collaborated with the far-right Russian organization "Eurasian Youth Union" led by Aleksandr Dugin and traveled to Russia to participate in the gatherings of this organization.

On February 9, 2009, the already outlawed "Donetsk Republic" organized, unhindered, another event in the downtown of Donetsk. The leaders of the organization set up a tent on Lenin Square and declared the "state sovereignty of the Donetsk Federative Republic." The leaflets distributed by separatists stated that the DFR succeeded the Donetsk–Kryvyi Rih Republic formed in 1918. The leaders of the "DR" included not only the Donbas but also the Kherson, Zaporizhzhia, Dnipropetrovsk, and Kharkiv regions in the territories of the new republic.

The action was a farce. No one in Donetsk took the fringe figures from the "Donetsk Republic" seriously. However, the organization's activities were evidently unofficially sponsored and encouraged by local authorities to rile the "orange" forces in Kyiv and once again threaten them with separatism. Supporting this version is the fact that after Yanukovych's victory in the 2010 presidential elections, the activity of the "republicans" sharply declined, and hardly anything about them was on the radar until the events of 2014.

In 2005, Roman Liahin made his first appearance and, just like Purgin and Khryakov, became infamous in the spring of 2014. After Yushchenko's victory, the future "head of the Central Election Commission of the DPR" created the movement "Us" in Donetsk, sponsored by politicians from the Party of Regions. Liahin's organization was even more fringe than the theatrical "Donetsk Republic" and was not remembered for anything significant except for a few statements. Liahin's activities, up to the beginning of the so-called "Russian Spring," were essentially limited to provocations of a rather small scale.

In 2006, he changed his name to Oleksandr Lukyanchenko to participate in the mayoral elections in Donetsk and confuse the voters by having the same name as the incumbent mayor. This maneuver was orchestrated by the influential Donetsk regional figure Oleksandr Bobkov, who was making Lukyanchenko's life a bit more difficult, as he himself aspired to take the position of mayor of Donetsk. In 2007, Liahin gained scandalous notoriety with an open letter to Viktor Yanukovych, urging the division of Ukraine and the accession of the eastern regions to Russia. Liahin proposed renaming the Party of Regions to the "Party of Southeastern Regions."

> "It is urgently necessary to coordinate the program provisions and the statute with the expectations of millions of party members and sympathizers, as well as change the name of the Party of Regions of Ukraine to the truthful name—the Party of Southeastern Regions of Ukraine. Disregard thoughts about how it looks; the matter is above all. Unlike the catastrophe of 1991, the fragmentation of Ukraine is a blessing. We will do it quickly and quietly. Dissenters, like thousands who died in vain 'for Ukraine,' will become heroes if need be," stated the appeal.

All activists of Donetsk separatist organizations were well acquainted with each other; moreover, they were all closely linked to the Party of Regions. Liahin was a member of the youth organization of the Party of Regions, "Young Regions," and also worked as a PR and public relations consultant for Andrii Kyseliov, the head of the Party of Regions faction in the Donetsk City Council. Oleksandr Khryakov was attributed by Donetsk media not only to Andriy Klyuyev but also to Borys Kolesnikov. **Pavlo** Gubarev, the future "people's governor" of the Donetsk region, who started his political career in the mid-2000s (we will discuss this in detail later), also collaborated with the Party of Regions. Typically, fringe elements were entrusted with organizing various provocations, from which the Party of Re representatives at the official level tried to distance themselves.

In February 2008, a deputy group, "Donbas Rus," emerged in the Donetsk Regional Council. The backbone of this group consisted of deputies from the Progressive Socialist Party of Ukraine (PSPU) of Nataliya Vitrenko, but representatives of the Party of Regions and the Communist Party of Ukraine also joined. The group was led by PSPU deputy Nataliia Bilotserkovska. Soon, a deputy group with the same name appeared in the Kuibyshev district council (in the corresponding district of Donetsk), where there was also a PSPU group. **Pavlo** Gubarev, a little-known figure at the time, was a deputy in this PSPU group.

The creation of the anti-Ukrainian association of deputies was supported by representatives of the Party of Regions from a group oriented towards Viktor Yanukovych. The emergence of "Donbas Rus" in Donetsk almost coincided with Yanukovych's resignation as prime minister (which occurred in December 2007). As always, the loss of power by the Donetsk group led to an escalation of separatist rhetoric and new calls for federalization.

In Luhansk, the role of the main militant separatist was assigned to Arsen Klinchaev, a deputy of the city and later regional council from the Party of Regions. This controversial politician benefited from the political patronage of Oleksandr Yefremov and always acted with his approval. In Luhansk, he did exactly what Khryakov, Liahin, and Purgin did in Donetsk—trolling the ruling party and President Yushchenko. For this purpose, Klinchaev registered a public organization called "Young Guard." Like

Donetsk's similar fringe organizations, it played a satellite role for the Party of Regions and was needed to voice various provocative messages that could not be articulated officially by Yefremov and his entourage.

The first project that brought Klinchaev scandalous popularity was the "Museum of Victims of the Orange Revolution." The "museum" (actually a rather mediocre exhibition) was opened in 2007 and was located in the regional art gallery. The "exhibits" included pages from newspapers with derogatory content about the "fascist Yushchenko," dolls in orange coats, boxes with "laced oranges," barbed wire, and other similar "creative" items. However, the weak execution was compensated by powerful promotion in the press controlled by the Party of Regions. In the same year, the unruly deputy made another vivid scandal—disrupting the screening of a film about Roman Shukhevych planned in Luhansk.

Klinchaev quickly earned the reputation of being the chief weirdo in Luhansk. From time to time, he participated in various brawls, poured paint on Yulia Tymoshenko's billboards during the election campaign, threatened journalists, and engaged in other minor provocations. In return, the regional authorities provided him with money and protection. In 2008, Klinchaev even managed to avoid responsibility for the deaths of two people who suffered fatal injuries on May 9 due to a malfunctioning carousel in an amusement park. The ill-fated carousel was Klinchaev's business, but he faced no punishment for violating safety regulations and presenting falsified documents.

Klinchaev's example vividly illustrated a significant difference in political life between Luhansk and Donetsk —pro-Russian radicals in Luhansk were not fringe figures but rather official representatives of local authorities. While in Donetsk, various small pro-Russian organizations were mainly involved in organizing roundtable discussions and conferences dedicated to opposing NATO and defending the Russian language, in Luhansk, local Party of Regions members and officials took the lead.

They also didn't neglect to lash out at "Westerners" on occasion.

Any event could serve as a pretext for attacks. For instance, in April 2009, after the Lviv Regional Council decided to dismantle monuments of the Soviet regime in the region, Luhansk Regional Council deputies promptly condemned their colleagues. The response statement of the Party of Regions faction was read out during the regional council session. In it, Luhansk deputies regarded Lviv residents' decision as the "beginning of overt fascism in the country" and demanded the "recall of the disgraceful decision." To that, a regional council deputy from the Progressive Socialist Party, Liubov Korsakova, went so far as to call for prohibiting residents of the Lviv region from entering the territory of the Luhansk region.

Unlike Donetsk, there were never prominent separatist movements like the "Donetsk People's Republic" in Luhansk. However, there existed a strong regional organization of the Communist Party of Ukraine (CPU), which was absent in the Donetsk region. Traditionally, Luhansk was considered the Communist Party's stronghold, but this party did not openly advocate for separatism. Instead, together with the Party of Regions, it promoted the idea of federalization.

PART FIVE

UNSUCCESSFUL MULTI-VECTOR POLICY OF YANUKOVYCH

The victory of Viktor Yanukovych in the 2010 presidential elections had the same effect as Leonid Kuchma's victory back in 1994. Instead of the promised decentralization of power, intense centralization began. The discussions about federalization were almost halted by the Party of Regions. The Donbas elite finally got what it wanted, and in this situation, calls for autonomy had no sense. Regional elites no longer needed to demand independence from Kyiv because Kyiv itself was in their hands. Now, it wasn't the Donetsk faction who had to live by Ukraine's rules, but the whole of Ukraine had to live by the rules of the Donetsk faction.

The activity of pro-Russian organizations in the Donbas decreased for a while. The goal was achieved. The "orange" President Yushchenko disgracefully lost the elections, and a pro-Russian politician returned to power in Ukraine. Yanukovych's voters had only to rejoice and wait for him to start fulfilling his promises. However, despite numerous expectations and fears, Ukraine under Yanukovych did not rush to become an unquestionable satellite of the Russian Federation.

Initially, it seemed that the country would follow the Belarus path. Already in April 2010, the new president pushed through the parliament the scandalous Kharkiv agreements, allowing the Russian Black Sea Fleet to remain in Crimea until 2042 in exchange for a gas discount. However, over time, it became clear that the majority of promises made by Yanukovych's team to its voters before the elections were not going to be fulfilled by the Party of Regions. They dropped the idea of federalization; they were in no hurry to grant Russian the status of national language, and the issue of joining the Customs Union of the Eurasian Economic Union quietly disappeared from the agenda. Instead, Yanukovych continued the course of European integration set by Viktor Yushchenko and engaged in negotiations for the signing of an Association Agreement with the European Union.

In essence, Viktor Yanukovych tried to implement the famous multi-vector policy of Leonid Kuchma, who had long balanced between the West and Moscow. However, if Kuchma managed to pull it off, Yanukovych quickly realized that it didn't work out so well for him. Firstly, he was a much less skillful politician himself. Secondly, Russia had changed, now behaving much more assertively and pressuring Ukraine to halt European integration.

In the fall of 2010, local elections took place in Ukraine. Once again, the Party of Regions easily won on the Donbas, taking full control of all local councils in the Donetsk region. In the Luhansk region, the Communists also achieved significant success. Other pro-Russian movements showed minimal results.

Interestingly enough, the nationalist party "Russian Bloc" received less than 1% of the votes in the Donetsk region. The Progressive Socialist Party of Ukraine, led by Nataliya Vitrenko, also failed. It appears that Donbas voters were not primarily supporting ideological pro-Russian parties but rather those who appeared as "their people," who provided them with illusions of returning to the past, to Soviet times, and clearly identified their enemies.

The pro-Russian camp was in crisis. Although Russian nationalists held the so-called "Russian marches" in Donetsk once a year, only a few dozen people would attend. The organization of these marches was handled by the "Russian

Bloc" party, which became more active in the Donbas during this period and sought to unite activists from various "anti-orange" organizations that had dispersed after Viktor Yushchenko left power. Some participants in the marches even came from the Rostov region. For example, in 2011, to march with Russian nationalists down the streets of Donetsk came out the leader of the Rostov branch of the "Eurasian Youth Union," Vladimir Prokopenko, We'll get back to him later.

The "Russian marches" brought some diversity to the dull political life of Donetsk but resembled more of a carnival than a political manifestation. The number of participants in such "marches" was a better indicator of the unpopularity of radical pro-Russian forces rather than of their strength.

In Luhansk, the pro-Russian agenda continued to be defined by the leaders of the Luhansk Regional Council and their circle. While Donetsk's Party of Regions, in keeping with tradition, displayed their pragmatism and focused primarily on financial matters after winning the elections, their counterparts in Luhansk continued their heroic struggle against the "caveman Ukrainian nationalists." Perhaps out of old Komsomol habit. The main spokesperson on ideological matters among the Yefremov supporters was Valeriy Holenko, the head of the Luhansk Regional Council, who had worked as the secretary of the city Komsomol committee in Soviet times.

To understand Valeriy Holenko's personality, consider the following example. In his capacity as the head of the Luhansk Regional Council, he held a press conference on the results of his trip to Moscow, and a significant portion of his speech was dedicated to describing the Hall of the Order of St. George in the Grand Kremlin Palace, where the Luhansk delegation was received. He detailed the interior so extensively that it was hard to hold back laughter: a mature man, managing an entire region, having visited many countries and seen European capitals, was fawning over the moldings, curtains, chandeliers, and carpets of some official delegation hall in the Kremlin. This story speaks more about him than any quotes from his speeches, which he always read from notes.

On May 8, 2010, in Luhansk, a solemn unveiling ceremony of a monument to the victims of the Organization of Ukrainian Nationalists (OUN) and the Ukrainian Insurgent Army (UPA) took place. The victims referred to here were the natives of the Luhansk region who perished at the hands of the Bandera supporters in western Ukraine. The decision to erect the monument was made in 2009 on the initiative of the local authorities. The "Young Guard" of Arsen Klinchaev formally acted as the organizer.

The entire Luhansk elite, including Oleksandr Yefremov, Viktor Tykhonov, Valeriy Holenko, and Russian State Duma deputy Konstantin Zatulin, was present at the opening ceremony. The monument was engraved with 18 names. Despite the fact that more people died every year in the region's mines, the perished miners were not honored with a monument in Luhansk. Similarly, the Luhansk authorities ignored the memory of thousands of victims of Stalin's repressions buried in Sucha Balka on the outskirts of the regional center.

In July of 2012, ahead of the parliamentary elections, the Verkhovna Rada adopted the controversial Law "On the Principles of the State Language Policy," better known as the Kivalov–Kolesnichenko Law. Its co-authors were notorious politicians known for their openly anti-Ukrainian views. The law did not challenge the fact that Ukrainian is the only national language in Ukraine but significantly expanded the possibilities for using the Russian language. The law itself did not appear to be a detriment to Ukraine, but its interpretation in Donetsk and Luhansk regions was problematic. The regional elites were not just defending the right of the residents of the eastern regions to speak Russian. The adoption of the law was portrayed by the media in the Donbas under the control of the regional authorities as a victory over the "fascists" from western Ukraine, with the intention to exacerbate existing interregional conflicts rather than smooth them over.

On July 6, during an extraordinary session of the Luhansk Regional Council, while discussing a statement in support of the language law, Rodion Miroshnyk, a deputy from the Party of Regions, stated that Ukrainian education turns Ukrainian children into "subhumans." He made such a statement during a discussion on the mandatory school curriculum in Ukrainian, suggesting that education in a non-native language adversely affects children's ability to learn and denies them access to knowledge and literature.

> "I don't understand the speeches happening in Kyiv today: 'they oppress the Ukrainian language, the Ukrainian language needs protection.' What kind of language is so frail that it needs protection from everything, that it has to grow in a greenhouse? It turns out that if we teach children this language, we deprive them of everything; we just raise subhumans! People who lack a vast amount of knowledge... With the support of the government, the Ukrainian language can develop, but not in a greenhouse, but by competing with other languages present throughout the entire territory of Ukraine," shouted Miroshnyk from the podium.

The reaction of patriotic citizens to the new law was understandably unfavorable. It wasn't because they were Russophobes, as pro-Russian politicians tried to portray them. People were put off not by the Russian language but by the methods employed by the regional authorities and the goals they pursued. For this reason, a significant number of

Russian-speaking citizens of Ukraine opposed the Kivalov–Kolesnichenko Law (the Party of Regions has always silenced and ignored this inconvenient fact).

The core of this problem was best articulated by the journalist Kostiantyn Skorkin from Luhansk:

> "While the truly interesting and complex issue of Ukrainian bilingualism is presented by certain politicians in a bundle with authoritarianism, Stalinist-style communism, anti-Western sentiment, and other reactionary nonsense that has nothing to do with today's Europe, as long as demagogues and freaks, not scholars, talk about it, there will be no language tolerance in our country," he wrote in 2010 on the "Vostochnyi Variant" website.

This was an overarching description of the "defenders of the rights of the Russian-speaking population." The guardians of the Russian language were driven not by a desire to protect people's rights but by mere Russian chauvinism.

Nearing 2013, there was growing confusion among Yanukovych's base supporters. The president spoke about European integration and prepared to sign the Association Agreement with the EU, while the Party of Regions officials at the local level took a pro-Russian position, insulting Ukrainians as "subhumans" and "freeloaders from Western Ukraine," repeating well-rehearsed theses about friendship with Russia. It looked like the government was suffering from a split personality.

Donetsk's Party of Regions members understood the absurdity of the situation and tried to navigate it as best they could. In 2012-2013, local authorities in Luhansk organized rallies with slogans like "To Europe without fascists," cleverly combining new aspirations with their traditional messages. By "fascists," they, as usual, meant anyone who wanted to see

Ukraine as Ukraine, not the UkrSSR.

Naturally, such a schizophrenic construction was appealing to very few, and it looked unviable from the start. Awkwardly balancing between two warring wings, Yanukovych failed to gain the trust of the national democrats and began to lose confidence of the pro-Russian camp, where anti-Western sentiment was one of the fundamental principles. The "Multi-vector" policy did not strengthen but weakened his power. Moreover, there was another problem —Russia strongly disapproved of such attempts to play both sides of the fence. Moscow had firm intentions to derail Ukraine from its European course. And to do that, it now needed to find new partners.

In addition to the "war on the ideological battlefront," a dramatic change in the structure of the regional economy was taking place in the Luhansk region. Financial pressure and the aggressive expansion of the Donetsk faction and Russian money into the region began in the mid-90s, and Oleksandr Yefremov, who tried to build his own financial-industrial group (FPG), could not keep up with the pace of neighbors on both sides. By 2011–2012, all major companies in the region were under the control of either Russians or pro-Russian and Donetsk oligarchs: "Luhansk Energy Association" was controlled by Kostiantyn Hryhoryshyn, Lysychansk Oil Refinery—by Russian TNK-BP, Sievierodonetsk Azot was owned by Dmytro Firtash, "Luhanskteplovoz"—by Russian "Transmashholding," "Luhanskvoda"—by Russian "Rosvodokanal," Alchevsk Metallurgical Complex and Coking Chemical Plant was owned by Donetsk ISD, later by Russian "Vniesheconombank," "Rovenkyanthracite" and "Svierdlovanthracite" was owned by Rinat Akhmetov's DTEK; "Krasnodonvuhillia"—by "Metinvest" of Rinat Akhmetov and Vadym Novinskyi. These enterprises formed local budgets in the cities where they were located, providing employment to hundreds of thousands of people. The change in their ownership had a significant impact, generating certain expectations and positive anticipations like "Russia will place orders at the plant, and there will be jobs." This only reinforced the popular belief that the region's economy heavily depends on Russian markets, and the "fate of the people" is tied to Russian business owners, by extension making many employees of these companies loyal to Russia and its policies, especially in Ukraine.

Moreover, this meant that the formation of a "Luhansk" financial-political clan became impossible. Yefremov himself did not become the owner of powerful plants and mines – his business was focused on intermediary and trading companies that received government contracts.

These circumstances created an important critical and mental distinction between the Donetsk and Luhansk groups. As a result of their economic policies, the Donetsk group began to control a vast number of productions and physically existing assets, while the Luhansk group did not.

"COSSACKS DOUBLE AGENTS"

Members of pro-Russian fringe organizations, organizers of marches and rallies, public speakers mentioned in previous sections, in the spring of 2014, led anti-Ukrainian forceful actions in the Donbas. It became evident then that the development of the system of influence agents, public figures who were supposed to provide political cover for the forceful takeover of the region, began long before the protests of the Euromaidan and the bloody Revolution in February 2014. Clearly, Yanukovych's escape was only a pretext, not the cause of the attack on Ukraine in the spring of 2014.

In addition to political structures promoting pro-Russian rhetoric, a paramilitary force named "Don Cossacks," affiliated with the "Almighty Don Host" (hereinafter referred to as ADH), was established in the Luhansk region.

A detailed history of Don Cossacks is not the focus of this book, and those interested can read about it in other sources. It is only worth noting that significant parts of the modern Luhansk region were part of the Don Cossack Host until 1919–1920. During the Communist takeover of power, Don Cossacks fought against them, and after the Cossacks' defeat, they were eradicated as a social group due to the so-called "de-Cossackization policy." During World War II, formations of Don Cossacks fought in the German army against Soviet rule, leading to organized repression against them even after 1945.

However, during the post-Soviet era, Russian propaganda changed its approach. Instead of branding them German collaborators, it began creating a powerful new myth of the revival of Don Cossacks as a support for the "new imperial power." In the Rostov region alone, hundreds of millions of rubles were allocated annually from state programs to support Cossacks. The budgets financed the work of Cossack patrols and provided funding for cadet corps, creative groups, and similar activities. Cossacks embraced the ideas of a unique modern version of imperial Russian nationalism.

In practice, the revived Cossack organizations quickly began to resemble paramilitary formations or unofficial private military companies (PMCs). They participated in various armed conflicts both within the territory of the Russian Federation and in neighboring hotspots.

> "In Russia, the revival of Cossacks took place under the strict control of the security service agencies. All reputable Cossack organizations are paramilitary entities that receive budgetary financing. Anyone who considered themselves heirs of Cossack history and could be considered 'unruly' was immediately incorporated into them. In Stanytsia Luhanska (up to 2022 was the demarcation line between the occupied and controlled territories of Ukraine. —A/N), they started with a museum. Then there were events aimed at educating 'in Cossack traditions,' followed by 'Cossack camps' for children, all of which led to contacts in Rostov at a high level. Initially, it was 'toasts with sabers,' and then suddenly became invisible. I believe that it was during this time that processes of structuring based on real propagandistic identity took place, preparing people and integrating them into Ukrainian government and security structures, like the border patrol service," says former head of Yanukovych's shadow headquarters in 2004, former deputy governor of Luhansk, and former member of parliament from the Party of Regions, Volodymyr Ivanov.

Since 2003, in Milove, a town in the Luhansk region, located in the northeast of the region and bordering the Russian town of Chertkove, a festival called "Friendship Street" was held. Before the war, the border between Ukraine and Russia ran directly along Friendship on Nations Street; houses on one side of the street were in Ukraine, and on the other side, in Russia.

Festivities were organized here "in Cossack traditions" – with vodka, songs, dances, and slogans like "we share common roots, common traditions, families, and history; no borders can divide us." If we consider this festival on its own, it was not inherently dangerous. However, in the context of the "struggle for the rights of Russian speakers" and the total economic expansion of Russian capital in the region, it served as the "icing on the cake," much like the Cossack song festival "Liubo," held since 2008 in the aforementioned Stanytsia Luhanska. Performing art collectives gathered at the festival to sing songs, dance, participate in horse races, and similar events. This cultural activity was widely covered in the media and, along with other ideological work directions, had a very noticeable propaganda effect.

Over the last 20 years, dozens of small, disjointed Cossack organizations have been created in the Luhansk region. For the most part, they were engaged in constant internal conflicts and political disputes. Typically, intensification "on the Cossack front" coincided with the approach of elections since all these organizations were involved in media support campaigns, acting as costumed performers. Those who identified themselves with Don Cossacks usually had a clear pro-Russian orientation. Attempts were made to create pro-Ukrainian Cossack organizations as a counterweight to them, but all these efforts were unsuccessful.

Approximately in 2008–2009, the development of a pro-Russian militarized organization began in the Luhansk region. It was carried out under the control of Russian special services and regional authorities.

In 2004, the ataman (head, commander) of the ADH and a deputy of the Russian State Duma, Viktor Vodolatskyi, ventured to support the Sievierodonetsk congress. In 2008, he planned to send units of Russian and Luhansk Don Cossacks to guard the monument to Empress Catherine II in Sevastopol. This monument was unlawfully installed at the initiative of local deputies and sparked negative reactions from Crimean Tatars. After this, the Security Service of Ukraine (SSU) prohibited Vodolatskyi from entering Ukrainian territory. On September 12, 2008, despite the entry ban, Ataman Vodolatskyi attempted to attend a meeting of the Permanent Inter-State Coordination Council of Cossack Hetmans of Belarus, Russia, Ukraine, and Transnistria in Sviatohirsk (the Donetsk region) but was stopped at the border. He was not allowed to enter Ukraine.

In early October 2009, the SSU also issued an entry ban for another high-ranking official of the ADH, Viktor Demyanenko. The Security Service had information that he intended to create "paramilitary formations" on Ukrainian territory. However, these bans did not prevent the leaders of the Luhansk Regional Council from actively engaging with Vodolatskyi on their territory and, moreover, officially participating in the subordination of Luhansk Cossacks to the "authorities" in Rostov.

In 2009, around 150 people gathered at the "Cossack Circle" in Luhansk. This was a significant event—never before had such a number of individuals considering themselves Don Cossacks gathered to make political decisions. The event aimed to elect an ataman and define his mission. But for some reason, the presidium committee was composed of the deputy head of the Luhansk Regional Council, Yevhen Kharin (some "Cossack" he was), and the deputy ataman of the ADH for ideology, Vladimir Voronin, and the chief of staff of the ADH, Viktor Mohylnyi (both Russian citizens). None of the actual leaders of Luhansk Cossack organizations were present. It turned out that the guests from Rostov had come to Luhansk to force Luhansk Cossacks to vote for the ataman they chose. The old and naive Leonid Ruban, who was considered the patriarch of this movement in Luhansk, did not suit them. Another candidate, a deputy of the Luhansk Regional Council from the Party of Regions and the deputy head of the Stanychno-Luhanske District State Administration, Pavlo Orlov, together with the head of the regional council, Holenko, secretly traveled to Rostov for a meeting with the head of the ADH, Viktor Vodolatskyi.

The attendees at the Luhansk "Circle" were quite surprised to be simply informed about this matter. They sincerely desired what they saw on television—Cossack self-government, democratic traditions, the election of leaders—but their friends from Rostov ordered them to shut up and listen.

Voronin directly suggested that Cossacks elect Pavlo Orlov as the ataman. When those present unequivocally expressed their disagreement, the Deputy Head of the Regional Council, Yevhen Kharin, intervened. He called those who were against Orlov "heretics," insisted that Holenko and Vodolatskyi had already decided everything, and if Luhansk Cossacks wanted to have good relations "with the Don," they should vote for Orlov. Since no one knew Orlov, he briefly talked about himself, emphasizing that he had participated in military actions in Ossetia on the Russian side.

> "I don't want to express my personal opinion on this; I want to say that there was a letter from the ataman of the ADH, Vodolatskyi. We know this person and deeply respect him, building relations with the ADH. We are accused of being the fifth column of the Kremlin;

some open cases against us for our statements and our position. There was a meeting with Valeriy Holenko, and it was decided that if there is such a recommendation from Vodolatskyi, to support the candidacy of our colleague Orlov," argued Kharin.

As a result, only 15 people voted for Orlov, while the majority elected Leonid Ruban as the ataman. However, the goals and tasks of Don Cossacks in the Luhansk region remained unchanged regardless of the winner's name. The Don Cossacks of Luhansk continued to be a branch of the Russian ADH, whether led by Ataman Ruban or Ataman Orlov.

Participation of regional government officials in the congress demonstrated that the Luhansk elites maintained close ties with paramilitary Cossack formations from the neighboring state despite their overtly anti-Ukrainian activities. Actually, the Luhansk authorities did not even attempt to conceal these contacts. All their interactions with Don Cossacks from Russia were open. For the Ukrainian state, this was a troubling sign. However, the Security Service did not respond to the actions of the Luhansk authorities. Despite the fact that Ukraine was still under the "orange" leadership at that time, they turned a blind eye to the flagrant cozying up with hostile forces in Russia.

The Luhansk authorities continued to regularly invite Cossack representatives to various rallies and roundtable discussions. They planned to allocate funding to the "proper" Cossack organizations. A few weeks before the start of the Euromaidan protests in 2013, the first meeting of the Coordination Council for the Development of Cossacks took place in the Luhansk Regional Council. The event was organized by the same Deputy Head of the Luhansk Regional Council, Yevhen Kharin. They planned to earmark allocations to support Don Cossacks and involve them in maintaining law and order as well as in the "patriotic education" of youth, but they did not manage to do this. The Maidan began, and after that, an armed conflict ensued.

During the revolutionary winter of 2014 and the "Russian Spring" that followed, Luhansk Cossacks joined the Anti-Maidan forces and were used by the authorities of the Luhansk region to provoke disorder and unrest. In mid-February 2014, before Yanukovych's escape, Leonid Ruban wrote an appeal to Russian President Vladimir Putin and Ataman of the ADH Viktor Vodolatskyi, requesting the introduction of Russian troops into Ukraine. This sparked outrage and a loud scandal throughout the country, but we will discuss this in detail later.

Both contenders for the position of Cossack ataman in 2009, Pavlo Orlov and Leonid Ruban, actively participated in the war. At the beginning of the war, Orlov sided with the militants against Ukraine, led the "Don" detachment, and was wounded near Metalist in May 2014. He then went on to serve in the so-called "People's Militia of "LPR." Ataman Leonid Ruban actively participated in organizing an illegal referendum in Luhansk and, in the spring of 2014, facilitated the delivery of "humanitarian aid" across the border from Russia to armed groups of militants, as he himself revealed in one of the interviews. In February 2016, Leonid Ruban passed away in Luhansk.

A favorable information context created around the paramilitary Russian Cossack movement and the cover provided by the regional authorities significantly influenced the perception of the region's residents. Don Cossacks and Russian nationalists presented themselves as "ours." It is impossible to determine the exact number of actual members of Cossack organizations and the extent of their funding, but there is no doubt that the support was substantial. In 2014, when the regional elite lost control over the situation in the

Luhansk region, power passed to Cossack leaders as well, who were joined by Cossacks from the Russian Federation. In May 2014, a group of armed individuals calling themselves "Don Cossacks" effortlessly violated the state border of Ukraine and seized the city of Antratsyt. The "Don Cossacks" also captured and controlled for some time the cities of Krasnyi Luch, Perevalsk, Stakhanov, and a number of others.

MEDVEDCHUK AND OTHERS

The victory of Yanukovych in the 2010 elections temporarily disarmed pro-Russian radicals. Playing on anti-Kyiv sentiments and accusing the government of neglecting the interests of Donbas became impossible. Among all notable Ukrainian politicians, Yanukovych was the most pro-Russian. So, when Moscow needed new allies in Ukraine to exert pressure on Yanukovych and make him more compliant on European integration issues, it turned out there was practically no one to rely on. In addition to the Party of Regions, there was the Communist Party of Ukraine on the pro-Russian flank, which, in Ukrainian realities, acted more as a right-wing rather than a left-wing Russian party. However, due to its archaic nature, it could not create full-fledged competition for the Party of Regions and, since 2006, existed only as its satellite.

The Kremlin needed a more reliable and potentially powerful ally, and such an ally was found. The former head of the Presidential Administration under Kuchma, Victor Medvedchuk, was best suited for this role. He maintained almost family-like relations with Vladimir Putin, who even became the godfather of his child, indicating a high level of trust. In 2012, Medvedchuk founded the movement "Ukrainian Choice," which was supposed to be a prototype of a new pro-Russian party, advocating for federalization, and blocking Ukraine's integration into the EU.

With Medvedchuk's assistance, the Kremlin aimed to create a counterpart to the Donetsk faction in the southeast of Ukraine. A force that could influence Yanukovych and keep him in check because after taking office, the new Ukrainian president had to reckon only with the powerful pro-Western opposition. On the pro-Russian flank, there was no one left who could exert pressure on him. This blunder had to be corrected.

On July 9, 2012, on his YouTube channel, Viktor Medvedchuk announced the launch of the "Federal Ukraine" project and emphasized that "Ukrainian Choice" aspired to play a leading role in promoting federalization ideas.

> "The public movement 'Ukrainian Choice' proposes to coordinate this activity, suggests creating an organizing committee to develop legislation for the federal structure of Ukraine," said Medvedchuk.

In his address, like other proponents of federalization in Ukraine, he cited successful federations, such as Germany and the USA, resorting to a manipulation we are already familiar with. Medvedchuk seemed to forget that the term "federation" means "union." He turned upside down the very essence of federalization—he proposed not to unite different territorial entities into one state but, on the contrary, to divide the existing unitary state. Moreover, Medvedchuk and other lobbyists of the federal system always mentioned wealthy federations but never mentioned disastrous examples. Somalia, Iraq, and Sudan were not protected from hunger, wars, and genocide by a federal system.

Of course, Medvedchuk also scared people with the division of Ukraine.

> "I am a supporter of a federal system, spending many years in big politics. And I believe that a federal system, federalization, is the only, in my opinion, possible remedy for the division of our country. The threat and the reality of such division exist. It exists considering the geopolitical situation of Ukraine and exists because

Ukraine is essentially artificially created from separate territories that had different histories, cultures, and humanitarian realms at different times," said the leader of the "Ukrainian Choice."

Russia was eyeing pro-Russian fringe movements that existed in various regions of Ukraine. In 2011-2012, Russians began attempts to unite small pro-Russian organizations in the Donbas into a single movement to more effectively lobby the idea of Ukraine's entry into the Customs Union with Russia and its affiliates.

In February 2012, at another roundtable in Luhansk attended by representatives from Russia, the announcement was made about the creation of the Ukrainian-Russian public initiative "Donbas for the Eurasian Union (EAU)." The Donetsk branch of this movement was led by one of the founders of the "Donetsk Republic," Andrei Purgin. In addition to him, other prominent figures from pro-Russian organizations in Donetsk and Luhansk also joined the movement, including Serhii Baryshnikov, Artem Olkhin, Yulii Fedorovskyi, and Roman Liahin. The Luhansk office of the "Ukrainian Choice" was represented by the already mentioned here regional council deputy Arsen Klinchaev.

From Russia to the creation of the new organization, activists of the nationalist organization "Eurasian Youth Union" and members of the pro-Russian organization "International Russia," led by the chief editor of the Russian information agency "Regnum," Modest Kolierov, played a role. In March 2012, the participants of "Donbas for the EAU" were already present in Rostov, where they held a roundtable titled "Ukraine and Donbas for the Eurasian Union."

The core idea of the EAU supporters' activities was not so much to promote the pro-Russian course as to create some kind of "Anti-Ukraine" in the Donbas. One of the participants in the Rostov conference, Yulii Fedorovskyi from

Luhansk, wrote in his blog that during one of the meetings, his colleagues suggested erecting a monument in Donetsk to the victims of the UPA, soviet special agent ("chekist") Lev Zadov, and Red Army soldiers who captured Kyiv in 1918. Of course, such rhetoric could only resonate with a limited number of overt chauvinists and radical Ukrainophobes. For others, this "advertisement" for the Customs Union was only alarming and repulsive.

In November 2012, members of "Donbas for the EAU" held a conference in Donetsk titled "Donbas in the Eurasian Project," where again guests from Russia were present, including the assistant to the State Duma deputy Yevhenii Fedorov. Interestingly, during this event, there was not so much criticism of Ukrainian nationalists as there was criticism of the Party of Regions and Yanukovych. The conference criticized the Ukrainian government for not actively pursuing rapprochement with Russia. Such rhetoric was atypical for Donetsk.

> "What we have now is more like a standstill than drawing closer to Russia or integrating within the Eurasian space. If with the 'orange' government, we moved as far away from Russia and the Eurasian space as possible, then with the current course and incumbent administration, we are not moving anywhere," lamented Kyrylo Cherkashyn, a lecturer at Donetsk National University.

> "The main obstacle is not from the nationalists, although they do have some manpower that they invest in resisting Eurasian integration, but the main opposition is in the governing party, in the Party of Regions," assured the attendees the assistant to the Russian deputy Fedorov.

At the end of the conference, its participants released a resolution demanding a nationwide referendum on Ukraine's accession to the Customs Union with Russia. Donetsk was referred to in the appeal as the "last stronghold and guarantee of unity between Ukraine and Russia."

However, despite the loud proclamations, the "Donbas for the EAU" movement had no impact on the political life of the Donbas and, even more so, the entire country. In essence, it went unnoticed by anyone. The media paid no attention to the meetings of these fringe figures, and outside the offices and conference halls, activists hardly made themselves known. Nevertheless, it can be argued that it was during this inconspicuous activity that pro-Russian activists in the Donbas actively established connections in Russia, and conversely, Russia formed a network of loyal organizations that could be tapped when needed.

LAND OF SHALE GAS

Having gained the highest office in the state, Viktor Yanukovych underwent rapid changes. Gone were the days when he was regarded as a protege and executor of the will of the oligarch Rinat Akhmetov. Now, the new president was in the process of becoming an oligarch and appointed his people to key positions. Quickly accumulating wealth and strengthening influence was Yanukovych's elder son, Oleksandr, who was responsible for the family business. The political weight of young politicians close to the Yanukovych family, Oleksandr Klymenko and Serhii Arbuzov, who had no previous ties to the Party of Regions and were relatively unknown in the mid-2000s, grew. At the same time, party veterans gradually moved into secondary roles, particularly representatives of the Luhansk elite.

In the press, the inner circle of the new president began to be referred to as the "family." The "family" quickly became a very powerful clan. However, Yanukovych almost immediately faced a fundamental problem—a shortage of assets over which he could establish control. Despite being a long-time top politician and one of the most influential figures in Ukraine, the leader of the Party of Regions did not own a large business. In 2010, when he finally assumed the presidency, it turned out that the best assets had long been divided and privatized.

In this situation, he had to make do with what was left. Primarily, the Yanukovych family turned their attention to the coal industry, where many state mines and enrichment plants were still operating, and there was also a significant shadow sector (illegal mines). In a short time, companies such as DRFC and MAKO became well-known in this industry; they were controlled by Oleksandr Yanukovych and made money through various corrupt coal schemes. But this was not enough for the "family." Just at this time, another attractive prospect appeared on the horizon. In the Donetsk region, there were reserves of shale gas estimated to be billions of cubic meters. Global prices for hydrocarbons were high at that time, and the development of these deposits promised enormous profits.

However, the Yanukovych family could not independently establish shale gas extraction. To achieve this, they needed to create from scratch a powerful company capable of extracting shale gas, and the "family" lacked such managerial talents. Therefore, they had to go a different, more familiar way. They decided to hand over the right to develop the deposits to major investors, and for their own needs, the "family" created the company "SPK-Heoservice," which was supposed to become a partner for transnational corporations and claim a share of the extracted natural gas.

In February 2012, Ukraine announced a competition for the development of two major deposits: Yuzivske in the Donetsk region and Oleske in the Lviv region. In May 2012, the government of Mykola Azarov identified the winners—two large international companies, Shell, and Chevron.

If these ambitious plans were to materialize, Ukraine could significantly increase its own natural gas production, and Yanukovych's inner circle would receive billions in profits. However, such a scenario was clearly against the interests of Russia, which was selling natural gas to Ukraine and did not want to lose such a significant consumer. It was not just about money. Energy independence also meant political independence, as natural gas had always been an effective tool of Russian influence on the Ukrainian government.

To put the arrogant Donetsk faction back in their place, before, in their pursuit of wealth, they could undermine the power of the Russian gas monopoly, Putin decided to use Medvedchuk. The "Ukrainian Choice" created by him in 2012 immediately joined the fight against shale gas extraction.

"As soon as the government moves from words to action, discussions about all these issues will arise, and I am confident that the population of these regions (where shale gas extraction was planned —A/N), local authorities will express their opinions on this matter. It is unlikely that the government will be able to establish production and shale gas extraction in Ukraine seriously," said Medvedchuk in his address published on his YouTube channel on May 28, 2012 (video title: "Shale Gas: Pros and Cons").

Medvedchuk didn't merely talk. Soon after, representatives of the Ukrainian Choice actively started fueling anti-shale hysteria and gathering people for rallies in the cities of the Donetsk and Kharkiv regions near planned extraction locations.

"Today, it's not enough just to talk about alarming signs; it's necessary to organize rallies against the actions of the government, which doesn't listen to any reasonable arguments against shale gas extraction in Ukraine. The public movement 'Ukrainian Choice' will do everything to prevent the approval by local councils of decisions by the central government on shale gas extraction in the territories of the Kharkiv, Donetsk, and Lviv regions of Ukraine," threatened Medvedchuk in January 2013.

Indeed, Medvedchuk's posse didn't waste any time. The wave of protests began to grow rapidly. This time, the populace was mobilized using scare tactics—convincing them that gas wells cause birth defects in children and the areas where gas would be extracted would turn into wastelands. All possible methods were used to intensify paranoia. Activists from the "Ukrainian Choice" movement even staged rallies wearing gas masks and chemical protection suits, aiming to draw the attention of the most emotionally vulnerable citizens.

Fear once again became a powerful mobilization factor. Activists spread gruesome videos and low-quality articles on social media portraying the harm of shale gas. New activists quickly joined the fight against multinational corporations. The American documentary "GasLand" by director Josh Fox gained popularity. In the United States, it was considered manipulative. Numerous articles claimed that this movie was made with money from "Gazprom" and that a Russian company had actively promoted it.

Terrifying internet tales found fertile ground. A country that survived Chornobyl had become accustomed to fearing technological disasters. Moreover, environmentalists skillfully used anti-Western stereotypes existing in society for their purposes. Residents of the Donbas were convinced that natural gas extraction companies pursued hidden sinister goals—they wanted to annihilate the Slavic population and even secretly import nuclear waste into Ukraine. This was mentioned, for example, in the popular article "Shale Gas Will Kill Donbas," which was circulated on forums, social media, and printed as leaflets. The publication can still be found online today. It is available, among other places, on the website of Nataliia Vitrenko and her Progressive Socialist Party.

> "According to the draft agreement available online, Ukrainian customs does not have the right to inspect containers, thousands of chemical tanks, and other cargo imported by American 'investors.' It is not excluded that inscrutable containers may contain radioactive waste, chemical, bacteriological, and even nuclear weapons. The clear intention of the Americans to mark their military presence near Russia is evident. By poisoning

the soil and surface waters, the Siverskyi Donets River, the Azov Sea, they condemn to slow extinction several millions of Slavs—the inhabitants of the Donetsk, Kharkiv, Luhansk regions, the lower Don," stated the article.

In this same material, a plan to fight shale gas extraction was proposed. It easily resembles the prototype of what happened in Donbas in the spring of 2014. In particular, people were urged to:

1. "Call friends, relatives, and neighbors. Send text messages with the text 'Watch Josh Fox's film 'GasLand' — you'll be shocked, a disaster is coming.' Shale gas is a real threat to life.

2. Record a thousand discs in AVI format (compatible with all DVD players) and distribute them for free, creatively packaging and signing them.

3. Send the movie to all known and unknown email and postal addresses, distribute leaflets, and submit articles to printed press.

4. Give your neighbor a disc or USB drive with a request to watch the film. Explain the threat in simple words.

5. Fences can speak if they say 'GASLAND won't pass!' or 'Stop fracking!'"

6 . Organize mass protests, pickets, marches, demonstrations, and concerts.

7. Engage deputies and public organizations in the fight. Write letters to the city executive committee, regional administration, and the president.

8. Arrange free screenings of the movie "Gasland" in theaters, followed by discussions.

9. Travel with a TV to villages, show the movie, organize meetings in clubs, and explain the scale of the tragedy.

10. Coordinate joint efforts with anti-shale groups, civic organizations, parties, and blocs.

11. Visit Orthodox churches, talk to priests, and pray to God for help.

12. Organize lectures, roundtable discussions, movie screenings, and debates in schools, lyceums, and technical schools. Rent out movie theaters.

13. Broadcast the movie on opposition cable and satellite channels. Purchase airtime.

14. Organize roundtables, conferences, and discussions involving knowledgeable experts.

15. Raise the topic of the environmental threat of shale gas extraction in the IT realm, on websites, blogs, and in groups.

16. Establish the production and distribution of an environmentally oriented newspaper. Purchase a mimeograph.

17. Provide legal assistance and support to anti-shale groups.

18. Organize groups to travel to the sites of drilling installations, lie under the bulldozer tracks, and chain yourself with handcuffs."

The anti-shale movement that unfolded in the Donetsk region in 2013 served as a kind of prelude to the "Russian Spring" of 2014. The coordinators of the protests gained valuable experience in organizing street actions, managed to build a certain base of active citizens, and learned to conduct mobilization PR campaigns. Scary stories about shale gas spread over the Internet at the same speed as panic news that "Pravyi Sector" ("Right Sector") militants advancing on the Donbas would circulate later. Activists posted flyers on poles and stops urging people to take to the streets against the "shale genocide." On September 26, 2013, anti-shale activists even blocked the Kharkiv-Rostov highway for several hours near the village of Khrestyshche near Slovyansk.

Protests unfolded mainly in the northern part of the Donetsk region since the Yuzivske shale play was located there. Well-attended rallies against natural gas extraction regularly took place in Kramatorsk and Slovyansk. Later, this fact would become the basis for various conspiracy theories about the connection between the war in the Donbas and shale gas. Moreover, supporters of this version would be found on both sides. Ukrainians would suspect that the Russian detachment of Strelkov-Girkin deliberately appeared in Slovyansk to disrupt gas extraction in this region. Supporters of the separatists would assure the populace that the war was happening because the West wanted to seize shale plays.

> "The real reason for punitive actions: Southeast sold to Western gas companies," would be written in social networks, leaflets, and newspapers in the spring of 2014.

The Communist Party, which had an established party structure in Donetsk, almost immediately joined the anti-shale protests. One of the leaders of the anti-shale movement in Slovyansk was Anatolii Khmeliovyi, the first secretary of the local CPU branch. In 2014, he became an active participant in the separatist movement and joined the pursuit of Igor Strelkov.

In other cities in the region, representatives of the Communists also coordinated mass actions. In Donetsk, deputies of the regional council from the Communist Party, Iryna Popova and Antonina Khromova, spoke out against fracking at rallies. In Horlivka, the leaders of the local CPU branch, Oleksii Karpushev, and PSPU activist Zoia Kolesnikova, were involved in organizing anti-shale protests. The coordination of rallies in the Donetsk region overall was overseen by Volodymyr Bidovka, a member of the Verkhovna Rada of Ukraine from the Communist Party. The individuals mentioned above combined their opposition to "shale genocide" with agitation against European integration and for Ukraine's accession into the Customs Union. Representatives of the "Ukrainian Choice" movement also advocated for federalization. In 2014, all these individuals willingly participated in the anti-Ukrainian uprising and supported the self-proclaimed "Donetsk People's Republic" ("DPR"). In 2018, Volodymyr Bidovka even became the head of the so-called People's Council (parliament) of the "DPR".

Communists and Medvedchuk's posse were quite openly lobbying Russian interests and persuading people in their speeches that Ukraine did not need to have its own natural gas extraction. Instead, they argued for pursuing a pro-Russian policy in exchange for discounts on Russian fuel.

> "During the three years of Azarov's government, the authorities have been making deliberately unprofitable for our country concessions to Western tycoons. In contrast, developing friendly and mutually beneficial relations with our brotherly Russia within the framework of the Customs Union, Ukraine would have preferences in the supply of Russian natural gas at a relatively low price," said Deputy Bidovka at a rally in Slovyansk in February of 2013. Other members of his party regularly expressed similar thoughts.

In all fairness, it should be noted that not only pro-Russian forces but also representatives of pro-Western parties participated in protests against shale gas extraction. The latter tried to use the protests against the Party of Regions to increase their own popularity. However, the main driving force behind the anti-shale gas protests was not them. At the forefront of the actions were representatives of pro-Russian forces.

In the spring of 2014, anti-shale gas protests turned into anti-Ukrainian ones. Former activists of environmental protests began to advocate for the Donbas to secede from Ukraine and organize an illegal separatist referendum. A strange metamorphosis occurred—the same people who had previously accused Yanukovych of conspiring with Western corporations and betraying the interests of the Donbas in March of 2014 essentially stood up to defend him. The grievances that were previously directed at Yanukovych were automatically redirected to representatives of the new government after his overthrow, even though they had no connection to the shale gas story.

On March 16, 2014, during a rally in Slovyansk, speakers combined anti-shale gas slogans with calls for separatism. The rally, initially organized as an environmental protest, turned into an anti-Ukrainian manifestation, with some participants carrying Russian flags. At the beginning of the rally, Valentyna Larina, a city council deputy from the CPU, proposed sending a demand to the government and the head of the regional administration to ban shale gas extraction in the Donetsk region. However, the next speaker, Larin's colleague Vira Kubrichenko (a city council deputy from the PSPU), urged people not to recognize the new government in Kyiv. She delivered a speech in support of separatism, shouted "Glory to Gubarev!" and called for a referendum on March 30 in the Donbas, "similar to the one in Crimea."

The issue of shale gas was mentioned in the speeches of separatists during the spring and summer of 2014, already after the start of hostilities. During this time, leaders of the anti-Ukrainian insurgency convinced the residents of Donbas that shale gas was one of the reasons for the declared anti-terrorism operation.

> "We will not allow turning the land of the Donbas into a testing ground for shale gas extraction by Western companies. We will not let Donbas become an ugly desert. We want to see our land green, flourishing, and abundant. This is what we are fighting for," said Pavlo Gubarev in August 2014, in the midst of the conflict.

However, there was no need to fight against Western companies at that time. After the start of hostilities, the shale gas story came to an unfortunate end. Western investors refused to operate near the front line. In 2014, projects were frozen, and in 2015, Shell and Chevron announced their withdrawal from the Ukrainian market.

SHATTERED HOPES

The course towards European integration caused serious discord within the regional elites. It contradicted both ideological beliefs and the economic interests of many of them. In private conversations, Donetsk and Luhansk politicians expressed dissatisfaction with the line chosen by Yanukovych but were not daring enough to openly oppose it.

However, Viktor Medvedchuk actively spoke out against European integration. According to an informed source, at some point, he began to count on rebellion and division within the Party of Regions. In September of 2013, Medvedchuk set out on a tour of cities in the southern and eastern regions to deliver "awareness talks" about the detriments of signing the Association Agreement with the EU. Accompanying Medvedchuk on these trips was Putin's adviser, Sergey Glazyev. In his speeches, he compared Yanukovych to Mazepa and threatened Ukraine with economic challenges should the Association Agreement with the EU be signed.

Each of these Medvedchuk's events became a gathering of pro-Russian forces. Billboard ads of the "Ukrainian Choice" were scaring people with the "horrors of the European Union." Citizens were being persuaded that "Association with the EU is the legalization of same-sex marriages" and assured that after signing the agreement, prices for Ukrainian necessities would supposedly skyrocket tenfold, "to the European level."

As the date of the Eastern Partnership Summit in Vilnius approached, passions escalated. Yanukovych's posse was insisting on the necessity of signing the Association Agreement, while "Ukrainian Choice" and the Communist

Party of Ukraine demanded a radical change in the foreign policy course. This was a bizarre confrontation as it involved political forces that were allies not so long ago. The Communist Party and "Ukrainian Choice" were now using the same rhetoric that the Party of Regions had relied on before 2010. They called for a referendum on Ukraine's accession to the Customs Union, claimed that integration into Europe was not beneficial for Ukraine, scared the public with stories of pornography lessons supposedly introduced in European countries, and promoted the idea of federalization. However, Ukrainian society, according to various polls, was largely unfazed by this. The majority of Ukrainians supported the country's European course. Supporters of joining the Customs Union with Russia and its allies were predominant only in the east and Crimea, but even there, there were no mass protests against Yanukovych's policies. It was evident that the efforts of the Communists and Medvedchuk were insufficient to change the situation.

However, their efforts were not needed. Before the signing of the Agreement between Ukraine and the EU, it became known that Viktor Yanukovych did not intend to sign the Association Agreement. On October 18, 2013, the Cabinet of Ministers approved the draft agreement between Ukraine and the European Union. After that, on October 28 and November 9, Yanukovych and Putin had two meetings. Then, on November 21, a government order was published on the Cabinet's website, suspending preparations for the signing of the document. It also mentioned the need to resume "active dialogue" with Russia and the Customs Union.

In an instant, Yanukovych reversed everything he had done and said in recent years. The preparation for the signing of the Association Agreement with the EU turned out to be a fake. The speed of Yanukovych and his associates' "rebranding" was astonishing. Officials and deputies who had assured the people of the inevitability of the European choice just yesterday now declared with the same fervent confidence that Ukraine was not ready to sign the Agreement, and the Association with the EU was not advantageous for the country's economy.

Such a sudden turnaround was perceived by the majority of Ukrainian society as a betrayal. If Yanukovych had not lied to the entire country and had not given citizens false hope from the very beginning, the uprising against him might not have started. However, the Party of Regions did the worst possible thing. By giving supporters of European integration hope, they cynically took it away at the last moment, waiting almost until the day of the Association Agreement signing. It was particularly significant that Yanukovych changed his course after another visit to Russia and a meeting with Putin. On October 28, information appeared in the press that the Russian president had promised to give Ukraine a $15 billion loan and a discount on natural gas in exchange for not signing the Association Agreement. Therefore, for the millions of Ukrainians, the withdrawal from European integration was justifiably seen as a sellout of national interests.

To have and to lose is worse than never having at all. The disappointment of society was immeasurable. There was a well-founded sense that the government was taking away the country's future. And for this, Yanukovych himself was primarily to blame. Throughout 2013, he had been persuading his fellow citizens that integration with the EU was an important and necessary step toward civilization and prosperity, only to later retract his words. People began to gather on Maidan in Kyiv. *(In Ukrainian language, maidan is both a main city square and a meeting of a large number of people at the square to discuss pressing issues. – T. Ed.)*

Initially, the protests didn't seem like a threat. However, on the night of November 29-30, militsiya special unit Berkut officers received an order to disperse the protesters. There was no need for this radical move at that moment. Those present on Maidan (mostly young people) were not harassing anyone, but the Berkut forces ordered them to disperse. Those who refused to obey were met with force, and the actions of the police were extremely brutal. Everything unfolded in front of journalists' cameras that captured the crackdown on protesters in every detail, and in the morning, the whole country saw it. The footage of the senseless beating of students, including girls, shocked Ukrainian society like an exploding bomb. On December 1, a massive rally took place in the capital, attended by one hundred thousand of people. Disturbances began near the walls of the Presidential Administration. It became clear that Yanukovych got a serious problem where he least expected it.

We won't go into a detailed description of the events of the revolution in this book; the Ukrainian history of 2013-2014 is a topic for a separate study. We are interested in the Maidan only from the perspective of its impact on subsequent events in the Donbas. Today, there is a widespread belief that the war in eastern Ukraine was a direct consequence of the clashes in the capital.

Was it really like that? Supporters of this version resort to a rather simplistic manipulation. They selectively pull out two convenient links from the chain of historical events and assert a simple thesis: "The war started after the Maidan. Therefore, it started because of the Maidan." Typically, such Anti-Maidan advocates don't like to talk about the reasons that led to the Maidan itself. However, it is clear that a revolution cannot spring out of nowhere without any preconditions. The main provocateur of revolutions worldwide is usually the government itself, and popular uprisings don't happen in stable and prosperous states. So, if anyone can be blamed for the fact that President Yanukovych couldn't complete his full five-year term, it is only the president himself.

The version that the Maidan was supposedly inspired by the "subterfuge of the hostile West" also doesn't withstand criticism. The West, undoubtedly, sympathized with the protesters and did not support Yanukovych. However, creating a revolutionary situation in a well-off state where there are no protest sentiments and the government holds great respect would hardly be successful, even for the most cunning conspirators. Interestingly, even opponents of the Maidan acknowledge this fact. For example, **Pavlo** Gubarev, in his speech on February 28, 2014, in the Donetsk City Council, stated that a significant portion of the responsibility for the Maidan lies with the Party of Regions itself.

> "One can talk endlessly about secret backstage directors of the Maidan, foreign intelligence, oligarchs, and other people who influenced it, but if there were no real problems, no one would have come out to Maidan," emphasized one of the leaders of anti-Ukrainian actions in Donetsk after the opposition's victory.

Two years after, in 2016, one of the leaders of the Luhansk political clan, Viktor Tykhonov, acknowledged in an interview with the Russian website "Politnavigator" that the "young reformers" from Yanukovych's entourage themselves provoked the revolution with their behavior.

> "Acting and not looking back, with their behavior, they were preparing and essentially justifying the new Maidan. They imposed tributes on everyone, did what worked best for them. We could already see the economy collapsing, and Azarov saw it, as did the people who worked under him. We tried to openly talk to Yanukovych about it, but he no longer listened. He removed everyone who spoke the truth to him," Tykhonov explained in 2016.

But on the eve of the revolution, everyone, understandably, remained silent, and not one of the Party of Regions representatives, including Viktor Tykhonov, had the courage for public criticism of the "family." On the contrary, they defended and supported Yanukovych until the last moment, even after the uprising had already begun, and the streets smelled of fire.

The 2014 revolution in Ukraine is often referred to as the Euromaidan. However, this definition is accurate only for the initial period, which lasted until November 30, 2013, when militsiya special unit Berkut brutally beat students. The mass rally on December 1 was caused not so much by the rejection of European integration as by the unjustifiably harsh actions of the police. Subsequently, every new attempt by the authorities to suppress the protest did not lead to the stabilization of the situation but rather swung harder the pendulum of violence. The revolution did not happen in an instant; it stretched out over almost three months and lasted throughout the winter of 2013–2014. During this time, the authorities had several opportunities to settle the situation. Initially, this could have been done by even two or three resignations. However, Yanukovych, as stubborn as a mule, did not want to compromise or give in to the protesters, even a tiny bit. He had a long and arduous rise to the presidency, expected an easy re-election for a second term in 2015, and did not entertain the thought of sharing power with anyone. He not only managed to fan the flames with his own hands but also was diligently adding more fuel to the fire for several months instead of promptly extinguishing the initial sparks.

The day after the massive rally in Kyiv on December 2, 2013, an emergency session of the regional council took place in Luhansk. The deputies supported Yanukovych.

> "We firmly oppose actions that lead to armed confrontation and people's suffering. We are confident

that the events on Independence Square on November 30 will be properly legally assessed. Ukraine has confirmed its course towards European standards. However, we need time and resources to reach this high benchmark, find a mutually beneficial format for partnership between Ukraine, the European Union, and the Russian Federation, whose cooperative ties ensure the development of the domestic economy and jobs for millions of our citizens," stated the resolution, adopted at the conclusion of the meeting.

On December 3, a similar session was held by the deputies of the Luhansk City Council, and then the order went down to the cities and districts of the region. All unanimously supported Yanukovych's decision to refuse the signing of the agreement with the EU.

In contrast to the protests in Kyiv, the Party of Regions decided to organize rallies in eastern Ukraine in support of Yanukovych's policy. However, supporters of the pro-Russian course did not rush to participate in mass actions of their own accord. Therefore, to ensure attendance, government representatives began using the usual and familiar method to them—through administrative resources. In Donetsk and Luhansk, pro-government rallies were mostly composed of public sector workers, students, and employees of enterprises belonging to deputies from the Party of Regions.

Like any compulsory attended event, such actions looked unconvincing and ridiculous. It was clear that the brought-in extras were just going through the motions and perceived what was happening as a "duty." People held premade posters and symbols of the Party of Regions in their hands and listened indifferently to the bland speeches of the speakers. The absurdity of the situation was evident. All participants understood that it was an imitation, but they still created the illusion of mass rallies in support of the government. It was unclear who the target audience of this performance was. Supporters of the Maidan just laughed at the pro-government rallies, realizing their phony nature, while the organizers and participants were aware that they were participating in the creation of a fake. However, no one could stop this absurd process.

For example, on December 4, the Party of Regions organized its own rally in Donetsk to support the president in response to the mass opposition rally in Kyiv. Several thousand people were brought to the building of the Donetsk Regional State Administration by buses and handed flags of the Party of Regions and banners with slogans like "Donbas is for stability," "Donbas supports the president," "Thousands are rallying – millions are working," "New Maidan—new deception," and so on. The Party of Regions essentially returned the political discourse to the state of 2003—as if there were no years of Yanukovych's rule, the "family," European integration, and everything else.

The crowd was again comprised mostly of state-owned mine workers brought on mining buses. Thus, the rally was practically financed from the budget. The essence of the speakers' speeches boiled down to the old slogans of the times of the Orange Revolution and the Sievierodonetsk Congress—they again began to fuel hatred towards residents of western regions. The Party of Regions once again tried to convince the Donbas that residents of other regions of Ukraine wanted to deceive them and live at their expense.

> "We can sing, dance, and have fun just as well as others. But we have a conscience! We work, we go to work in hot workshops and in the mines. Are we ready to continue enduring so that freeloaders and idlers live at the expense of the Donbas? Are we ready to feed loafers?"- bellowed the host of the rally, Oleksandr Sulaiev, into the microphone. The crowd responded with dissatisfied

murmurs.

On December 9 in Luhansk, the Congress of Deputies at All Levels took place. Its delegates supported Viktor Yanukovych, and during the event, all the propaganda messages that had been hammered into the heads of the residents of the eastern regions for years were voiced.

"The parliament did not vote on a law on sexual minorities, which legalizes same-sex relationships," said People's Deputy from the Party of Regions Volodymyr Medianyk, attributing this fact to the current government. The head of the regional administration, Volodymyr Prystiuk, stated that the participants of the congress would not oppose if Yanukovych "takes harsh measures" against protesters "to restore order."

Oleksandr Yefremov already then called the events on Maidan a "revolution," although, at that moment, a revolution was still far off. Only a mass rally was taking place, where citizens expressed their dissatisfaction.

"We must understand that the fate of our enterprises, the future employment of our children depends solely on our actions. If we sign the Agreement with the EU, we won't get new jobs. I promise to defend the interests of our region until the end," said Yefremov in a phone call. Representatives of the Cossack organization also appeared for the first time at the congress, entering into a scuffle with journalists.

On December 17, Viktor Yanukovych flew to Moscow, where he signed several agreements with Vladimir Putin. As anticipated earlier, Russia provided Ukraine with a discount on natural gas and agreed to invest $15 billion in Ukrainian securities. Ukrainian media commented, "Viktor Yanukovych exchanged European integration for Russian money and cheap natural gas." Supporters of the Maidan sadly noted that the debt would still have to be repaid, and the cheap gas would mostly benefit oligarchs from Yanukovych's inner circle—Rinat Akhmetov and Dmytro Firtash.

Wishing to demonstrate support from the population and convey that Yanukovych was fulfilling the will of the people, the authorities organized another rally in Donetsk on the same day. It took place in the workshop of the "Nord" plant, owned by Party of Regions Deputy Valentyn Landyk. Secretary of the Donetsk City Council Serhii Bohachov and representatives of the regional organization of the Party of Regions came to meet with the workers. However, the event was organized so poorly that it had a reverse effect. Instead of confirming the high rating of the government, it demonstrated the impotence and foolishness of the officials.

The statement released by the "Nord" press service after the meeting resembled low-quality propaganda, reprinted from some Brezhnev-era newspaper:

> "We support the nationally elected President Viktor Yanukovych and the government in their efforts to stabilize the situation in Ukraine. We call on the president to resume trade volumes with Russia so that Ukrainian goods can smoothly enter traditional export markets. We give Viktor Yanukovych a mandate of public trust to sign all documents in Moscow that contribute to this goal," the statement said.

Photographs taken at the meeting instantly spread on the internet and became the subject of ridicule. Weary factory workers stood in a dark and cold workshop, dressed in dirty robes and coats. In their hands, people held signs like "Donetsk supports the President's course" and "Donetsk will not allow a state coup," brought to the plant by officials. At first glance, it was clear that people were participating in this not of their own free will, and politicians were simply using their subordinates to create the appearance of popular support.

The assembly at "Nord" of Valentyn Landyk prompted recalling the statements of his brother Volodymyr (a well-known Luhansk businessman-regional, former head of the regional organization of the Party of Regions) when, back in 2010, he explained the difference between the West and East of Ukraine in an interview with Gazeta.ua:

> "Look at how a steelworker, a machinist works in the East. These are awful conditions. They earn 200–300 dollars. And a guy from the West of Ukraine says, 'I wouldn't work like that for such money! I'll go to a Pole, chop wood for him, he'll give me 100 dollars, and I'll come back to him again.' This is a mentality. We wanted to launch the 'Nord' plant in Ivano-Frankivsk. But we barely got out of there. We brought our own people there by train because the locals didn't want to work, even though they were paid the same as in Donetsk. Everyone should work. We need to close the borders and produce our own goods, build farms. We will try to do this in 10 years," Volodymyr Landyk explained a few years before the onset of revolutionary events.

This revelation vividly illustrated the logic that the Party of Regions followed in its actions. For the first time, a representative of one of the industrial groups in eastern Ukraine publicly acknowledged what was previously only spoken about by opponents of the Donetsk group. The Donbas elite was interested in a powerless and cheap labor force and even dreamt of closing borders to prevent people from seeking better-paying work abroad. Naturally, after Yanukovych's sharp geopolitical turn, Volodymyr Landyk's admission could not be forgotten. The disdain with which the Party of Regions member spoke about the inhabitants of western Ukraine, whose only fault was the desire for fair compensation for their work, only added energy to the protest.

However, it wasn't just Landyk who spoke disparagingly about migrant workers. During the Maidan period, Ukrainian workers going abroad for employment in the EU were presented by the propaganda of the Party of Regions as enemies of the state, alongside radicals and nationalists. Rare were the meetings in eastern Ukraine without mention of "Western Ukrainians who scrub toilets in Europe." Hearing such condemnation of migrant workers from supporters and even representatives of the authorities was, at the very least, strange. After all, people went to work abroad not because of a good life—unemployment pushed them to it. In the fact that millions of Ukrainian citizens were forced to go to other countries and engage in hard labor, the government could only blame itself. However, officials and local council deputies implanted into the minds of ordinary people from the Donbas that their fiercest enemies were the same laborers from Galicia and Volyn, tilers, welders, and caregivers, who were guilty only of not finding decent work at home.

AGONY

The unwillingness of Yanukovych to listen to protesters increasingly fueled passions in the capital. The Party of Regions claimed that mainly fringe individuals and nationalists, acting on Western instructions, were opposing the government. Such an attitude only fueled the protest and pushed people towards radical actions. But instead of trying to cool down the situation, the authorities decided to tighten the screws.

On January 13, a person from the inner circle of Oleksandr Yefremov, the deputy head of the Luhansk Regional State Administration, Eduard Lozovskyi, essentially called on the Security Service of Ukraine (SSU) to "clear out" the protesters.

"Bands of thugs have seized the center of the capital, and only a month after the attack by nationalist stormtroopers on Bankova Street, finally, 'the police had the right to shoot.' Or perhaps, should we handle it like Zhukov did in Odessa in '46?" wrote Lozovskyi. *(After WWII Marshal Zhukov was stationed in Odesa and in successful attempt to crack down on organized crime allegedly gave his officers permission to shoot to kill, no court, no trial. —T. Ed.)*

On January 16, 2014, the ruling coalition openly and fraudulently adopted the so-called "dictatorship laws" in the Verkhovna Rada, which significantly strengthened the regime. In particular, concepts such as "extremist activity" and "foreign agent," clearly borrowed from Vladimir Putin in Russia, were introduced. The legislation prohibited the activities of media without state registration and imposed criminal liability for libel.

The situation was complicated not only by the adoption of the laws themselves but also by the manner in which it was done—without a discussion or a real vote count, just a show of hands. Moreover, the raised limbs were not even genuinely counted. During each vote, Deputy Volodymyr Oliinyk simply called out a pre-determined number: "235."

Such blatant arrogance crossed all lines. There was a usurpation of power, and Yanukovych lost any legitimacy in the eyes of opponents. Clashes erupted on the streets, the first casualties occurred, and in regions where Yanukovych was unpopular, a real uprising broke out. Frightened members of the Party of Regions realized they had made a mistake and tried to turn the tide, but it was already too late.

Throughout the winter, the actions of the government were chaotic and disorganized. Obviously, Yanukovych did not understand the true nature of the popular uprising and did not know how to quell it. Other top officials were not particularly smart or savvy either. In response to opposition protests, the Party of Regions organized the so-called Anti-Maidan, but the mass pro-government rallies were completely underwhelming compared to the opposition's protests. In Kyiv, Yanukovych had almost no support, so people had to be brought to the capital from other cities for the Anti-Maidan.

In the Donbas region, people were brought to pro-government rallies for free but with the use of administrative resources. Thousands of workers from mines, factories, and plants were transported by buses to the squares, where representatives of local authorities—officials and deputies— spoke on stages set up in advance. Speakers did not spare opponents, and sometimes explicit calls for violence were heard. Anti-Maidan activists demanded that Yanukovych brutally suppress the protests.

But the Kyiv Maidan was far away. Therefore, all the hatred of the speakers was directed at local opponents of Yanukovych, who gathered at small local Maidans in Donetsk and Luhansk. In the eastern part of the country, opposition supporters were in an obvious minority and, therefore, did not pose a serious threat to the authorities but were well suited to vent their anger. Supporters of the Maidan in the Donbas region were constantly subjected to attacks, not only by ordinary supporters of Yanukovych, who might genuinely be moved by emotions, but also by "titushky" - hired young men, sometimes athletes, serve as hooligans, provocateurs during political rallies.

Initially, protesters in Donetsk had the opportunity to gather undisturbed. The gathering place was the Shevchenko monument, located not far from the regional administration building. In November and December, gatherings there were peaceful, but on January 19, 2014, the situation changed abruptly. On that day, Donetsk supporters of the opposition decided to drive in a car convoy to Yanukovych's estate in the village of Kalinkino-2 and picket it in protest against the adoption of dictatorial laws. The president himself was not in Donetsk that day, but according to the organizers' plan, he was supposed to find out about the picket from the press. They were attempting a publicity stunt. Indeed, after the organizers of Donetsk Automaidan announced their action, the news spread instantly in the media. Such a move by opposition members in Donetsk, who were in the very "den of the enemy," looked quite daring.

Viktor Yanukovych apparently perceived this action as an intrusion on his territory. According to a source in the Donetsk Regional State Administration, upon learning about the planned trip to the estate, the president's elder son became angry and tasked his people with "dealing with" the opposition and preventing the car column from leaving. The task was assigned to the "influential businessman" Armen Sarkisian from Horlivka, known in the city as the "overseer" for Yuriy Ivanyushchenko.

On January 19, opposition members in Donetsk gathered at the parking lot near the regional administration to head from there to Yanukovych's residence. However, their departure was quickly blocked by cars belonging to Sarkisian's posse. The Automaidan car convoy was not even allowed to leave the parking lot. Activists were surrounded by thug-looking young men who began insulting Maidan supporters, pushing them, and yanking Ukrainian flags from their hands. The police present at the scene stood aside and did not intervene.

The "titushky" were led by Armen Sarkisian himself, who stood behind them wearing a cap pulled down over his eyes, as well as his associates Hahik Ahavelian and Eduard Poliepkin. Another notable figure who participated in the confrontation was the shaven-headed tough guy Oleksii Petrov, who later, in 2014, became one of the leaders of the militants in the so-called "Donetsk People's Republic" ("DPR") in Horlivka. The mercenaries achieved their goal – the trip to Yanukovych's residence did not take place.

After the "battle" on January 19, government-hired "Tonton Macoutes" attempted to disrupt almost every opposition action in Donetsk. "Titushky" poured zelenka (green antiseptic liquid) on participants of the Donetsk Euromaidan, threw eggs at them, and took away or broke their flags. There were also incidents involving "titushky" themselves. On January 26, a curious incident occurred in Donetsk: near the Shevchenko monument, two groups of "titushky" mistakenly took each other for Maidan supporters and engaged in a brawl.

In Luhansk, the local authorities demanded harsh measures. On January 20, the Party of Regions faction in the Luhansk Regional Council issued a statement calling on Yanukovych to use force to suppress the confrontation on the streets. In addition, Luhansk deputies demanded the ban of the "Svoboda" party and the imposition of a state of emergency in Kyiv.

> "The Euromaidan as a peaceful action ended in the evening of January 19, when it transitioned into a phase of violent confrontation, pushing the country to the brink of civil war. Those who call themselves peaceful demonstrators and activists of the Euromaidan took to Hrushevskyi Street with a clear purpose: to use force, organize unrest leading to bloodshed," claimed the statement by Luhansk regional officials.

The utter cynicism of this statement was staggering. As known, on January 19, the first casualties among the protesters appeared, and the Luhansk authorities not only showed no sympathy for the deceased but expressed sentiments of "they brought it upon themselves," without mentioning the culpability of law enforcement officers.

Against the backdrop of escalating events in Kyiv, the situation further intensified in regions predominantly supporting the opposition. On January 23, thousands of Lviv residents blocked the square in front of the Lviv Regional State Administration. People stormed the building, demanding a meeting with the governor, Oleh Salo. They informed him that "from now on, they take control of the government." Under pressure, Salo wrote a resignation statement. Following suit, Volyn governor Borys Klymchuk also resigned. In several regions of western and central Ukraine, supporters of the Maidan took control of regional administrations.

On January 25, the Party of Regions organized another large-scale rally in support of Yanukovych in Luhansk. The majority of those present were workers from the "Marshal" and "Avtomotozapchastyna" plants, owned by two well-known Luhansk members of the Party of Regions, People's Deputy Serhii Horokhov and regional council deputy Andrii Niedovies. Speakers again demanded to "restore order" and take "harsh measures." The events in Kyiv were labeled a "coup d'état."

> "We appeal to the President of Ukraine as the guarantor of the Constitution, to the deputies we elected to the Verkhovna Rada, to all representatives of state power, demanding the immediate restoration of order in Kyiv and the reinstatement of legality across the entire territory of the country. To show firmness and consistency in defending the constitutional order of Ukraine. To protect the residents of our state from civil confrontation, using all necessary lawful actions and harsh measures, up to the imposition of a state of emergency," said the resolution of the rally.

Simultaneously, on social networks like "Odnoklassniki" and "VKontakte," rumors began to circulate about the "secession of eastern regions from Ukraine" and their accession to Russia. In all these posts, a well-known deputy of the Luhansk Regional Council, Arsen Klinchaev, was mentioned. Essentially, he was the first to voice these ideas in his own name.

> "We don't want the country to split, and we won't allow it. But I am convinced that if the power in the country falls into the hands of fascists, the East of Ukraine won't tolerate it. The East is waiting, although many are on the edge of their seats. Many are ready, so to speak, to 'have some fun.' And I do not rule out the possibility that the eastern regions, if the power in the country falls into the hands of protesters, will not want to live in such Ukraine and will reunite with Russia," Klinchaev said in an interview with the publication "Vostochnyi Variant."

By the end of January, it became clear that the power was gradually slipping from Yanukovych's hands. However, despite resolute calls from fellow countrymen to deal with the Maidan, the president hesitated. This hesitation frightened officials in the Donbas. In the current situation, they, as in 2004, tried to mobilize their electorate using old, proven methods. They began to scare people with radicals and fascists from western Ukraine, who supposedly planned to come to the Donbas and stir up unrest in the region. And the residents of the eastern regions, frightened by the events in Kyiv, once again believed in these scare tactics.

One of the politicians deliberately fueling hysteria in Donetsk was the city council secretary, Serhii Bohachov. On the morning of January 27, he made a statement that was immediately broadcast on local television channels controlled by the Party of Regions. Bohachov claimed that eight buses with members of the "Right Sector" were heading towards Donetsk, supposedly planning to overtake the building of the Donetsk Regional State Administration. Almost immediately after this statement, buses with miners from state mines began to gather near the administration building. Together with special militsiya unit Berkut, the miners were supposed to defend the building from the assault of nonexistent "invaders." When journalists asked the Governor of Donetsk region, Andrii Shyshatskyi, who gave the order for the miners to come to the Regional State Administration, he replied that he did not make such a decision, and the miners were sent according to the decisions of labor collectives.

Throughout the day, hundreds of miners in orange helmets wandered aimlessly around the administration building. Some residents of Donetsk, frightened by rumors about buses with fascists, mistook them for activists of the "Right Sector." The authorities fueled hysteria, but in the end, the "Banderites" never appeared in the city. Serhii Bohachov explained their absence by claiming that the buses with nationalists allegedly did not reach the destination and turned back at the border of the Donetsk region.

In Luhansk on the same day, January 27, 2014, an official order from the head of the regional administration, Volodymyr Prystiuk, created a "Headquarters for Ensuring Public Order and Stable Operation of Enterprises." Prystiuk was seriously afraid of the "arrival of other people" in the region and even instructed to control the sale of baseball bats in stores. No one directly mentioned where they expected "guests" from, but from the overall vibe of the informational arena, it was implied that it was about the same "Right Sector" portrayed in the Russian and Ukrainian pro-government regional press as a powerful and numerous organization. To combat radicals, local authorities began to create so-called "people's militia squads."

> "Due to the attempts to storm the regional administrations in the Kharkiv and Zaporizhzhia regions, a number of civic organizations in the Luhansk region have put forward an initiative to take on the responsibility for ensuring public order and protecting fellow citizens from radicals who are committing lawlessness. Members of the Luhansk Regional Council fully support this initiative of civic organizations," said the statement of the regional council on this matter.

> "I would like to address those "travelers" who are trying to enter Luhansk land. You should know that we have very honest, hospitable people here. We love to welcome guests, we will always share a meal and a drink with them, we love to sing songs, and we also give gifts. But besides loving to relax, we also love to work. All enterprises are currently working steadily here because people understand the need to feed their

families, their country, and, unfortunately, freeloaders. I'm just warning you that if some guys try to come to the Luhansk region and establish their own order, create turmoil, chaos here, we'll work them over and it won't be pretty. Because our patience is also coming to an end," warned Governor Volodymyr Prystiuk on January 28, 2014.

On January 31, the head of the Party of Regions faction in parliament, Oleksandr Yefremov, also began to scare the residents of Luhansk with "visitors."

"I spoke today with a saleswoman in one of the large stores in our city. And she tells me: 'Oleksandr Serhiiovych, some people, some strangers have appeared in our city.' I say: 'Maybe it's just your imagination?' She says: 'No. I have worked in sales all my life, and I can easily tell apart locals and visitors. I'm telling you that there is some group of 'not our' people in our city today, they go to the stores, they keep warm there, and it's quite obvious,'" - narrated Oleksandr Yefremov.

From the context, it was understood that Yefremov, like Prystiuk, meant "tourists" from western Ukraine. And if those words seemed like a lie then, in the context of subsequent events, it is entirely plausible that the saleswoman from Yefremov's story did indeed notice visitors —except they were from Russia.

On February 8 in Donetsk, participants from two rallies clashed again. Supporters of Maidan gathered near the regional prosecutor's office to honor the memory of those who died in Kyiv. Opposite them, a larger pro-government rally assembled. Its participants, mostly the same hired "titushky," shouted threats and insults at Yanukovych's opponents. At the Anti-Maidan rally that day, a veteran of the anti-Orange movement and one of the future "ministers of the "DPR," Oleksandr Khryakov, appeared.

"Viktor Fedorovych Yanukovych! We chose you, we fought for you at the polling stations with this filth since 2004, we held the tent city 'For Ukraine without Yushchenko.' We marched in Russian parades across Donetsk. How much longer can you ignore our wishes? Give Berkut the order to clear out this filth. And we will help, give you a hand. Our Cossacks, our soldiers, our Soviet warriors, and our Russian fighters haven't forgotten the serial number of their weapons, recorded in our military ID!" rambled Khryakov.

His speech was an explicit call for murder and civil war. The video recording of Khryakov's speech spread in the media and shocked opposition supporters. However, as is often the case in such situations, the threats had the opposite effect. Calls like these only fueled and convinced the protesters that there was no turning back. Stopping the revolution was already impossible, but Yanukovych did not make much effort to do anything about it.

By February 9, a no-name community "Luhansk Volunteer Brigade" with 50 subscribers on "Vkontakte" announced a "March against the Maidan scum." "Activists of Russian Orthodox gatherings, the Union of the Russian People, the Novoaidar Yurt of Don Cossacks, the literary and historical club Rusych, the Russian Union, the Russian community of Sievierodonetsk, as well as the Luhansk Volunteer Brigade named after General Denikin, will take part in the march," the announcement said. In reality, these organizations did not exist.

It was a test: how many people would come out for an anti-Ukrainian or openly pro-Russian rally without administrative resources and the government's order? It showed that by the beginning of February, there was no real anti-Ukrainian movement in the region; only 20 people attended the rally, and they were mere civilians who could not engage in violent actions. For example, on that day in Luhansk, Anastasiia Piaterikova appeared at a rally for the first time—a dancer from a nightclub who would later become the main public speaker for the anti-Ukrainian movement on Russian television in February-March.

On February 12, a forum of representatives of regional councils took place in Crimea, attended by regional officials, including Valeriy Holenko from Luhansk and Andrii Fedoruk from Donetsk. Given that the forum occurred two weeks before the start of the Russian invasion of Crimea, there is no doubt that it had a deliberate nature. Discussions there went beyond the necessity to stop all hostilities in Kyiv. They talked about fundamental changes to the Constitution and the actual transition to a federal system, as well as the need to adopt an effective law on local and national referendums. Few paid attention to this detail at the time, but subsequent events confirmed the significance of this assembly. Its content indicated that scenarios of secession from Ukraine were being considered by the regional elites of the southern and eastern regions of Ukraine even before Yanukovych fled.

On the same day, February 12, the first truly menacing forewarning happened in Luhansk. The known ataman of the Luhansk district of the Cossack ADH, controlled by Russian special services, Leonid Ruban, the first one from the Luhansk region, appealed to Vladimir Putin and the Russian ataman of the ADH, Viktor Vodolatskyi, with a request to "provide military support to the people of Ukraine."

> "Opposition leaders call for protests involving radical nationalists who have seized the downtown of the capital and control in western regions of Ukraine. They provoke civil war, stating that they will seek NATO's assistance. We address you as concerned citizens who respect the laws of Ukraine and international legal acts to which our state has joined, urging you not to abandon

us to the mercy of heartless Western Herods. But, in the event of further escalation of the political crisis and attempts to bring in NATO troops to Ukraine, to provide military support to the people of Ukraine," stated the appeal, which received wide resonance in the media.

The regime's agony continued until the twentieth of February and ultimately ended in mass killings. On February 18, street fights erupted in the capital. From the 18th to the 21st of February, 77 people were killed on Maidan. On the night of February 22, the president realized the game was lost and fled Kyiv. Almost all the top officials of the country followed suit.

THUNDER IN THE EAST

On February 22, 2014, a Congress of Deputies from the Southern and Eastern Regions, Sevastopol, and the Autonomous Republic of Crimea took place in Kharkiv. It was expected that the leadership of the country, which had fled from Kyiv, would speak at the congress. However, neither Yanukovych nor Azarov appeared at the congress, although they arrived in Kharkiv. In addition to Ukrainian politicians with pro-Russian beliefs, there were also Russian "guests" at the congress: State Duma deputy, head of the international relations committee Aleksey Pushkov, Senator Mikhail Margelov, governors of the Bielhorod, Rostov, and Voronezh regions, as well as the Consul General of the Russian Federation in Kharkiv, Sergey Semenov. The presidium of the congress included all the heads of the regions that supported Yanukovych during the Maidan. It all started the same way as in Sievierodonetsk in 2004.

In content, the congress was absolutely reactionary, but it ended up being remarkably "toothless." Speakers expressed outrage, argued, threatened, but did not articulate radical calls for secession or the establishment of some kind of "republics." On this day, the leaders of the regional Party of Regions organizations realized that Yanukovych was already de facto not the president and that there was no one to demand "order in the state" from. From Kharkiv, the Luhansk delegation immediately went home, where a session of the regional council was planned for late in the evening. Just before its start, a rather strange event occurred in the city, the meaning of which remains unclear to this day. Around 6:00 PM, a group of about 50 people gathered in the square in front of the regional council building, armed with baseball bats. Shouting "Glory to Ukraine!" the unknown individuals began to simulate storming the building. They seemed like real "titushky" with identical bats and medical masks. Someone fired several shots in the dark.

This pseudo-storming was led by the well-known Luhansk politician Vyacheslav Serpokrylov (at that time, the head of the local branch of the UDAR party), who had a reputation as a provocateur in the city. For many years, Serpokrylov had been organizing various actions and commissioned rallies, creating fake civic organizations and movements. He was involved with regional branches of different political forces, working either against the Party of Regions or in their interests, depending on the situation. He had collaborated with Arsen Klinchaev in the past as well.

In 2009, together with Klinchaev, Serpokrylov created the civic association "SSSR" (the idea was in consonance with the abbreviations of the Union "Social Justice and Development" and Union of the Soviet Socialistic Republics (USSR) in Russian.) During the presentation of this organization, Klinchaev willingly participated in a staged fight with fake "Ukrainian nationalists," deliberately hired to add drama to the event.

Serpokrylov's attempt on February 22, 2014, to organize a strange and senseless pseudo-storming of the Luhansk Regional State Administration, apparently, was also a provocation that ultimately led to the escalation of anti-Ukrainian sentiments in Luhansk. Essentially, the leader of the Luhansk UDAR and his people played the role of the same bloody radicals that Yefremov and Prystiuk had been scaring the people of Luhansk with for a month. Serpokrylov was never seen at the Luhansk Euromaidan, and its leaders immediately distanced themselves from his involvement in this raid.

The building of the regional administration was "guarded" by several activists from the "Luhansk Guard," a pro-Russian public organization founded in January 2014 and financed by local Party of Regions members. Whether there was an actual clash between Serpokrylov's posse and the activists of the "Luhansk Guard" who were trying to "protect the building of the regional administration" is unclear. The available video recordings are challenging to interpret, so it is highly likely that both sides were merely simulating the brawl. In the dark, shots were fired, but it was impossible to determine who was shooting and where.

Eyewitnesses claim that the "assaulters" did not even approach the building of the regional administration and stayed in the square across it the entire time. Ultimately, the "assault" ended with nothing; Serpokrylov's people dispersed through the alleys. However, the goal was achieved: news agencies published reports of a "radical attack on the Luhansk Regional Council," which quickly spread across social media.

After this incident, panic rumors spread through the city that the "Right Sector" had finally arrived in Luhansk and instigated bloody disturbances. Serpokrylov's "assault" mobilized radical pro-Russian locals. People armed with chains, baseball bats, and rebars gathered in front of the regional administration building. Soon, Oleksandr Yefremov triumphantly appeared before them, promising to "defend Luhansk from lawlessness."

The deputies of the Luhansk Regional Council gathered for an emergency session. The Party of Regions members looked bewildered. Everyone already knew that Yanukovych had fled, and they were waiting to hear what Yefremov would say. The headliner of the event was a deputy of the Luhansk Regional Council and the owner of the "Avtomotozapchastyna" plant, Andrii Niedovies. He attacked the bankrupt president.

"I have been saying one thing for the past few years:

Mezhyhirya *(Yanukovich`s palace in Kyiv suburb – T. Ed.)* and the 'family' will drive this country into a pit from which we will not be able to escape. Both the 'family' and us, the people who put him on the throne, will be taken out with pitchforks. We are on the brink of this situation," he said.

However, immediately after this confession, Niedovies began urging regional council deputies to engage in acts of civil disobedience. The essence of his speech was that opponents of the Maidan should start fighting against Maidan activists using their own methods.

"Look at the list of those killed. Look at the addresses and names. Nine out of ten are people from the west. There were no Kyiv residents there. Central, and mostly western Ukraine. Respect to them for that. They were able to do what they considered necessary. Now we must learn from them the acts of civil disobedience," Niedovies said from the podium.

However, his words about "nine out of ten" were an outright lie. To establish this, it is enough to look at the addresses and names of the deceased, which are available in open sources. For example, out of the 23 killed on February 18, only four were natives of western Ukraine (Volyn and Galicia). Seven of the deceased, including journalist Vyacheslav Veremii, were residents of Kyiv and the Kyiv region. Two were from Donetsk region. Out of the eight killed on February 19, only one was a native of western Ukraine. Of the 47 killed on February 20, 25 were "westerners." Needless to say, Niedovies knew the real state of affairs. However, the facts contradicted the worldview that Luhansk politicians had been carefully building for so long, so they decided to simply ignore them.

Niedovies stated that the police of the Luhansk region should "submit to the authorities where we live."

"We must become the only legitimate authority that can say something. And there must be people who will raise the flag—our flag, the flag of our region—and say that we want to live the way we want. And that's it. And if they try to break us, we must show our teeth in a snarl, not a smile," Niedovies continued.

Another regional council deputy, Rodion Miroshnyk (who would later become a representative of the so-called "LPR" in the Minsk Contact Group,) urged colleagues to create all conditions for people who "want to defend themselves" and help them organize tent camps. The mayor of Luhansk, Serhii Kravchenko, even more explicitly called on colleagues to resist.

"If each of you gathers your teams and says, 'Who's willing?' hundreds of thousands will come. Not a single scoundrel will come here. They will know that Luhansk is strong!" - shouted Kravchenko from the podium.

After long and heated speeches, the Luhansk Regional Council declared that it assumed full authority in the region. Deputies appealed to the Verkhovna Rada, demanding the right to create municipal police and local law enforcement, and also announced the formation of people's self-defense units. The regional council recommended that city and district councils in Luhansk do the same.

In fact, the emergency session of the Luhansk Regional Council became a prelude to the events of spring 2014. Everything that Miroshnyk and Niedovies called for soon began to be implemented. In Luhansk, groups of people did appear, as if summoned, who quickly armed themselves and, with the full support of local authorities and the police, took power into their own hands. The Donbas was frightened by the very fiction it had fabricated. Supporters of the Maidan, portrayed as Nazis and killers by propaganda for several months, struck fear into the local population. A significant number of Donbas residents truly believed that foretold buses with fighters from the "Right Sector" were about to arrive to the region and retaliate against its residents for supporting Yanukovych.

On the next day, February 23, when information about Yanukovych's flight had already reached the media, the head of the Party of Regions faction in the Parliament, Oleksandr Yefremov (he was practically the only public speaker from the government who did not flee or go into hiding), made a dramatic statement. On behalf of the party and the parliamentary group, he acknowledged mistakes, disowned the fugitive president, and accused him of committing crimes.

> "Ukraine has been deceived and plundered, but even this is nothing compared to the tragedy faced by dozens of Ukrainian families who lost their loved ones on both sides of the confrontation. Ukraine was betrayed, and people were set against each other. The entire responsibility for this lies with Yanukovych and his closest circle. We, the parliamentary group of the Party of Regions in the Verkhovna Rada of Ukraine and our fellow party members, strongly condemn the criminal orders that led to human casualties, an empty treasury, enormous debts, disgrace in the eyes of the Ukrainian people and the world. As a result, our country found itself on the brink of the abyss, facing the threat of division and loss of national sovereignty. Any attempts to influence the situation, persuade the president, went unheard. The party of millions essentially became a hostage of one corrupt 'family.'
>
> The group of the Party of Regions represents the interests of over 10 million voters and more than one million party members. The Party of Regions

consists of regular, hardworking people who love their land and their people. These include industrialists, scientists, workers, doctors, and teachers. We came to parliament to serve Ukraine and its people. The Party of Regions parliamentary group declares that differences in opinions, sometimes in ideology, are not obstacles to working together for the good of Ukraine. There may be different views, but our goal is a common one—a united, strong, and independent Ukraine. We condemn Yanukovych's flight and recklessness; we condemn betrayal; we condemn criminal orders that put ordinary people, soldiers, and officers in jeopardy.

However, attempts at total intimidation and vigilantism, destabilizing the situation in the regions, are unacceptable in democratic societies. Dear fellow party members, I address all of you—deputies from the Party of Regions in the Verkhovna Rada, regional, municipal, and local councils, and all patriots of our party. We will do everything to protect you and shield you from the mistakes and crimes made at the highest level," said Oleksandr Yefremov.

Headless, the Party of Regions members now had to adapt to new realities and figure out how to exist going forward. The bitterness of political defeat was compounded by the realization that Yanukovych and those around him had committed a heinous crime for which someone would have to be held accountable. In a matter of days, the Party of Regions, which had always prided itself on internal discipline and monolithic unity, fragmented into separate factions, each of which had to grapple with the need to find new patrons. Not necessarily within the country. A few days after Yanukovych's escape, unidentified military personnel appeared in Crimea. The annexation of Crimea by the Russian Federation began.

The prospects for Viktor Yanukovych himself remained unclear until the end. There was a possibility that, with the support of his Russian partners, he might attempt to return and continue the struggle for power. After leaving Ukraine, the ousted president showed up in Rostov and held a press conference on February 28. His speech left a mixed impression. Yanukovych stated that he remained the legitimate president and supreme commander but did not issue any orders to anyone. Moreover, he claimed to be against Russia's military intervention in Ukraine, although it had already begun, with Russian forces appearing in Crimea. Yanukovych's supporters were bewildered and even more disappointed. Many expected, some with fear, some with hope, that he would seek assistance from the Russian government, triggering a full-scale invasion of Ukraine. At that time, the Russian leadership pretended to have no involvement in the events in Crimea.

In such confusion, each of the Party of Regions members acted at their own discretion. Some waited in anticipation of some stabilization, while others made timid attempts to negotiate with the new authorities. Some decided to play the old game called "Donbas separatism." Moreover, the conditions for this had become highly favorable once again.

PART SIX

BLOODY SPRING IN DONETSK

After Yanukovych's flight, Donetsk was in disarray for several days. Officials, local deputies, organizers, and participants of the Anti-Maidan could not believe that it was all over. Just like ten years ago, after the Orange Revolution, they thought that the victors would seek revenge. In various parts of the city, small gatherings of Anti-Maidan activists occasionally took place, but no more than 200-300 people participated in these actions. All this activity resembled a fist waving after a fight and initially did not cause much concern. The attention of the entire country at that moment was focused on the situation in Crimea, where the main dramatic events were unfolding.

On February 22, near the monument to Hrinkevych in Donetsk, a rally took place, featuring a speaker from Kharkiv representing the organization "Oplot." This organization, created in Kharkiv by former Interior Ministry employee and businessman Yevhen Zhylin, gained notoriety during the events of the winter of 2014 in Kyiv, where Zhylin's posse clashed with Maidan supporters. In Donetsk, a representative of "Oplot" openly urged residents to take up arms and use them against political opponents.

> "I am more than confident that half of you here have weapons. You are Donbas. I know how people live here and how resolutely they speak. Half of you may have illegal weapons; well, now is the time to use them. It will be a legal use!" called out Zhylin.

At that moment, there were no enemies against whom weapons could be used in the city, excluding, of course, local supporters of Eurointegration who behaved absolutely peacefully. No one planned to travel to Donetsk from other regions of Ukraine and foment unrest there. There was no sense in it, as the goal of the uprising had been achieved—Yanukovych and his team ceased resistance and fled Ukraine. However, the Donetsk authorities continued to mislead and stir up the people. Representatives of various organizations affiliated with the Party of Regions convinced Donetsk residents that a war was about to begin, that they needed to arm themselves and fight against Maidan supporters, whom they referred to as nothing but "fascists" and "radicals." Day after day, speakers lied about buses with "Maidan militants" and "Right Sector" approaching the Donbas, and these alarming rumors circulated through the city, accumulating various details and specifics. Stoked by propaganda, people would believe any horror story. Taxi drivers recounted tales to passengers about radicals who had come either to Horlivka or Selidove to topple the local Lenin monument.

On February 24, with the support of the city authorities, a small tent city appeared on Lenin Square in Donetsk. The formal organizers of this event were newly created organizations "Defense of Donbas" and "Eastern Front." The organizers of the tent city declared that they intended to protect the Lenin monument from nationalists and urged people to join the people's militia squad to defend the city. Above the tents flew the tricolors of the separatist organization "Donetsk Republic."

The leaders of the organizations told journalists in comments that they intended to simply maintain public order because they feared an increase in crime. However, it was clear that this was just a cover story. During the rallies, speakers were more candid and stated that these squads were being formed to fight against Maidan supporters, "radicals," and "nationalists" who allegedly were preparing to come to Donetsk.

Eduard Akopov, who called himself the commander of the "Eastern Front," did not hide the fact that he planned to create paramilitary formations and even appealed to the city authorities for assistance in this matter.

"Taking this opportunity, I would like to ask the city authorities for help in allocating premises for a formation of 500 people, to put them into a barracks state so that they remember what discipline and army life are. I wanted to ask for instructors who could teach people a bit, remind them of disassembling and assembling the Kalashnikov rifle, and combat tactics," Akopov said during an expanded meeting with the heads of district councils and representatives of law enforcement agencies on February 25.

The mayor of Donetsk declined this request. However, no one did anything to stop the 'Eastern Front' and the 'militia squads either. Officials took an ambivalent position, trying not to cross certain red lines, but at the same time, encouraging public hysteria.

The governor of the Donetsk region, former top manager of one of Rinat Akhmetov's plants, Andrii Shyshatskyi, publicly supported the organizers of the tent camp.

"Unfortunately, if there is a threat and aggression coming from the Maidan, both on social media and on television, citizens have to self-organize for protection," quoted the head of Donetsk Regional State Administration, the newspaper "Siegodnia."

But, in fact, the tents in the square were not a self-organization. In addition to the governor himself, the creation of the tent city was also undertaken by members of the Donetsk branch of the Communist Party of Ukraine, as well as the secretary of Donetsk City Council, Serhii

Bohachov, who personally came to Lenin Square, interacted with activists, and provided comments to journalists.

The formation of units for future defense took place not only in downtown Donetsk in those days. Governor Shyshatskyi urged the mayors of cities in the Donetsk region to create self-defense units to resist the "Right Sector." He proposed involving people with registered weapons in these units. Cities reacted differently to the governor's task. It is known for sure that the mayor of Khartsyzk, Valerii Dubovyi, indeed summoned members of the local hunter's community and proposed creating an armed unit. In some cities, Shyshatskyi's initiative was ignored.

Two years later, during the trial regarding Shyshatskyi's order, the mayor of Slovyansk, Nelia Shtepa, also mentioned the meeting, as she, along with other city heads, attended it.

> "At the meeting, Shyshatskyi said that aggressive radicals from the 'Right Sector' might come to Donbas. He mentioned how many people they had already killed, and, therefore, it was necessary to create local self-defense units to combat the 'Right Sector.' For this, we were supposed to gather everyone with weapons, hunters, and propose to them to form self-defense units," she explained.

But the main roles in the upcoming confrontation were supposed to be played by completely different organizations: the "Donetsk Public Formation for Protecting Public Order and State Borders," where the then-unknown Oleksandr Zakharchenko was listed, and the "People's Militia of Donbas" led by Pavlo Gubarev, which was being formed precisely in those days. On February 25, the "People's Militia" appeared on social media, and an "Appeal of Pavlo Gubarev to the Donbas Militia" was published on the internet.

"For the local authorities to dare to act, they must feel pressure from the residents of Donetsk. Therefore, the task of the patriots is to create such a civic movement that could, on the one hand, protect the city from incoming nationalists and, on the other hand, force the authorities to listen to the people of Donetsk, not the illegal 'government' in Kyiv. To achieve this, we need to gather 10,000 people in front of the Regional State Administration. And I know that there are three times as many of us," was stated in the appeal.

WHERE DID PAVLO GUBAREV COME FROM, AND HOW DID HE BECOME THE "PEOPLE'S GOVERNOR"

To better understand what happened in Donetsk in March 2014, we need to go back to the mid-2000s when the future "people's governor" of the Donetsk region took his first steps in politics.

In the book "The Torch of Novorosiia," which was released during the heat of the conflict, Gubarev barely mentioned his involvement in regional politics. He only hinted that in his youth, he spent some time in the ranks of the nationalist organization "Russkoie Natsyonalnoie Yedinstvo," ("Russian Nation Unity") which openly proclaimed its goal of fighting against "foreigners" and imitated the NSDAP. However, this part of Gubarev's biography was not well-known in Donetsk. He first appeared in 2005 in the public organization called the "Antivolokitny Komitet" (AK, "Anti-red tape committee"), created by another young Donetsk politician, Mykola Levchenko.

Levchenko created this project for the mayoral elections in the interests of the city head, Oleksandr Lukyanchenko. The public activists fought against paper pushing and bureaucracy. Gubarev was chosen as one of the leaders of AK, and Levchenko became the honorary president of the organization. Another future participant in the events of March 2014, Gubarev's friend Myroslav Rudenko, also emerged during that time. However, the "Antivolokitny Komitet" existed for a short time and was hardly remembered for anything significant. Pavlo Gubarev quickly left this project and soon began working in the headquarters of another mayoral candidate, Serhii Beshulia.

Beshulia was a mid-level official, heading the executive committee of the Kyiv district, and had no noticeable influence or significant business in the city. Behind his nomination stood Vadym Bondarenko, who was then relatively unknown in Donetsk (future head of the Donetsk Tax Office and a member of the "family"). At that time, Bondarenko controlled the Donetsk branch of the Socialist Party of Ukraine (SPU) and intended to lead the party faction in the city council. It was he who invited Gubarev to work in Beshulia's headquarters and proposed that he become a deputy from the SPU in the Kuibyshev District Council. The party program of the SPU, which claimed to be anti-fascist but essentially adhered to Russian national socialism, perfectly matched Gubarev's views.

Vadym Bondarenko headed Serhii Beshulia's headquarters and was involved in organizing his election campaign. It's hard to say if he really hoped to lead his candidate to victory —Beshulia's ratings did not exceed a few percent, and his chances of winning against the incumbent mayor were slim. More likely, Bondarenko wanted to assert himself as a strong player in Donetsk politics in this way, but he failed. Beshulia, at the end of the day, was simply not allowed to participate in the elections. However, Bondarenko himself became a deputy in the city council on the lists of the Socialist Party of Ukraine. Gubarev also managed to become a district deputy.

How did Vadym Bondarenko come from, where did he get the money for the elections, and how did he obtain the Donetsk franchise of the SPU? He got help through connections with people who would later be referred to as the "family." According to Donetsk businessman Vladyslav Dreher, who was well acquainted with Bondarenko, his success was due to one of the managers of the "family"— Oleksandr Sychynava. Thanks to Sychynava, after the 2006 elections, Bondarenko experienced an incredible career takeoff. First, he was appointed as the head of the organizational and regulatory department of the State Tax Administration in the Donetsk region, although at that time he had no relevant education. Then, in 2008, Bondarenko headed the tax office of the Kalininsk district. In 2011, he became the head of the tax office of the Donetsk region. After the creation of the Ministry of Revenues and Duties as a joint entity of the State Tax and Customs Service, Bondarenko took the position of acting head of the Main Department of the Ministry of Revenues and Duties in the Donetsk region.

At that time, only a person from the "family" could hold such a position, as the Minister of Revenues and Duties, Oleksandr Klymenko, who was known to be close to Yanukovych, headed the organization. Making such a career in just five years and in a region like Donbas was not easy for a random person. However, Bondarenko had influential patrons. His connections were not limited to Sychynava alone. Vadym Bondarenko's namesake, Eduard Bondarenko, who was a member of the SPU faction along with him from the early 2000s, was a partner of Vitalii Bieliakov, who headed the "family" company DRFTs. In 2012, Eduard Bondarenko himself took over the "family"-controlled company "Donbasenergo." These facts suggest that **Pavlo** Gubarev was not a "nobody," as initially believed, but was always connected to Yanukovych's inner circle.

After the 2006 elections, Gubarev got involved in the advertising business. However, according to insiders, this was more of Vadym Bondarenko's business, and Gubarev was just a junior partner. In 2008, Gubarev became the director of the company "Rekkom," founded by Vadym Bondarenko's mother, Nina Ivanivna. Later, Gubarev registered his own company, "Patyson," which was involved in advertising placement. He took a break from politics for a while. Before his sudden appearance on the political scene in 2014, he had hardly ever been in the public eye.

According to Maksym Rovinskyi, the former press secretary of Donetsk Mayor Oleksandr Lukyanchenko, Vadym Bondarenko was behind the sudden appearance of Gubarev in March 2014, serving as the shadow organizer nomination of his longtime associate as a "people's governor."

> "I have no evidence, but I am confident that Bondarenko contributed to how Gubarev would later play out. Whether he provided him with money or Russia financed Gubarev through him. But something definitely was going on," Rovinskyi explained in his comments for this book.

According to Rovinskyi, Gubarev became more active during the revolutionary confrontation in Kyiv. The political crisis engulfing the country could not have left him unmoved. As a Russian nationalist-Eurasianist, Gubarev, of course, could not sympathize with Ukrainian national democrats and their European aspirations.

> "When all these processes started on Maidan, at some point, Gubarev emerged. I used to attend the rallies of Donetsk Euromaidan at the Shevchenko monument, and I remember that at one of these events, he just showed up and was filming something on his camera. I hadn't seen him for a long time before that. We said hello. He was cracking jokes, looking relaxed, and didn't announce any special plans," recalls Maksym Rovinskyi. "Around that time, he somehow got in touch with [Donetsk City Council Secretary] Bohachov, presenting him a project

for a pro-government internet television. He brought a proposed budget with him. And Bohachov decided to consult with me, as he didn't understand anything about internet media. He asked me if I knew enough about it and how realistic the estimates Gubarev had brought to him were. It was a relatively small amount, around 200 thousand hryvnias. I looked at it and said that this much money would only buy equipment. But to keep it running, we would need to spend a similar amount every month. Paying people's salaries and so on. As far as I understand, based on my verdict, Bohachov ultimately declined Gubarev's request for financing."

After this meeting, Gubarev disappeared for some time. It's unclear what the future leader of the pro-Russian conspiracy was doing during this period. **Pavlo** Gubarev himself wrote almost nothing about it in his book. He only mentioned that he was present at the Congress of Deputies of All Levels in Kharkiv on February 22, 2014. However, after Yanukovych's ousting, a week before spring, Gubarev reappeared in Donetsk. According to Maksym Rovinskyi, who met him at that time, he was already a completely different person.

"He showed up a few days before that session of the city council where he came out and read his ultimatum (referring to the events on February 28, details later on —A/N). It was the end of February when Yanukovych had already fled. A friend then asked me to go with him to some meeting where he didn't want to go alone. We arrived at the Hotel "Shakhtar Plaza." Gubarev was there with three armed guards. He already behaved completely differently. It was a striking difference from the day I last met him at a rally. Now, he was the way everyone later saw him at the rallies. His facial expression, speech, habits—everything about him had changed. Later, there was a lot of talk about him being on something. I don't know if it was true. But he behaved very strangely.

He began to say that this country would no longer remain the way it was. He said that Russia supported him, that the police and the SSU were behind him, and he intended to become the people's governor. I thought him insane at that time. He was talking nonsense, saying that a separate state would soon be established here, that everything would be demolished, and he told us to ask him questions about what this state would be like. I immediately asked, tongue in cheek, about his thoughts on private property. It was trolling, but he didn't understand, and he started explaining seriously that private property would be preserved. At that moment, Gubarev said he wanted to speak at the city council session, and for our own good, we should let him speak; otherwise, he would take the floor himself. When I met with Lukyanchenko and told him about this, the mayor refused. So, when Gubarev came to the session, it was decided not to give him the floor," Rovinskyi recounted.

According to Rovinskyi and other eyewitnesses who saw Pavlo Gubarev during this time, he freely moved around the city with three armed individuals and had no problems with law enforcement. He attended meetings with people holding automatic weapons. It was evident that Gubarev had influential backers, and for this reason, he was not afraid that someone would report him to the SSU or the police.

Gubarev never said who these backers were. In his interviews and in the book, he always portrayed what was happening in Donetsk as a grassroots movement. He depicted himself as the main organizer of this movement. However, only an extremely naive person could believe that the relatively unknown Gubarev managed to independently create a mass movement, find weapons, people, and finances in just a week. Until Yanukovych fled Ukraine, Gubarev never appeared or spoke at any of the Anti-Maidan rallies, unlike

Purgin. He did not even have a fringe organization of his own, did not participate in roundtable discussions, and was not noticed at "Russian marches." However, by March 1, he had at his disposal, at a minimum, several hundred trained fighters, some armed.

According to one well-known Donetsk businessman who requested anonymity, Yanukovych's team, which fled Ukraine, planned to play an age-old bandit combination—first, create a conflict, and then offer their services for its resolution to return to the country. When it became clear that the elites of the southeastern regions were not going to support Yanukovych, the only tried-and-true method left was Donbas separatism. It was much easier to organize unrest in this particular region than to instigate a coup in other eastern and southern regions. Perhaps Gubarev was chosen as the organizer of the coup simply because, at the right moment, he turned out to be the most convenient candidate willing to participate.

Were the Donetsk authorities complicit in this plan? Did they assist Gubarev, or did they just idly watch him, knowing well whose interests he served? It's difficult to say. Proving a conspiracy involving officials and Gubarev is challenging, as none of the participants in those events will speak the truth. According to the official version maintained to this day by both the self-proclaimed "people's governor" and the Donetsk authorities at that time, Gubarev acted solely on his own initiative. But how can one explain the behavior of officials who not only did not hinder him but actively helped him?

On February 28, 2014, as promised earlier, Pavlo Gubarev attended the session of the Donetsk City Council. The mayor and deputies did not plan to give him the floor, but People's Deputy Mykola Levchenko, who also came to the session from Kyiv, insisted that Gubarev be allowed to speak.

"I've known **Pavlo** for a long time; he's a guy who

genuinely cares about the fate of the country. He helped us in election campaigns," persuaded Levchenko.

In this way, he practically ensured that his long-term acquaintance's speech did take place. Everything looked as if Levchenko was interested in Gubarev's speech and helped him get to the podium. Why Levchenko did this, whether he was in cahoots with Gubarev or just playing democracy, there are different theories about that.

Talks about Mykola Levchenko's connections with Russia had been circulating in Donetsk for a long time. This politician never hid his pro-Russian views and made openly anti-Ukrainian statements more than once. According to a source in the Donetsk SSU, in 2007, a meeting between Mykola Levchenko and an FSB general was documented at Donetsk airport. The meeting took place in the VIP terminal, and from the conversation, it was understood that Levchenko was an FSB agent working for Russia. At that time, the recordings of the negotiations were allegedly delivered to the higher-ups, which ordered the destruction of these materials because, formally, it was subordinated to the "orange" head of the SSU in Kyiv, but in fact, it was connected with the Party of Regions.

According to the source, one of the first tasks for Levchenko was to organize an information campaign in support of Russia's actions in Georgia in 2008. In September 2008, Levchenko did travel to the Russian-occupied South Ossetia, and after his return, he organized a propaganda photo exhibition in Donetsk dedicated to the "atrocities of the Georgian aggression." Given this information, the Deputy's support of Gubarev was clearly not accidental.

Donetsk businessman Vladyslav Dreher believes that Levchenko and Gubarev were not in conspiracy, but Levchenko decided to use his long-time acquaintance, thinking that he would be able to control him in the future.

"Gubarev was not under Levchenko's control. The fact that he was once in Mykola's orbit did not mean that Mykola could control him. Levchenko's mistake was thinking that Gubarev was his project, while Gubarev did not think so. He worked with other people, most likely in Russia. We remember the situation when on March 1, the rally started slipping out of the control of the Party of Regions, and when Mykola wanted to bring it back under control, he couldn't do it," said Dreher.

In his speech, Gubarev demanded that the Donetsk City Council declare the parliament, the Cabinet of Ministers, and the Donetsk Regional Administration illegitimate and also cease transferring taxes to Kyiv. In case of refusal to comply with these demands, Gubarev promised to "delegitimize" the deputies.

"In case of non-compliance with our demands, the 'People's Militia of the Donbas' will consider the Donetsk City Council and all its deputies illegitimate. We are ready to take adequate measures to delegitimize the city council, as well as each deputy individually, with all the consequences that may arise from it," stated Gubarev. He concluded his speech with the words, "Whoever didn't hide is not my fault." *(This is a hallmark phrase in a head-and-seek game, announcing the start seeker's search, similar to "Ready or not, here I come!" Sometimes used figuratively to forewarn of readiness to make a move. —T. Ed.)*

Gubarev's speech was interrupted several times by outraged exclamations. In his address, he criticized the Party of Regions multiple times for their perceived lack of firmness and ability to maintain control. Deputies clearly were not accustomed to such an attitude and did not expect such words. Obviously, the majority of them did not take Gubarev's words seriously. Many of the deputies knew **Pavlo** from before, having dealt with him in political matters, and therefore did not consider him an independent player capable of achieving anything.

Later, Gubarev claimed that after his speech, Levchenko offered to meet, and during this meeting, he threatened him with a gun. However, whether this episode was real or if Gubarev and Levchenko fabricated it to provide the latter with an alibi is hard to determine. Regardless, it was Levchenko who arranged for Gubarev to become the focus of media attention.

Following these events, even stranger incidents unfolded. On March 1, the day after Gubarev's speech in the city council, a rally organized by the city authorities was scheduled to take place on Donetsk's main square. Gubarev had already announced that he and his supporters would seize the stage, but despite knowing this, the organizers did not cancel the rally and did not take any additional security measures.

> "Tomorrow, at the rally organized by the Party of Regions (near the Regional State Administration building), some important issues will be raised, but this should not distract us from the main task, from condemning the state coup, from the illegitimacy of the central government bodies, and other issues raised in the Ultimatum of the 'People's Militia of the Donbas.' It is important for us to bring our speaker to the stage and address truly crucial issues that determine the safety of the region's residents and our lives," reported the Gubarev supporters in their public statement on February 28.

Despite Gubarev's threats and ultimatums, the authorities, in fact, did everything to give him the podium. Everything looked as if the rally was organized precisely to allow Gubarev to take over it.

"On March 1, the rally took place at Lenin Square,

where everything in Donetsk began. I was categorically against this rally and argued with Bohachov, who was its organizer. Gubarev did not hide that he would overthrow the authorities and was preparing to declare himself the people's governor, so his plans for Donetsk's leadership were known. I yelled at Bohachov in his office, "What the hell are you doing? You're gathering a crowd for him!" But Bohachov acted like a rapt idiot. Throughout the spring of 2014, he couldn't decide whether he was for or against Ukraine, attempting to sit on the fence. Once I directly asked him at a meeting: what is your position? You know mine; I don't want Russia here. And what about you? Tell us privately, at least, so that we know. But he never said anything. He avoided the answer," says Maksym Rovinskyi.

The Secretary of the Donetsk City Council, Serhii Bohachov, was considered a member of the "family." This circumstance also raises doubts about the "rapt idiot" behavior of Bohachov being accidental. During the confrontation in Kyiv, the Secretary of the City Council intimidated the Donetsk population with buses from the "Right Sector" and did everything to escalate the situation. On March 1, despite colleagues' warnings, he ordered a large number of people to be brought to the downtown of Donetsk, thereby playing into the hands of pro-Russian radicals. The mass gathering, which Gubarev could not have organized independently, was assembled by the Donetsk authorities for him.

On the day of the rally, Gubarev's plan worked. On March 1, together with several hundred of his supporters, he arrived at Lenin Square. His group partially consisted of Russian citizens. In late February, calls started appearing on social media urging residents of adjacent Russian regions to travel to cities in the south and east of Ukraine under the guise of tourists to participate in the uprising against the Ukrainian government. Those coming to Donbas mainly arrived from neighboring Rostov.

In this city, dispatching Russians to Ukraine was handled by the activist of the "Eurasian Union of Youth," Volodymyr Prokopenko, who had previously come to Donetsk for "Russian marches." Working on this matter was also another well-known Eurasian activist from Rostov, a friend and associate of Pavlo Gubarev, Oleksandr Prosielkov. (Later, he would hold the position of "Deputy Minister of Foreign Affairs" in the self-proclaimed "DPR", and in the summer of 2014, he would be killed by unknown assailants while in the rear of the separatist fighters).

The rally began as an ordinary event organized by local authorities. Serhii Bohachov took the stage, calling on the crowd to honor the memory of those who died in Kyiv and the "betrayed by the authorities" special militsiya unit Berkut fighters. Bohachov's speech was openly disliked by the crowd. Shouts and whistles were audible. Someone angrily shouted from the crowd, "You betrayed them yourselves!"

At some point, a group of Gubarev supporters moved toward the stage from the Coal Mining Ministry building where they had initially gathered. However, the Party of Regions did not want to let Gubarev onto the stage. A brief scuffle ensued, in which Gubarev's supporters gained the upper hand. The fight unfolded right in front of the crowd, which angrily shouted and demanded that the speaker be allowed to speak. The vague and meaningless speeches of the Party of Region clearly did not match the mood of the people. The attendees wanted more radical actions and calls.

When Gubarev took the microphone and began to sound off the same statements he had voiced in the City Council a day before, the crowd responded with joyful roars. Gubarev knew well what the attendees expected from him. At the time, Russian forces were already present in Crimea, and pro-

Russian residents of Donetsk, fueled by officials' statements and media propaganda, anticipated the appearance of "little green men" in the Donbas as well. From the stage, the "commander of the people's militia" declared the new Ukrainian government illegitimate, called for a referendum on the independence of the Donetsk region, and demanded its accession to Russia. After this speech, one of Gubarev's associates suggested the crowd "elect him as the people's governor."

In an instant, an unknown 30-year-old resident of Donetsk soared to fame, transforming into the leader of the pro-Russian movement in Donetsk. Gubarev was not a great public speaker, but he said exactly what the supporters of the Party of Regions and Yanukovych wanted to hear at that moment. The crowd in the square immediately expressed readiness to follow the new leader.

ZAKHARCHENKO VS SEPARATISTS

However, not everyone in Donetsk liked this scenario. While Gubarev was gathering people and preparing for the role of "people's governor," another structure with a long and awkward name, the "Donetsk Municipal Public Formation for Public Order and State Borders Protection," was gaining strength in the city. For simplicity, its participants referred to themselves as "people's volunteer squads," declaring their assistance to law enforcement. The leader of the volunteers was retired police officer Ihor Melnykov, and one of his closest assistants was the future leader of the so-called "Donetsk People's Republic" ("DPR"), Oleksandr Zakharchenko.

Ihor Melnykov's organization emerged before the revolutionary events began. The decision to revive "people's volunteer squads" in Donetsk was made suddenly in the summer of 2013. The first district headquarters of the volunteer squads were opened in the Kirovskyi district of the city, as reported by the Donetsk Ministry of Internal Affairs at the time. Ihor Melnykov became the head of the city headquarters.

Did the authorities anticipate back then that the volunteer squads might soon be needed as "titushky"? Were these formations for public order protection created with the aim of specific events (a possible revolution) or just as a precaution—it's unclear. We have no evidence for this, so let's not delve into conspiracy theories. However, the fact remains that volunteer squads did not limit themselves to maintaining order on the streets. Soon, they found their first reason to participate in a political action. After the incident in Vradiyivka (where several Ministry of Internal Affairs officers raped and attempted to kill a local resident, leading to civil disobedience actions in the village), protests against police brutality erupted throughout Ukraine. In response to these protests, Melnykov and his people decided to organize a rally in Donetsk in support of the police.

"In light of recent events in Kyiv, where police officers find themselves in real danger, facing attacks, we have decided to speak out in defense of law enforcement under the Donetsk Regional Council," stated Melnykov.

The announced rally took place on July 18. Political slogans were used at the gathering, with squad members holding signs that read "Provocateurs from Svoboda and UDAR—go away" and criticizing the opposition.

During the revolutionary events, Donetsk volunteer squads were keeping a low profile. However, after the victory of the Maidan, they reminded people of their presence. Melnykov deployed his people to patrol the streets of Donetsk alongside the police. On February 24, in a comment to the newspaper "Viesti," Ihor Melnykov stated that his people were on duty at seven checkpoints near Donetsk to prevent "armed militants" from entering the city.

An article titled "Volunteer Squads Came Out to Guard Donetsk" appeared on the "Viesti" website on February 25. There were no "militants" near the city at that time, but, at the instigation of local authorities, rumors of activists from the "Right Sector" planning a visit to Donetsk had circulated in the city since January. Referring to Melnykov's people as "volunteers" is not really precise, as the people of the "People's Brigades" were created with the support of the administrative resource, had a clear political position, and, in fact, were a formation-oriented towards the Party of Regions.

Unlike **Pavlo** Gubarev's "People's Militia of the Donbas," the "volunteer squads" claimed that they were assisting the police, which, in turn, officially stated that they were subordinate to the new head of the Ministry of Internal Affairs, Arsen Avakov. Thus, Ihor Melnykov's people, including Oleksandr Zakharchenko, formally found themselves on the Ukrainian side at the beginning of the anti-Ukrainian coup. According to Maksym Rovinskyi, in reality, the volunteer squads were reporting to the city authorities rather than the police and were not acting independently. After **Pavlo** Gubarev appeared, Melnykov and Zakharchenko immediately tried to assume control of his "People's Militia."

> "When the rally gathered on March 1, I stood aside near the theater and didn't even approach the stage. I understood that there would be huge trouble because a day before, I met with Oleksandr Zakharchenko at the 'Sun City' cafe. Zakharchenko warned me that Gubarev was planning to stir up unrest. He told me that Gubarev had a lot of money, that he was paying people, and that he had 300 individuals who would help him get on stage and incite the crowd. Zakharchenko said: Give me any other name except Gubarev, and we'll have the crowd chanting for him to let our person speak," said Maksym Rovinskyi.

In March 2014, Gubarev and Zakharchenko were on opposite sides of the barricades. At that time, Donetsk was in a rather chaotic situation, with the "volunteer squads" defending the government against the "people's militia," but both groups held anti-Ukrainian positions. The only difference was in the degree of radicalism. While the Party of Regions talked about budgetary federalism and the expansion of regional autonomy within Ukraine, the Gubarev supporters called for the secession of the Donbas and incited Donetsk residents to riots and destruction of administrative buildings.

One episode of the confrontation between the

"volunteer squads" and the "people's militia" can be seen in a video that is still in open access. On March 17, supporters of Gubarev attempted once again to break into the Donetsk Regional State Administration, and Melnykov's people stood in their way, preventing them from reaching the administration. An interesting aspect of this episode was cameras caught the future leader of the militants, Oleksandr Zakharchenko, silently standing in the crowd near the Administration. Gubarev's supporters insulted Zakharchenko and Melnykov, calling them fascists. Gubarev, who was already arrested at that moment, was replaced by a strange individual named Robert Donia, who declared himself Gubarev's successor.

The video with Oleksandr Zakharchenko later gained wide popularity on the internet under the title "Zakharchenko—titushka." Zakharchenko's appearance was scrutinized only after he became the leader of the militants. By the way, Ihor Melnykov, who then led the "volunteer squads," did not disappear either and eventually accepted the position of "Deputy Minister of Internal Affairs" in the self-proclaimed "DPR".

The career of "People's Governor" Gubarev turned out to be very short-lived. On March 3, Gubarev led his supporters to the Donetsk Regional State Administration building again, where a session of the Regional Council was taking place that day. Without support of the administration, no more than 3000–4000 people came to support Gubarev. The attendance record of the March 1 rally was never repeated throughout the turbulent spring of 2014.

The majority of those who came were the electorate of Communists and the PSPU: retirees, former Afghan War veterans, Cossacks, excitable women of indeterminate age, and openly antisocial elements. However, in the vanguard of this crowd were strong young men who formed the backbone of the "people's militia." Some of them were Russian citizens, and some didn't even hide that they came from Russia. In particular, the head of the executive committee of the Russian Sverdlovsk regional branch of the "Another Russia" party, Rostyslav Zhuravliov, openly wrote about his adventures in Donetsk on social media and posted photos with Gubarev from the captured Administration.

The chief of Donetsk police, Roman Romanov, went out to meet the crowd, agreeing to escort Gubarev to the building and allow him to speak in the session hall. There, Gubarev reiterated his demands, which he had put forward in Donetsk City Council on February 28: urging the deputies to recognize the government and parliament as illegitimate authorities, vote for a referendum on the status of the Donetsk region, and recognize him as the people's governor. From the podium, Gubarev claimed that his supporters had managed to gather 800,000 signatures across the Donetsk region in support of him, which was undoubtedly a falsehood.

Gubarev's plan was simple. With the example of Crimea in mind, where armed individuals seized the local parliament building and coerced local deputies into voting for a "referendum" on the peninsula's status, the leader of the "people's militia" intended to repeat this move in Donetsk. According to his plan, under the pressure of the crowd, Donetsk deputies were supposed to appoint him as the head of the region (similar to the appointment of Aksionov in Crimea) and announce a referendum on the region's future. However, Gubarev's plan had one significant difference from the events in Crimea—there were no armed "little green men" in Donetsk. Therefore, becoming the "Aksionov of Donetsk" was not in the cards for him.

As a result of a tumultuous and tense session, the Regional Council deputies voted for holding a "referendum" in the Donetsk region (without specifying the issues on the ballot), recommended local self-government bodies to consider the issue of creating formations to maintain public order, and even declared the unacceptability of increasing rates for housing and utilities. However, Gubarev's main demands were ignored. No one was willing to cede power to him.

The appeal that the regional council decided to send to the parliament accurately reflects the position of the Donetsk authorities, or more precisely, the lack of any coherent position. In the same document, the deputies initially demanded from Kyiv to allow the Donbas to decide its fate independently through a local referendum, and then spoke about the impermissibility of actions aimed at the division of Ukraine.

> "We appeal to the Verkhovna Rada of Ukraine with an urgent demand to promptly adopt a law on local referendums, which would allow the residents of the Donetsk region to express their will. We advocate for the Russian language to have the status of a regional language in the Donetsk region, which will enable our citizens to communicate freely, choosing the language that is more convenient for them. We stand for an economically thriving, unique Donbas as part of a united and strong Ukraine! We condemn divisive statements or calls for the separation of the Donetsk region from Ukraine! In conditions where the region's economy is in crisis, and the financial situation of the majority of residents of the region is rapidly deteriorating, regional authorities should have the opportunity to make a wider range of decisions," stated the appeal of the regional council.

Deputies tried to use the turmoil to once again attempt to negotiate more powers for themselves from the center. However, this yielded nothing. The decision of the Regional Council angered the Gubarev supporters. The crowd of "people's militia" burst into the building and began smashing everything in its path. Deputies had to escape through emergency exits. Former governor Andrii Shyshatskyi was almost stabbed as he pushed through the ranks of enraged pro-Russian supporters.

Representatives of the authorities suddenly became victims of their own policies. For years, they had been promoting regional hostility, frightening residents of the Donbas with fascists, and convincing them that in western Ukraine, there were subhumans and enemies. However, when all this propaganda finally spilled into mass hysteria on the streets of Donetsk, the officials suddenly found themselves as enemies. Gubarev's supporters called them traitors and lackeys of Banderites for not having a radical enough position. In an instant, the Donetsk Anti-Maidan, which was created by the Party of Regions to fight political opponents, became as much a threat to them as the Maidan in Kyiv.

The number of the Gubarev supporters was small, but the police did not stop them and did not defend the Regional Council. Separatists managed to break the doors of the regional administration, occupy the first floor, and enter the session hall. This passivity of law enforcement became a reason to accuse the leadership of the Donetsk office of the Ministry of Interior of sabotage and sympathy for the rioters. Police chiefs explained the inaction of their personnel by demoralization and unwillingness to confront protesters after the Maidan events. In reality, perhaps both factors played a role.

After the regional council dispersed and refused to support Gubarev's demands, it became clear that his plan was not working. The situation reached an impasse. The pro-

Russian activists' hope was pinned on the Crimean scenario, but the Russian leadership had different plans for the Donbas. Local authorities, recognized as legitimate by separatists, tried to serve two masters but they were not willing to submit to radicals. The radicals themselves did not fully figure out what is it they wanted.

The author of these lines personally attended almost all pro-Russian rallies in Donetsk during the spring of 2014 and vividly remembers the atmosphere of these events. Speakers, taking turns at the microphone, roared passionate calls and put forward mutually exclusive demands. Some insisted on the need for a referendum on federalization, while others demanded secession from Ukraine and accession to Russia. Some called for the "legitimate president" Yanukovych to return, while others cursed him for cowardice and betrayal and did not want his return. From the podium, Pavlo Gubarev promised to raise everyone's salaries by 40% when he became governor and then claimed that soldiers in military units in Donetsk had joined his side. Several times, speakers at the rallies announced that Russian military equipment had already crossed the border of the Donetsk region, but this information was never confirmed.

Within a few days, it became clear that Gubarev's performance was gradually losing its meaning. Russian forces did not appear in Donetsk, and the number of protesters decreased. Several times, the Gubarev supporters captured the building of the Regional Administration and raised the Russian flag over it, but they did not try to stay inside and eventually dispersed. On March 6, Gubarev was arrested and taken to Kyiv. Only a few hundred people gathered for a rally in his support outside the SSU office in Donetsk.

CONFRONTATION IN LUHANSK

Meanwhile, the situation in Luhansk unfolded differently. There was no strong, consolidated anti-Ukrainian organization like the "People's Militia," but there was a much more pro-Russian-oriented regional elite. The local authorities openly supported anti-Ukrainian actions from the very beginning.

Several civil organizations and political groups organized protest actions, first simultaneously and then jointly.

Let's start with the regional branch of the Communist Party of Ukraine. Around 2005, while the CPU's indicators were declining nationwide, and its activists were steadily aging and dying, the situation in Luhansk developed in the opposite scenario. At that time, Spiridon Kilinkarov took over the regional branch of the CPU. He managed to mobilize the loyal electorate to the CPU and prevent it from switching to the Party of Regions. In 2006, he became a Member of Parliament from the Communists for the first time on the party lists. Quickly, the CPU became something akin to local quasi-opposition—often opposing the Party of Regions on tactical issues regarding the management of local property but having no ideological contradictions with them. Moreover, through active involvement in economic processes, the CPU became increasingly influential, and it was evident that the organization had good funding.

Spiridon Kilinkarov did become king of the hill in 2010 when he faced off against the Party of Regions in the mayoral elections in Luhansk and, in fact, won. During the campaign, he managed to secure significant financial, media, and administrative resources from all the "offended" and former Party of Regions members who had conflicts with Oleksandr Yefremov and his circle. The Party of Regions then once again nominated a weak and powerless candidate, Serhii Kravchenko, who was essentially Yefremov's underling and followed his orders. When it became evident that Kilinkarov would win the mayoral elections in the regional center, then-President Viktor Yanukovych and the head of the Communist Party of Ukraine, Petro Symonenko, intervened in the situation. According to sources from the Party of Regions, during the meeting between Yanukovych and Symonenko, a decision was made to instruct Kilinkarov to step down, rewrite the protocols, and hand over the mayor's seat to Kravchenko. In return, the Party of Regions agreed to appoint a communist as the secretary of the City Council, handed over illegal financial flows from municipal transport, and a substantial amount of money in cash to Kilinkarov. Serhii Kravchenko became the mayor for the second time with a humiliating result, "outperforming" Kilinkarov by 21 votes, earning him a derogatory nickname. However, it was most challenging to come to an agreement with Spiridon Kilinkarov. He sought power, won the elections, but he argued and haggled for a while. Since then, people in Luhansk began to speculate that Kilinkarov would become the next leader of the Communist Party of Ukraine, as he demonstrated his potential in real elections and vast ambitions for the first time. And in many ways, Spiridon Kilinkarov's actions in 2014 were conditioned by the results of the 2010 elections.

In the spring of 2014, the Luhansk Communists, led by Spiridon Kilinkarov and Yurii Khokhlov (we have already mentioned him in the section on the looting of coal enterprises), were among the first to start organizing and shielding various events of the "Russian spring." Closer to

April, as will become evident later, they received funding for these activities.

At the end of January, old and new small civic formations of an Anti-Maidan nature, controlled by the Party of Regions, began to intensify in Luhansk. By March–April, they took the lead in the anti-Ukrainian insurgency in the region.

One such formation was led by the organization "Young Guard," headed by Arsen Klinchaev, a deputy of the regional council closely associated with Yefremov, whom we have mentioned several times before. The name of the organization was an allusion to Oleksandr Fadieiev's Soviet novel about the Komsomol underground during World War II, which resisted the Nazis in the city of Krasnodon during the German occupation and was eventually destroyed. Throughout Soviet times, there existed a peculiar cult of the "Young Guard" in Luhansk, which was regularly reinforced by ideological actions and was primarily directed toward the older generation. However, in reality, the "Young Guard" of 2014 was just a formation of "titushkas" who followed the instructions of the local authorities.

In early February, a more radical pro-Russian group, the "Luhansk Guard," emerged. It was formed based on the local branch of the PSPU led by Nataliia Vitrenko, and its leader was elected the secretary of the Luhansk city committee of the PSPU, Oleksandr Kharytonov, who worked as a loader at the central market. Another "prominent activist" of the organization was 21-year-old Anastasiia Piaterikova, a dancer from a night club who became a host of pro-Russian rallies and quickly gained fame through explicit photos on social media. Already in February, representatives of the "Luhansk Guard" set up a small tent city in the center of Luhansk, where young sporty guys with bats, knuckledusters, and rebars took turns guarding the administrative buildings. They declared their goal as protecting these buildings from radicals. The tent city was funded by Luhansk's Party of Regions, which the latter did not try to hide.

The first large-scale pro-Russian rally in Luhansk, like in Donetsk, took place on March 1, 2014. On that day, up to ten thousand people gathered in the city center, which was a significant number for Luhansk. Similar to the neighboring regional center, the crowd was filled with hatred towards the supporters of the Maidan. The organizers of the rally did everything to heighten these emotions even more. The meeting was hosted by Rodion Miroshnyk, a deputy of the Luhansk Regional Council from the Party of Regions. Initially, he gave the floor to the head of the Regional Council, Valeriy Holenko, and then invited the leader of the "Luhansk Guard," Oleksandr Kharytonov, to the microphone. Kharytonov began spouting utter nonsense.

> "I rarely get to be on the internet. But absolutely by chance, my son found it. Two copies of 'Mein Kampf,' each priced at 65 million dollars. So, after so many years, these books have such value! Fascism is raising its head again!"

The crowd greeted this stream of consciousness with joyful cheers. At that moment, those present were ready to believe anything – as long as these claims fit into the narrative of the "treacherous Ukrainian fascism rising in Kyiv."

Members of the "Luhansk Guard" Harytonov and Piaterikova, demanded that the deputies of the Luhansk Regional Council not recognize the new government, prohibit Ukrainian political parties of the national-democratic camp, grant Russian the status of the second national language, and hold a referendum on the federal structure of Ukraine. And unlike the deputies of the Donetsk

Regional Council, Luhansk deputies immediately agreed to the radicals' demands and fully supported them the next day.

The overall informational context was extremely negative. On February 23, after Yanukovych's escape, the Verkhovna Rada voted to repeal the controversial Kivalov-Kolesnichenko Language Law. Crimea was seized by the "little green men." On March 1, the Federation Council in Russia supported President Vladimir Putin's appeal to use the Armed Forces of the Russian Federation on the territory of Ukraine "until the normalization of the socio-political situation in this country." Officially, this was justified by "the extraordinary situation that has developed in Ukraine, the threat to the lives of Russian citizens, our compatriots, and the personnel of the military contingent of the Armed Forces of the Russian Federation stationed in accordance with the international treaty on the territory of Ukraine." These events significantly influenced the mood in Luhansk. After that day, protesters were already raising Russian tricolor flags.

On March 2, 2014, a session of the Luhansk Regional Council took place, which became a turning point in the region's history. The building was surrounded by an aggressive, anti-Ukrainian crowd. Organized groups of Russian-speaking men were noticeable, and political representatives of the crowd included leaders of the local PSPU and CPU.

The session was held under the threat of the building being stormed, and representatives of the protesters were allowed to enter the hall. They tried to force the deputies to vote for an anti-state resolution.

The first part of the session ended inconclusively: deputies started to disperse, but physically couldn't leave. A crowd of several hundred people surrounded the building, the doors were blocked, and protesters threatened deputies and especially journalists. Some representatives of the media were allowed out of the building, making them pass through the "corridor of shame." The crowd could start storming at any moment, and no one would restrain it. The level of aggression was critical, and many feared for their lives and well-being.

Deputies were forced to return to the hall and continued their work practically without media coverage. After lengthy debates, the deputies adopted a resolution not to recognize the new authorities and appealed to the Verkhovna Rada with their demands. Among other things, they demanded giving the Russian language the status of a national language, protecting the population of Luhansk from" illegal armed formations", stopping the persecution of special militsiya unit Berkut personnel, and not blocking Russian TV channels.

> "If our demands are not met, and there is a further escalation of civil confrontation and a direct threat to the lives and health of the population of the Luhansk region, we reserve the right to seek assistance from the fraternal people of the Russian Federation," stated the resolution of the Luhansk Regional Council session, which was read from the porch to the pro-Russian activists present by Valeriy Holenko. The Deputy from the Party of Regions, Arsen Klinchaev, raised the Russian flag above the regional council building, thereby solidifying the act of state betrayal committed by his colleagues.

In the regional council, only one deputy publicly opposed the separatist resolution. It was Andrii Shapovalov, a representative of the "Strong Ukraine" party. Speaking in the hall, he urged his colleagues not to allow war in Ukraine.

> "Why are you doing this? The average age of a regional council deputy is 59 years, you won't go to war, your children and grandchildren will. I won't vote for this

appeal," said Shapovalov. Activists from the "Luhansk Guard" tried to drown out his words with jeers and whistles.

On March 2, the Acting President of Ukraine, Oleksandr Turchynov, appointed new governors for the Donetsk and Luhansk regions. The multimillionaire Serhiy Taruta became the head of the Donetsk region, while the relatively unknown Mykhailo Bolotskykh took charge of the Luhansk region. Bolotskykh had a military and civil defense career, serving as the head of the State Emergency Service from 2012 to 2014. While there were high expectations for Taruta, Bolotskykh was a clearly unsuccessful candidate. He had not lived in Luhansk for a long time and lacked stable political connections there, especially with those who could actually affect the situation. His authority and recognition in the region were practically non-existent.

In response to these appointments, on March 5, the "Luhansk Guard" declared its leader, Oleksandr Kharytonov, as the "people's governor" during a rally. In just a few days, events in Luhansk escalated.

On the morning of March 9, dozens of residents of the regional center with Ukrainian symbols gathered at the Taras Shevchenko monument to celebrate the poet's birthday. However, the peaceful memorial rally was attacked by Anti-Maidan activists. Some Anti-Maidan supporters, predominantly fit men, arrived in the city in an organized manner, by buses. Those were parked on nearby streets. And in one of the yards not far from the Regional State Administration, young people changed clothes and received instructions under the guidance of Arsen Klinchaev. Within a few days, the Security Service of Ukraine made a statement that Klinchaev had recruited around 150 "titushkas" to storm the Administration, promising each of them $150 for the job.

The number of attackers significantly exceeded the

number of pro-Ukrainian citizens, and people had to flee. The police did not intervene in the clashes and indifferently observed what was happening.

At this point, the Anti-Maidan activists, under the leadership of Kharytonov and Klinchaev, did not stop, and they moved to storm the regional administration. Similar to Donetsk, the appointed governor from Kyiv was declared the main enemy of the separatists. So they decided to overthrow him. Breaking into the building, representatives of the "Luhansk Guard" and "Young Guard" vandalized the reception area, entered the office of the head of the Luhansk Regional State Administration, and forced Bolotskykh to write a resignation statement. The Russian tricolor and red flag were raised again on the flagpole in front of the building. After this, Anastasiia Piaterikova addressed Yanukovych and Putin, requesting them to "save the southeast of Ukraine from terror."

> "Dear Presidents Viktor Fedorovych Yanukovych and Vladimir Vladimirovich Putin, we, the citizens of Ukraine, the Luhansk region, and practically the entire southeast of Ukraine, call on you to take measures to protect us from the terror initiated by the Kyiv junta!" the appeal stated.

The specific terror mentioned was not explained. At that moment, the new government had not done anything remotely resembling terror. However, the "guards" in Luhansk had their own worldview, which did not align with reality. As experience has shown, the leaders of anti-Ukrainian actions were not concerned with what the new Ukrainian government would actually do. Calls for disobedience did not require a real reason.

By the beginning of spring, it became clear that Ukraine had lost informational control over the region. The population completely stopped trusting Ukrainian media but easily believed any nonsense from the social media network "Odnoklassniki." The most absurd rumors spread on social networks at an astonishing speed. In early March, someone came up with the idea that the new government was supposedly planning to withhold part of the salaries of budget workers for the "restoration of Maidan." Despite the obvious absurdity of this news, it instantly spread, circulating by word of mouth as a fait accompli.

On March 10, representatives of the protesters began collecting signatures under an appeal to Russian President Putin to send troops to the Luhansk region. On the same day, Anti-Maidan activists seized the building of the "IRTA" television company, which belonged to local Party of Regions member Volodymyr Landyk. In this way, they sought revenge for a criticizing story about the capture of the Luhansk Regional State Administration, which journalists had aired the day before.

> "At first, we endured a barrage of insults, obscene language directed at us by individuals whose behavior cannot be described as appropriate. Especially when combined with a strong smell of alcohol emanating from them. They dragged us through the corridors, humiliated us, demanded a live broadcast, so that we would kneel in a live broadcast and apologize for what we were showing. Personal belongings of employees were stolen—wallets, mobile phones. It was outright looting. But we did not comply with any demands of the invaders," described the situation Karolina Poltavska, the director of "IRTA".

On the evening of March 10, Ukrainian law enforcement finally began to take action. Initially, SSU officers detained and transported Arsen Klinchaev to Kyiv. On March 13, they also arrested "People's Governor" Oleksandr Kharytonov. These arrests somewhat sobered up the Luhansk separatists. There was a sense that the new Ukrainian government was gaining control over the situation in the Donbas, and Putin was not rushing to send the "little green men" to the Donbas. On March 13, the head of the Luhansk Regional Council, Valeriy Holenko, abruptly changed his militant rhetoric and stated that he did not intend to declare a local referendum, which the regional council had previously threatened.

"There is no law in Ukraine regarding local referendums. We simply cannot declare it. Even if the deputies gather and adopt such a decision, it will be annulled immediately, instantly. An illegal decision by the deputies will be the basis for adopting a resolution of the Verkhovna Rada of Ukraine, for example, on the early dissolution of the Luhansk Regional Council," came round Holenko.

Deputy Mayor of Luhansk, Oleksandr Tkachenko, distanced himself from the use of force. Initially, he actively and publicly supported actions against the Maidan.

"At first, civic formations like the 'Luhansk Guard" emerged on a sound basis as a counterbalance to ultranationalist movements that gained momentum in the country. At that stage, I supported their creation and defended the possibility for citizens to express their position peacefully. However, the events of March 9 and 10, related to the occupation of administrative buildings, hoisting Russian flags, open confrontation, and calls for the intervention of Russian forces, placed these formations on the edge of the law and, in many ways, beyond it," he noted.

This episode vividly demonstrated why the regional authorities created organizations like the "Luhansk Guard." At the right moment, they could distance themselves and shift responsibility for all illegal actions onto them. However, there was no single coordination center for protest actions, and the monopoly of the local Party of Regions leadership on regional politics was destroyed. The process continued with the support of other anti-Ukrainian forces.

On March 15, the district administrative court banned any rallies in Luhansk until March 30, 2014. However, the very next day, separatists freely organized a so-called "people's referendum" in the city center. On the central square, a tent was set up by the "Young Guard" movement, where people were invited to vote with "ballots" for federalization and accession to the Customs Union. The organization of the "people's referendum" was led by the well-known local figure Iryna Hotman, who was associated with the orbit of People's Deputy Volodymyr Struk from the Party of Regions. In interviews with journalists, Hotman claimed that she did not violate Ukrainian legislation because she applied to conduct a sociological survey.

The place of the arrested "people's governor" Kharytonov was briefly taken by Yurii Khokhlov, a regional council deputy from the Communist Party of Ukraine, who, despite the court ban, also organized pro-Russian rallies in Luhansk on March 16 and 23 under the guise of a "deputy's reception for citizens."

In these turbulent days in Luhansk, another interesting formation emerged called "Luhansk Self-Defense," which was different from other similar organizations. Its creator was businessman Sergiy Korsunsky, who claims to have cooperated with the Ukrainian authorities and tried to take control of the pro-Russian movement in Luhansk in April 2014. When it became clear that this was not possible, Korsunsky left Luhansk for the territories controlled by Ukraine.

"Luhansk Self-Defense" positioned itself as a moderately pro-Russian organization, declaring its main goal to be the support of order on the streets. In reality, the "self-defense" consisted of ordinary "titushky" who worked for money and were willing to carry out assigned tasks. Other pro-Russian formations immediately sensed something amiss and suspected that "self-defense" was playing a double game. In the "Luhansk Guard," they started calling the self-defenders the "Right Sector," leading to a conflict between the organizations."

The leader of the "Self-Defense," Dmytro Volosovych, emphasized in an interview with Luhansk journalists on March 15 that his people had no connection to the "Luhansk Guard," and he called the capture of administrative buildings by the "guards" outright "provocations":

> "Our goal is order on the streets, not referendums, flags, captures, and other things that the 'guard' is involved in. We have had a conflict with them recently. Four guards, being drunk, tried to get into our tent. A 'conversation' started. When the noise attracted the police, well, we helped the police detain them. Three were restrained, one escaped. They are already looking for him. When they were capturing 'IRTA,' we were against it too. We wanted to go and defend, but then they would say that we were protecting Landyk (the owner of the TV channel. —A/N), so we didn't go, stood here, near the administration," he explained.

Volosovych promised to fight against mass unrest, not allow attacks on Maidan supporters, and even declared that he was ready to fight with Russians if they "come with weapons." Such a statement clearly contrasted with the general mood of the pro-Russian movement, where no one intended to fight with Russians, of course. On March 22, members of the "Luhansk Self-Defense" clashed with representatives of the "Luhansk Guard" and destroyed the tent camp of the "guards." After that, the "guards" called

Volosovych and his people "mercenaries of the Kyiv regime." The publication of the Luhansk Regional Council, "Nasha Gazeta," describing this conflict, openly sided with the "Luhansk Guard."

Sergiy Korsunsky claims that some pro-Russian groups in Luhansk were willing to cooperate with the Ukrainian authorities and abandon separatist slogans, but the authorities in Kyiv failed to seize the opportunity to negotiate with them. This was due to a poor understanding of local specifics, failure to listen to advice, and arrests of individuals who should not have been arrested.

"At first, I communicated with Kharytonov, the 'people's governor.' He was ordered around by deputy mayor of Luhansk Oleksandr Tkachenko—he was constantly pulling him aside at rallies, suggesting what to say, advising on the best course of action. I saw that Kharytonov was a completely normal, easy-to-manage person, not a fanatic. He wanted power, and it wasn't difficult to reach an agreement with him. Initially, when the Security Service of Ukraine took him, I said that he should be released. I proposed my plan—to remove the uncontrollable radicals and create a party like 'Federative Ukraine' with figures like Kharytonov, which would operate within the law and never align itself with Russia. I went to Petrulevych (head of the regional SSU), Huslavskyi (head of the regional Ministry of Internal Affairs), talked to them, saying I could reach an agreement, solve everything peacefully, but there were people who incited seizures and unrest, like Khokhlov and Kachura (a deputy of the regional council from the Communist Party and an activist of the "Luhansk Guard," respectively). I asked them to neutralize them, but instead, for some reason, they neutralized Kharytonov," Korsunsky explained.

According to him, the local branch of the Communist Party of Ukraine was primarily interested in radicalizing the protests and conducting an anti-Ukrainian referendum. If Korsunsky's words are to be believed, at the end of March, the Communists tried to bribe his people from the "Luhansk Self-Defense," pull them to their side and organize the seizure of administrative buildings with their help.

> "They summoned my guys who were guarding these rallies to the party office. Chalenko, a city council deputy from the CPU, and Kilinkarov took them there. They opened a safe full of money, took out three bundles of 60,000 hryvnias each, and offered them to seize the SSU building. They replied that it was not their function; they stood for order, guarded monuments from the 'Right Sector,' and ensured that the rally proceeded peacefully. Then I took my guys, brought them to the Petrulevych's deputy head, Andrii Zhyroid. There, one of them wrote a statement that the People's Deputy tried to hire him to capture the SSU building and requested action. Kilinkarov promised them Russian passports and life in Crimea if something went wrong. He promised protection. But even after we reported this, law enforcement did not take action," Korsunsky explained. However, there is no credible evidence to confirm his words.

At the end of March, videos started appearing online from the so-called "Luhansk partisans." A group of armed individuals wearing masks called themselves the "Army of the Southeast" and promised to start armed resistance against Ukrainian authorities in the Luhansk region. The mysterious "partisans" claimed that their goal was to conduct a referendum on the "self-determination of the Southeast." Initially, few took these statements seriously. Anyone could record such a video and upload it to YouTube.

However, on March 22, correspondents from the Russian newspaper "Komsomolskaia Pravda" published an interview with them. After the release of this material, it became clear that some armed formations were indeed being created in the Luhansk region.

In an interview with Russian correspondent Oleksandr Kots, the leader of the "Luhansk partisans," Valery Bolotov (at that time, he did not reveal his name and gave the interview wearing a mask), stated that he decided to rise in defense of his land because Kyiv allegedly sent several hundred fighters from the "Right Sector" to the Luhansk region. This information, like dozens of similar statements, was an outright lie. However, such simple tricks had the desired effect, instilling fear among the population and garnering support. Bolotov claimed that he intended to fight for granting the Luhansk region the status of a federal subject within either Russia or Ukraine, provided that Ukraine itself became a federation.

In their next video, the "partisans" demanded that the Ukrainian government cancel the upcoming presidential elections in the Donbas and set a specific date for a federalization referendum by April 5. Otherwise, they threatened to launch an armed uprising on April 6.

> "We demand the cancellation of the presidential elections and the designation of a specific date for a referendum on the Southeast. In case our demands are not met by April 5, 2014, the People's Army of the South-East will be mobilized on April 6. We declare a full-scale popular mobilization for all those ready to defend their rights to life and freedom. If our demands are not met, we will announce the gathering of the people's militia in the downtown squares of our cities on April 6 from 10 am to 12 pm. Bring identification, a daily ration, any personal weapons, and means of individual protection.

The advance to regional centers will be organized in columns," said Bolotov in another address from the "Luhansk partisans."

On March 17, the first public address of another future prominent insurgent leader, Oleksiy Mozgovoy (who controlled Alchevsk and its surroundings and was killed in 2015), appeared online. The video message was recorded in the square near the building of the Luhansk Regional State Administration against the backdrop of the slogan "Ukraine, Russia, Belarus—Holy Rus." Mozgovoy did not hide his face from the beginning and addressed "his fellow countrymen from the eastern region":

"Enough of sitting at home, enough of thinking that someone will do something for you. Don't worry about your own skin, worry about your honor... Go out into the streets and demand, no one will do anything for you."—He spoke about the fact that the "unfriendly' ones have been given a chance that cannot be lost.—"I choose Russia, I am for Russia."

The topic of partisan units was quickly picked up by Russian propaganda media. A story aired on the channel "Russia," in which the "leader of the unit" claimed to have 300 assault rifles, anti-tank grenade launchers, and plans to destroy the enemy's vehicles. The enemies were referred to as "radicals from the Right Sector gang."

The actions of law enforcement in Luhansk in the spring of 2014 remain unclear and have yet to be fully understood. It was not possible to determine the principle by which the SSU officers chose whom to detain and whom not to. Why did the security services almost immediately arrest Klinchaev and Kharytonov but did not touch the Communists Chalenko and Khokhlov, who were doing essentially the same things as their arrested associates, remains a mystery. However, the main events in Luhansk were still ahead, and the decisive role in them was to be played by people whose names were unknown to anyone until April 2014.

CHAOS AND VIOLENCE

The arrest of Pavlo Gubarev did not lead to the cessation of anti-Ukrainian protests in Donetsk, but it multiplied the chaos and turmoil within the ranks of Donetsk separatists. Gubarev's associates began to fight among themselves for the right to lead the pro-Russian movement in the city. Additionally, alongside the "People's Militia of the Donbas," other groups and their leaders began to emerge. The Ukrainian state almost did not intervene in these events. During this period, it practically did not perform its functions in the Donbas, and the situation was left to unfold on its own.

After the "people's governor" was sent to pretrial detention in Kyiv, a struggle for leadership unfolded within the "People's Militia." One of the associates of the "people's governor," named Robert Donia, immediately emerged as a contender for the leadership. He appeared next to him on the podium in early March. At a rally on March 9, Donia actively gave interviews to Russian journalists, calling himself the "deputy governor" and positioning himself as Gubarev's successor. However, such a development of events did not suit another group of Gubarev's supporters, which included **Pavlo**'s wife, Kateryna Gubareva, as well as his longtime friends Myroslav Rudenko and Serhii Tsyplakov. They perceived Robert Donia's self-nomination as an attempt to take over their organization.

Meetings of separatists took place every weekend and were essentially "marathons of hatred." Never before had Donetsk witnessed such outbreaks of widespread animosity. From the first days of the spring turmoil in 2014, it was clear that the protest was taking a destructive path, and its leaders were doing everything to provoke violence. Insults, hysterical curses against Ukraine and the USA, calls for riots and pogroms were hurled from the podium. No one spoke to the people in Lenin Square about the economy and how the Donbas would live without Ukraine. Rational arguments were not wanted by anyone. The crowd craved emotions, adrenaline, the ecstasy of unity, and anything that hindered this euphoria was immediately perceived as betrayal. Any calls to stop and think about what would happen to the economy of the industrial region if it lost control and became an unrecognized state immediately provoked aggression. Anyone who urged prudence was declared a provocateur and an "agent of the junta."

A pro-Russian segment of society was in a state of delirium. Even though in the spring of 2014, Ukrainian TV channels were still broadcasting in the Donbas, and Ukrainian media were freely operating, separatists did not want to hear any arguments from the Ukrainian side. Information that did not suit them was declared lies and slander, while the biased stories from Russian media, which met the expectations of the crowd, were not critically perceived. In turn, Ukrainian media made numerous strategic and tactical mistakes in covering events in the east, which had extremely negative consequences.

The echo chamber effect emerged: a situation in which pro-Russian citizens and participants in separatist movements were only willing to hear themselves and arguments that confirmed their point of view. This phenomenon is quite common. The desire to see in the surrounding world only what confirms our initial views is a well-known trait of the human psyche. Even the English philosopher Francis Bacon wrote in his work "Novum Organum": "The human understanding when it has once adopted an opinion...draws all things else to support and agree with it. And though there be a greater number and weight of instances to be found on the other side, yet these it either neglects and despises, or else by some distinction sets aside and rejects."

This Donbas echo-chamber did not pop up in 2014. It had been constructed for many years with active involvement of local politicians. Election campaign propaganda, stories on local TV channels, and publications in local newspapers had long demonized and ridiculed residents of western and central Ukraine who disagreed with the pro-Russian course. They reinforced and perpetuated old myths and superstitions dating back to Soviet times. When the political crisis occurred, citizens having had this ideology ingrained in them, now maintained their comfortable echo-chamber on their own without any coercion. All attempts to dismantle it and convince separatists that they had chosen a destructive path failed.

Supporters of Ukraine's territorial integrity in Luhansk and Donetsk did not remain silent. They also decided to make themselves heard and took to the streets because they understood that pro-Russian activists had seized the initiative and were trying to speak on behalf of the entire Donbas. However, it was not the entire region that supported the separatists' demands, and hundreds of thousands of citizens had a different opinion. To ensure that this opinion was heard, it was necessary to express it loudly and publicly.

On March 5, supporters of Ukrainian unity held the first rally in Donetsk. Several thousand people gathered in Lenin Square under yellow-blue flags to express their protest against the country's division. On the opposite side of the square, supporters of the Russian Federation with Russian tricolor flags and flags of the "Donetsk Republic" were separated from the pro-Ukrainian rally by a police cordon. They shouted insults, threw eggs at opponents, but did not dare to attack. Clashes were avoided that evening.

The event ended peacefully but angered the separatists. The yellow-blue flags challenged their established narrative, which excluded Ukrainian Donetsk. Supporters of Russia claimed that almost the entire Donbas was against Ukraine, that the entire region was eager to join the Russian Federation, but the large pro-Ukrainian rally refuted these claims. Although the pro-Ukraine rally was less forceful and vocal than the separatist actions, ignoring it was impossible.

At that time, there was still a belief among the separatists that Putin would send "little green men" to the Donbas if they showed him the appropriate image of total support for Russia. The rally for the unity of Ukraine disrupted this plan. And the impact would have been much greater if the local authorities had at least morally, verbally, supported the pro-Ukrainian actions. However, the Donetsk authorities ignored the Ukrainian rally. The city mayor, city council members, and regional council deputies pretended that there were no actions in support of Ukrainian unity. No one attended, gave a speech, or expressed opposition to the country's division. Similarly, hundreds of supporters of Ukraine were ignored by the authorities in Luhansk, where deputies openly sided with the separatists and spoke at their rallies.

On March 13, in Donetsk, the first serious clash between supporters of Ukraine and Russia occurred, resulting in the beating of Ukrainian activists and the murder of "Svoboda" Party member Dmytro Cherniavskyi. The day before, separatists openly called for violence on social media and threatened to attack the Ukrainian rally, but neither the authorities nor law enforcement did anything to prevent bloodshed. Ukrainian activists hesitated until the last moment about whether to proceed with the rally, but ultimately decided not to cancel it. Canceling would have meant that Ukrainian Donetsk surrendered and accepted the course toward the country's division.

The rampage occurred in Lenin Square and was the first of its kind in the city's recent history. On that day in Donetsk, armed fighters with knives, bats, and rebar appeared for the first time, beating and maiming supporters of Ukraine, trying to inflict severe injuries. The forces were unequal. The Ukrainian side was not prepared for armed confrontation, and the police basically did not intervene in the events and made no effort to protect unarmed people.

The brutal beating of Donetsk residents and the murder of a Ukrainian activist who came unarmed to a peaceful demonstration was a shock to the city. Prior to this, skirmishes sometimes broke out at rallies in Donetsk, but there were no killings. To justify their own brutal actions, the pro-Russian side immediately resorted to a tried and true tactic—they accused the Ukrainian activists of being nationalist outsiders from other regions. The fact that the deceased Dmytro Cherniavskyi was a native of the Donetsk region did not faze them.

The bloody rampage exacerbated the contradictions within the ranks of the "people's militia." Gubarev's entourage was frightened by what had happened and blamed Robert Donia for organizing the disturbances.

> "Taking advantage of **Pavlo** absence, some radical elements and provocateurs, using his name as a cover, are attempting to take the protest upon themselves and steer it toward riots and destruction. Pavlo never assigned us such tasks. We are not Nazis, we do not destroy our city, we do not kill people. I have contacted the organizer ‚Robert Donia. He said he has left our ranks, left the 'People's Militia of the Donbas.' Now, he has his own organization. He takes full responsibility for organizing these events," said Kateryna Gubareva in her

video statement.

In the wake of the events, Oleksandr Khodakovsky, now infamous but at the time the commander of the Donetsk unit of the SSU "Alpha," commented as well.

Khodakovsky gave an interview in which he placed all responsibility for what happened on the police. He accused law enforcement of negligence and inaction.

"Early in the morning, the 'Siren' plan is announced, placing the entire garrison of Donetsk law enforcement on high alert. Theoretically, on this day, all law enforcement officers were supposed to be focusing on identifying and detaining such actors—aggressive individuals engaged in unlawful activities. However, in reality, there were no significant changes observed in the actions of the police. The police were operating in standard mode, and this plan was only formally declared. Strangely, two rallies with clearly opposing goals and tasks were announced practically at the same time. Here's the question! Why was there no attempt at coordination to separate them by location and time? It seemed like these groups were deliberately accumulated in the same place, which was meant to become a battleground. According to our data, more than one hundred plainclothes law enforcement officers were present in the square. These were people engaged in visual observation and reporting to their leadership. Preparation for the clash was in full swing. But law enforcement officers observed this from a distance, even though they knew that the 'Siren' plan had been announced. Right there, in the square, people were arming themselves. What is a piece of rebar? It's a blunt weapon. People deliberately brought it with them," Khodakovsky recounted.

Interestingly, he actually placed responsibility for

the rampage on the separatists. "The main aggression came from the pro-Russian side. The provocateurs, for the most part, were on the pro-Russian side," said the future field commander of the self-proclaimed "DPR".

The situation in Donetsk was getting out of control. Nobody knew what to do. The law enforcement nominally obeyed Kyiv but did not perform their duties, sabotaged orders, and accused each other of inaction. The local authorities formally advocated for a united Ukraine but, in reality, sympathized with and played into the hands of the separatists. The authorities in Kyiv, instead of extinguishing the separatist rebellion at the initial stage and neutralizing its leaders, took a strange, half-hearted approach. After the arrest of **Pavlo** Gubarev, a whole month passed before they arrested and took his deputy, Robert Donia, to Kyiv (this happened on April 4). At the same time, they left alone other leaders of the "people's militia"—Myroslav Rudenko, Serhii Tsyplakov, and Oleksandr Kofman—and they continued to lead the protests unhindered.

As usual in such cases, there were those who tried to take advantage of the confusion and "raid" the pro-Russian movement to steer it in the desired direction and improve their own situation. One of these "tricksters" was the People's Deputy from the Party of Regions, Oleksandr Bobkov—a low-profile figure little known outside Donetsk but with some influence in the city. In March 2014, Bobkov realized that it was a favorable moment for him to finally step into the spotlight and occupy the vacant position left after the leaders of the Donetsk clan dispersed.

GODFATHER OF THE "DPR"

Oleksandr Bobkov was a classic stereotypical representative of the Party of Regions. When he was younger, he was involved in criminal circles in the Budonivskyi district, later transitioning from crime to politics and officially heading the local council in the same district.

At the beginning of his "career," Bobkov was a member of the well-known Donetsk criminal group led by Givi Nemsadze. According to businessman Vladyslav Dreher, who was well acquainted with Bobkov, the future people's deputy was known by the nickname "Bobik" in his youth and engaged in extortion at the Budonivskyi market. Later, he was appointed by the elders to the position of director of the same market. In the early 2000s, when criminal wars subsided and bandits began to merge with the authorities, Bobkov started working for the Budonivskyi district council and began his career in the Party of Regions, which was just emerging at that time.

"Budonnivka" was considered one of the most criminal districts in Donetsk. The Nemsadze group, originating from there, was responsible for several dozen deaths. Another figure from this district who gained notoriety was Mykhailo Liashko, better known as "Misha Kosoi." Bobkov himself was implicated in several high-profile murders, including that of the head of the district CPU, Ilya Morozov. A day before the local elections held on March 26, 2006, unknown assailants threw a Molotov cocktail through his window. Morozov suffered severe burns. Doctors fought for his life for a week, but on April 4, Morozov died.

Since the mid-2000s, Oleksandr Bobkov already controlled the Budonivskyi and Proletarskyi districts, where he had managed to establish businesses and privatize some valuable assets. However, Bobkov's interests were not limited to this area. His goal was much more ambitious—he dreamed of taking control of the entire Donetsk and becoming the mayor of the city. People close to Bobkov said that he was greatly inspired by Yanukovych's example. Bobkov was of the same mold—a large, unpretentious guy with a criminal background, a classic "manager." Looking at Yanukovych, he understood that such a type was in demand in Donbas, and he planned to rise to the top. However, his plans were hindered by the interests of the unofficial ruler of Donetsk—Rinat Akhmetov, who already had his own mayor and had no intention of replacing him with Bobkov.

> "Bobik" had a fixation—to become the mayor of Donetsk," Vladyslav Dreher recounted. "There was a period when the mayor of Donetsk, Oleksandr Lukyanchenko, was seriously ill and didn't want to run for another term. However, Rinat Akhmetov insisted that he should still run for the elections. Bobkov knew about this situation, waited for it, and counted on becoming the mayor instead of Lukyanchenko. In preparation for this, he secured his appointment as the head of the Donetsk city organization of the Party of Regions. The formal decision to nominate a candidate for the mayor of Donetsk from the Party of Regions had to be made by the city party organization, so Bobkov took over as its head as a guarantee of his future mayoralty. Then there was one curious incident. In 2005, Borys Kolesnikov spent some time in pre-trial detention, and after his release, he tried to spend less time in Ukraine just in case. His family lived in Moscow, and he himself spent most of his time in Russia. In 2006, there were local elections in Ukraine, and on their eve, Bobkov entered into an open conflict with Akhmetov's people. At the party conference, he, in the absence of

Kolesnikov, approved the list of candidates for the city council according to his own wishes. Bobkov placed his people at the beginning of this list and the people of the current mayor Lukyanchenko (that is, of Akhmetov and Kolesnikov) at the end. Bobkov himself nominated himself as a candidate for the mayor of Donetsk from the Party of Regions.

Lukyanchenko was alarmed by what was happening. He rushed to call Kolesnikov, who was at the airport at the time. Kolesnikov urgently arrived at the conference after it ended and demanded a re-vote on the results. As a result, the list was turned upside down, and Lukyanchenko's people ended up back at the top. And Bobkov was never confirmed as a candidate for the mayor's position."

Bobkov was offended by such treatment. He performed well in the 2004 elections in Donetsk, working to get results for Yanukovych in his district, and believed that he should be rewarded for it.

"Viktor Yanukovych came to Donetsk for a meeting with the activists at the press center of the Shakhtar Hotel. I was sitting in the front row at the meeting with Oleksandr Khryakov. It seems that Volodia Molchan stood up and said, 'Viktor Fedorovych, today we still don't consider it a loss. The whole struggle is still ahead, but in the distribution of mandates and seats, don't forget those who stood on the barricades, including Oleksandr Bobkov.' Viktor Fedorovych replied, 'Bobkov is a hero of our time, and we will remember all the heroes.' But I never made it to the lists of the Verkhovna Rada, I wasn't invited to the Cabinet of Ministers when Viktor Yanukovych headed it, they didn't support me as a candidate for the mayor of Donetsk," Bobkov later grudgingly complained in one of his interviews.

After the humiliating incident for Bobkov at the party conference, his conflict with Akhmetov's wing began. Like all other conflicts within the Party of Regions, it was not public, but the city was aware of the strained relations. At one point, Bobkov even wore a bulletproof vest, fearing an attack. To spite the Akhmetov supporters, he began undermining their protege—the young secretary of the Donetsk City Council, Mykola Levchenko, whose position he wanted to overtake.

"The rivalry between Bobkov and Levchenko began after Levchenko became the secretary of the city council. Bobkov was also vying for this position, so their conflict sometimes took on bizarre forms. It got to the point that during the presidential elections in 2010 in Levchenko's district, where he was responsible for the results, on Bobkov's orders, all the pens at the polling stations were replaced with pens with disappearing ink. It was a desperate move. The Party of Regions members were given strict orders at that time: to forget about all in-fighting during the elections and work to get results for Viktor Fedorovych. Bobkov ignored this order and decided to sabotage the elections in Levchenko's district to undermine his opponent. However, Bobkov miscalculated in his scheme. In Levchenko's district, there was a different system of falsifications. Unlike Bobkov, he didn't cast ballots into the ballot boxes; he simply falsified the protocols by entering the desired results. In Bobkov's understanding, pens with disappearing ink spoiled the ballots. But for Levchenko, it didn't matter what was in the boxes. He entered numbers in the protocols that did not depend on the number of votes. Therefore, Bobkov's plan ultimately did not work out," Vladyslav Dreher recounts.

After Yanukovych's victory in the elections, Donetsk immediately became the arena of confrontation between the representatives of the president's team (the "family") and the people of Akhmetov-Kolesnikov. The region was decided to be divided as follows: the governor would be from Akhmetov, the head of the regional council would be from Yanukovych. Quickly assessing the new realities, Bobkov approached the "family" and soon became one of the main pillars of Yanukovych's team in Donetsk, as the latter did not have such a strong backup team as Akhmetov did. As a token of gratitude for his support, Bobkov was given the garbage business. At that time, waste disposal in the city was handled by the company "Hrinko Don," but it was quickly pushed out of Donetsk, and Bobkov's controlled LLC "Hromada" took its place. However, the power in the city still belonged to Akhmetov. Bobkov ruled only in his own area of Budonnivka and in the neighboring Proletarka. These peripheral districts seemed to symbolize the periphery of political life to which "Bobik" was relegated.

In the parliamentary elections of 2012, the majoritarian system returned, and Bobkov got the 41st district, which covered the areas of Donetsk under his control. He easily won the elections in this district and became a people's deputy in the parliament, fabricating getting 80% of the votes. In those elections, it was an all-Ukrainian record among majoritarian candidates.

In 2013, Bobkov was considered by Yanukovych's team as a candidate to replace Volodymyr Rybak, the Speaker of the Verkhovna Rada, who seemed insufficiently tough to the "family." However, for some reason, this reshuffle never happened. Yanukovych's downfall was a severe blow to Bobkov. After the president fled and the Party of Regions collapsed, the people's deputy found himself in a very precarious situation. In Donetsk, he turned into one of the generals of a defeated army, which was left without a supreme commander. At the same time, the new government in Kyiv was entirely hostile towards the Donetsk faction, while in his hometown, the unfriendly Akhmetov clan held sway. In the face of instability, Bobkov decided to rely on the third force—pro-Russian groups. His calculation was to harness the protest, become one of the speakers on the topic of federalization, and gain new positions through this. To achieve this, Bobkov began to create a group in Donetsk called "Oplot," the core of which consisted of the people of Ihor Melnykov and Oleksandr Zakharchenko. Bobkov considered Pavlo Gubarev and his "People's Militia" as people of his longtime rival Mykola Levchenko. Presumably, this is why Bobkov's people clashed with Gubarev's posse from the very beginning.

According to a person who worked with Bobkov before the war, Oleksandr Zakharchenko and Oleksandr Tymofieiev (Zakharchenko's right-hand man, known as "Tashkent", and essentially the second person in the "DPR" until September 2018) were acquainted with the people's deputy and worked with him long before the war. It's difficult to confirm or refute this information. However, there is no doubt that by March 2014, the future leader of the separatists was already familiar with Oleksandr Bobkov and worked in his interests.

Bobkov himself did not hide his connections with Zakharchenko, Melnikov, and Tymofieiev. In one of his interviews published in 2016 on the Donetsk website "Komitet," he admitted that he had met with Zakharchenko several times and had assisted his armed formation.

> "I wholeheartedly supported the protesters in my hometown, and I believe my meeting with Zakharchenko and Tymofieiev was only natural. So, during our first meeting with the guys in the square during the rally, we agreed to meet regularly—either I would find them upon arrival, or they would come to my home, and we exchanged thoughts on the events. I provided support to the protesters in Donetsk," Bobkov recounted.

On March 19, together with representatives of pro-Russian movements in Donetsk, Bobkov held a press conference at the "Shakhtar Plaza" hotel, during which he called for a referendum on federalization and granting regional autonomy to Donbas. Alongside Bobkov sat a representative of Oleksandr Khodakovsky's organization "Patriotic Forces of Donbas," and in the hall, among the journalists, then little-known Tymofieiev and Zakharchenko silently observed the conference.

Bobkov addressed the new Ukrainian government, urging them to fulfill the demands of the pro-Russian rallies. What exactly was demanded at these rallies was not entirely clear. So, Bobkov himself compiled a list, interpreting the calls heard in the streets the way he deemed necessary. Bobkov demanded that the governor of Donetsk region not be appointed from Kyiv but be elected locally, that the Verkhovna Rada urgently adopt a law on local referendums, and that Russian be granted the status of the second national language.

> "In case our demands are ignored by the authorities in Kyiv, we reserve the right to raise the issue of preparing legislative proposals regarding the federalization of Ukraine," stated the resolution distributed by Bobkov to journalists.

At first glance, there was nothing criminal about Bobkov's demands. But just a few days later, speaking at the Proletarsky District Council before the district administration employees, Bobkov stated:

> "It's time, indeed, to break up this country, to create five confederations, five free states, and develop further."

One of those present recorded the speech of the Member of Parliament on the mobile phone and uploaded it to the internet. After that, there were no doubts left about true intentions of Bobkov and his associates. Soon, words turned into concrete actions.

On April 6, another pro-Russian rally took place in Donetsk, after which pro-Russian activists again seized the building of the Donetsk Regional Administration. Law enforcement officers guarding the administration offered almost no resistance. It seemed then that the separatists would again wreak havoc and disperse, as had happened before, but this time, everything unfolded differently. Supporters of Russia demanded the immediate convening of an emergency session of the Donetsk Regional Council to adopt a decision on the referendum and began to barricade themselves inside the building. An ultimatum was issued to the regional council: to gather in the session hall by the end of the day on April 6. Otherwise, the separatists threatened to dissolve the regional council and replace it with their own "people's council."

According to the press secretary of the Donetsk mayor, Maksym Rovinskyi, the actions of the separatists on that day were not coordinated. Some of them opposed storming the building and considered the seizure of the Regional Administration an act of provocation.

> "On the day when they finally seized the regional administration, I called Roman Liahin to find out from him about their plans on that side. In addition, I communicated with the Communist Lytvynov, who also willingly maintained contact. I asked them what they were going to do, and they replied that they were preparing documents, forming a political position to subsequently lead a dialogue within the framework of Ukraine on autonomy or federalization. Then, the seizure happened. Soon after that, I received a call from a friend of one of the leaders of the 'people's militia,' Oleksandr Kofman, who relayed that Kofman was not

involved in this. Many from their circle then regarded the seizure of the Regional Administration as a provocation and denied their involvement in it," recalled Rovinskyi.

During the night from the 6 to the 7 of April, truckloads of tires were brought to the administration for barricades. No one stopped the vehicles, and there were no reinforced traffic police checkpoints in the city. The state didn't even attempt to resist. On the morning of April 7, the building of the Regional Administration was surrounded by barricades made of logs, tires, sandbags, and barbed wire along its perimeter. During the day, separatist leaders announced the creation of the "Donetsk People's Republic" and scheduled a referendum for independence on May 11 for the "DPR."

It was a clumsy imitation of the events in Crimea. After the legitimate regional council refused to comply with the demands of pro-Russian insurgents and to engage in unconstitutional actions, the separatists themselves took seats and played the role of deputies. This performance did not even remotely resemble a legitimate process. It was impossible to imagine that anything could come out of this farce. However, the helplessness of the Ukrainian state, which at that time was only formally present in the Donbas, allowed the insurgents to gradually fill the power vacuum. Neither the Security Service of Ukraine, nor the police, nor the military from local units intervened in the events. Initially, the authority of the new "government" was limited to the captured building and its adjacent territory fenced off by barricades. However, within a week, a wave of seizures of administrative buildings spread across the entire Donetsk region, indicating that the Ukrainian government had definitively lost control over the region.

The separatist leaders announced the creation of a "temporary government of the "DPR." Formally, there were several co-chairs in the "government" from the start, but de facto, the first person of the self-proclaimed "DPR" became Denis Pushilin. His career rise was incredibly rapid, even compared to the careers of other separatist leaders. Only on April 5, at yet another pro-Russian rally, Pushilin was declared the new "deputy people's governor," thus replacing Robert Donia, who had been arrested the day before. Within a few days, he then took over the new "republic." Like the previous "people's governors," Pushilin was unknown to anyone and seemed to come out of nowhere. Besides him, the "temporary government" also included veterans of Donetsk separatism: Roman Liahin, Andrei Purgin, and Oleksandr Khryakov. However, the Gubarev`s supporters who precipitated the whole situation were effectively sidelined. After April 6, people who had long and consistently collaborated with politicians from the Party of Regions and had a reputation as provocateurs in Donetsk emerged in prominent roles in the pro-Russian movement.

Pushilin, unlike the fanatical Gubarev, appeared to be a pragmatist. Previously, he had not actively participated in pro-Russian movements, nor had he been noticed at rallies and round tables dedicated to Russian-Ukrainian friendship. As it later became known, Andrei Purgin, after recommendations from acquaintances, introduced him to the pro-Russian movement in the spring of 2014. Before these events, Pushilin earned a living from the financial pyramid MMM, essentially engaging in fraud. Given these circumstances, it seemed that he joined the anti-Ukrainian uprising for some mercenary reasons, simply sensing a favorable opportunity. The new leader of the separatists spoke not so much about joining Russia as about regional autonomy.

> "All we want is a referendum. For me, the ideal option, which I insist on, is sovereignty. A good example is Bavaria. They are not seceding, although they could vote for it, but they don't exercise that right. They pursue

their foreign economic relations without consulting the center, and they do so quite successfully. What prevents us from doing the same?" he told journalist Kateryna Serhatskova in an interview with "Ukrainska Pravda" shortly after his appearance as "co-chair of the government."

These considerations about Bavaria strangely coincided with what Oleksandr Bobkov used to say, as he also liked to mention this German region as an example. Indeed, Bobkov very soon appeared in the captured building of the Donetsk Regional State Administration. On April 11, he held a meeting with the "temporary government of the "DPR," during which he announced that he had submitted a bill "On Local Referendum" and would seek its adoption by parliament. The idea was immediately approved by the "DPR" government," and there was nothing surprising about it, as most of the people there were well acquainted with Bobkov.

Despite the open support of Donetsk separatists, Bobkov remained a member of the Verkhovna Rada and continued to work calmly in parliament, where he indeed promoted a law on a local referendum. His plan was to achieve the legalization of separatist movements and then lead them. At the same time, the new Ukrainian government, which the Donbas separatists accused of horrific bloodthirstiness, did not pose any obstacles to Bobkov.

"In fact, Bobkov himself began to stir up the conflict in order to eventually resolve it on his own terms and thus advance to new positions. He tried to promote a bill on local referendums on behalf of the Party of Regions, but Borys Kolesnikov eventually blocked this project. After that, Bobkov announced that he no longer had common ground with the Party and left the Party of Regions group in parliament. He joined the parliamentary group of Vitalii Hrushevskyi, "For Peace and Stability," where many loyal deputies of Yanukovych from the Party of Regions faction also went. The group existed for some time on Kurchenko's money, but Hrushevskyi attempted to outsmart him. He decided to bypass Kurchenko to reach those who supported him directly and receive money from them, but Kurchenko found out about it immediately. After that, they quarreled, Kurchenko stopped providing money, and the group fell apart. Some of the deputies from this group soon went to Russia and began to speak out sharply against the Ukrainian Anti-Terrorist Operation in the State Duma there," businessman Vladyslav Dreher recounted.

On April 16, armed individuals with bands bearing the inscription "Oplot" appeared on the premises of the Donetsk City Council. The group of militants was commanded by Oleksandr Zakharchenko, who immediately announced to journalists the main demand of the occupiers - to adopt Oleksandr Bobkov's bill on local referendums. Zakharchenko promised that his people would not obstruct the work of the city council but also would not leave the building until the parliament fulfilled their condition.

"We want to present our demands to the Verkhovna Rada regarding the adoption of Oleksandr Bobkov's bill on local referendums. It has been submitted, and they refused to adopt it in the faction," explained Zakharchenko.

This was Zakharchenko's first public appearance as one of the leaders of the pro-Russian movement, as well as the first appearance of militants with firearms in Donetsk.

"Zakharchenko was Bobkov's man. Before taking over the city executive committee, he would come to Lukyanchenko to warn him about the seizure and explain his actions. When they entered the city council, they explained to us that they took it to prevent the invaders from the Donetsk Regional State Administration, those who called themselves the "DPR," from coming there. According to Zakharchenko, in such a case, the work of the city council would have been paralyzed, just like the work of the regional council, and the city hall itself would have been defeated and looted," Maksym Rovinskyi recounted the events of April 16.

The collaboration between Bobkov and Zakharchenko was openly disclosed by "people's governor" Pavlo Gubarev:

"The clans of Yanukovych and Ivanyushchenko participated (in the creation of armed units of the "DPR" —A/N). They formed their units to protect their assets. The 'Oplot' unit was created by these forces. Oleksandr Mykhailovych Bobkov stood behind Zakharchenko and helped build this unit. I know that the 'Kalmius' unit was also created with the support of wealthy individuals," Gubarev recalled in an interview with Russian writer Maksym Kalashnikov in 2020.

The seizure of the city council organized by Bobkov was indeed an open-armed blackmail against Kyiv. However, the people's deputy not only did not hide from law enforcement but also continued to work in the Verkhovna Rada. What negotiations he conducted with the Ukrainian authorities at that time is anyone's guess. The regional administration headed by Governor Serhiy Taruta, which was subordinate to Kyiv, also acted quite paradoxically. People who worked in the Donetsk Regional State Administration in the spring of 2014 say that Taruta initially chose the wrong path and started paying money to Donetsk separatists, hoping to buy them and quell the coup in this way. That is why, reporting on the situation in Kyiv, the Donetsk governor assured that he fully controlled the situation.

The separatists didn't refuse money, but they also weren't

in a rush to submit to Taruta. Moreover, there was simply no unified headquarters among the pro-Russian plotters, and an agreement with one group did not mean control over the entire movement. However, when the cities of the Donbas began to come under the control of Russian fighters, Taruta finally lost even a remote chance of handling the situation.

The governor himself openly stated that he was cooperating with "Oplot" led by Zakharchenko and considered this organization an ally.

> "This is the wing that is ready to help us protect key objects today. This is the 'Oplot' group, and they are currently helping to ensure security, including for the 'Donbas' TV channel. They have joint actions (with the "DPR" —A/N), but there are also stark contradictions concerning aggressive, unlawful actions. Therefore, we have found dialogue with them; we have agreed with them that they will not participate in seizures," Taruta said at a press conference on May 8, when battles were already underway in the Donetsk region.

Obviously, at that time, the governor believed in what he was saying. Undoubtedly, he knew where the "Oplot" came from and who stood behind its creation, so he did not consider Zakharchenko and his militants as true separatists. As we discussed, initially, "Oplot" opposed radicals from Gubarev's "People's Militia" and held relatively moderate positions. However, just three days after Taruta's press conference, the separatists conducted an illegal referendum, declaring the Donetsk region's secession from Ukraine. Soon, the "Oplot" militants became the most active participants in the armed conflict.

The situation in eastern Ukraine was changing rapidly. From the beginning, controlled movements and groups quickly slipped out of control or passed from one curator to another.

The separatist leaders of the spring of 2014 were only caliphs for an hour, and no one could predict who the wave of anti-Ukrainian conspiracy would lift tomorrow and who would dissolve in the dirty froth. After the capture of Slovyansk by Russian saboteurs, a force appeared in the region that neither Oleksandr Bobkov nor anyone else from the Party of Regions could sway. The appearance of Russians radically changed the situation and destroyed the influence of the local elite.

Bobkov left Kyiv only in the summer, in the midst of the military actions in the east of the country, when control over events in the Donbas had definitively shifted to the Russian side, and his protege Oleksandr Zakharchenko began to submit to Russian curators. Bobkov did not succeed in realizing his dream and heading the "Donetsk Republic." However, unlike his former colleagues from the Party of Regions, he turned out to be more fortunate. By the beginning of 2019, Bobkov still retained control over his assets—the Donetsk Coke and Chemical Equipment Plant and the Horlivka Coke and Chemical Plant. The "nationalization" declared by the leaders of the so-called "DPR" did not affect these enterprises.

SECRETS OF THE LUHANSK SSU

On April 5, an officer of the Russian GRU named Bannykh was detained in the Luhansk region. He "arrived for inspection," as the head of the Security Service of Ukraine in the Luhansk region, General Oleksandr Petrulevych, later recounted. Bannykh was supposed to coordinate the activities of local separatist groups, which were planning to overthrow the authorities in the southern and eastern regions of Ukraine. All communications of Bannykh were monitored by the SSU, and he reported to Moscow that "they were more or less prepared in the Luhansk region, but in the Donetsk and Kharkiv regions, they were not ready, not to mention Odesa or Mykolaiv."

According to Petrulevych, the Russian special services were preparing to seize several regions in Ukraine in May, but it all started earlier because Luhansk experienced a sort of false start.

"All the planning for the explosion in the Southeast was conducted in Luhansk, not even in Donetsk," revealed Oleksandr Petrulevych a few years later.

On the same day, April 5, 2014, employees of the Security Service of Ukraine detained a group of saboteurs in the city of Stakhanov, who were planning a forcible takeover of power in the region—the same "Luhansk partisans" who recorded video appeals and promised to launch an armed uprising on April 6. Among those detained were Oleksii Rielke and Oleksii Kariakin—future leaders of the pro-Russian coup. In addition, the SSU seized a whole arsenal of weapons: 300 rifles, an anti-tank grenade launcher, and a large number of grenades.

However, not all the militants were arrested. On the same day, the leader of the "partisans," Valery Bolotov, who avoided arrest, recorded a new video in which he called on pro-Russian citizens to take to the streets. At the end of his speech, Bolotov removed his mask and revealed his identity.

"I call on the people of the Southeast to come out in open confrontation; everything planned for April 6 must be implemented. We must not retreat; this is our land," he said.

The next day, in Luhansk, a car convoy and a rally were planned, and the head of the Regional State Administration, Mykhailo Bolotskykh, was very nervous. He went to General Petrulevych to consult on further actions. Petrulevych assured the governor that the Security Service of Ukraine was working and everything should be fine. But what happened next was far from "fine."

On April 6, as expected, another pro-Russian rally gathered in the downtown of Luhansk. This time, the participants demanded not only the resignation of the new authorities and a referendum on federalization but also the release of the arrested "Luhansk partisans" from the day before. From early morning, hundreds of people gathered near the SSU building. Around noon, a crowd of protesters from the adjacent square joined them, and the situation immediately escalated—activists began throwing stones into the windows of the SSU building, hitting and pushing Interior Troops soldiers who were surrounding the building. People demanded the release of the detained militants, and the head of the regional branch of the Ministry of Internal Affairs, General Volodymyr Huslavskyi, started negotiations with them. Law enforcement officers—SSU agents themselves, as well as the police—were supposed to defend the building from the crowd. However, neither side made much effort to stop the crowd. Disputes about who was more responsible for the surrender of the Luhansk SSU—the police or the Security Service itself—continue to this day. Each side accuses the other of negligence and inaction.

The Chief of the Security Service of Ukraine in the Luhansk region, General Oleksandr Petrulevych, is convinced that the head of the regional Ministry of Internal Affairs, General Volodymyr Huslavskyi, acted on the side of the separatists.

"Around 4:40 pm, Huslavskyi, accompanied by two unidentified individuals, entered the SSU building and began demanding the release of the six detainees held in the temporary detention facility. The crowd let him pass without hindrance, shouting, 'The police are with the people.' Huslavskyi assured everyone that after the detainees were released, he would take the people away from the SSU building and personally bring the detainees to court on Monday (April 7) for the imposition of preventive measures." Petrulevych later recounted during his interrogation in court.

General Volodymyr Huslavskyi refused to take responsibility for the seizure of the SSU, stating that the SSU building was "insufficiently protected," for which he blamed Petrulevych. He claimed that General Petrulevych himself decided to release the detainees, and this step was "coordinated with the leadership" at the time. What actually happened is hard to say, but the fact remains: for some reason, the "partisans" were brought to the Luhansk pre-trial detention center instead of being taken to Kyiv, as was done with other detained organizers of the unrest, and then, under pressure from the rioters, they were simply released.

This action not only did not calm the passions but further agitated the crowd, which immediately stormed the SSU building. However, it was not a storming event, as we might imagine. The crowd simply pushed back the internal troops and broke down the doors. The Internal Troops soldiers hardly resisted. SSU employees also did not attempt to stop the attackers and allowed them to enter.

On the same day, the insurgents gained control of the armory of the SSU, which contained a whole arsenal —several days prior, weapons had been brought to the SSU headquarters from regional branches of the Service. In a matter of hours, "pro-Russian-oriented activists" transformed into armed "to the teeth" militants, and the rally turned into an illegal paramilitary formation. The SSU armory contained 44 grenade launchers, 69 machine guns, 887 AK rifles of various modifications, and around 1,000 pistols (TT, PM, APS). In total, over 2,000 weapons, 680,000 rounds, 370 grenades, TNT, plastic explosives.

How did such a large stockpile of weapons end up in the hands of separatists without a single shot being fired? Who is truly to blame for what happened? It is quite obvious that both the employees of the Ministry of Internal Affairs and the SSU share equal responsibility for the failure on April 6. From the very beginning, everything seemed as if law enforcement deliberately played into the hands of the separatists.

Bolotov and his associates also openly announced their uprising in their video messages, scheduled for April 6, which was a compelling reason for the Security Service of Ukraine to take additional security measures. This particularly concerned the weapons stored in the armory. Obviously, if the head of the regional SSU, Oleksandr Petrulevych, doubted the ability of his subordinates to protect the weapons, he should have relocated the arsenal elsewhere. But instead of doing so, Petrulevych didn't even consider mining the entrance to the armory. Instead of real explosives, the doors were "mined" with dummies on his orders. As Petrulevych later explained, this was done "to avoid casualties among the civilians." However, Petrulevych did not explain how exactly these "civilians" could have ended up in the SSU building.

Realizing that the armory was not properly secured, the separatists easily opened it and seized the weapons.

> "We, the joint headquarters of the 'Army of the Southeast,' address the people of our regions. We promised that if our demands were not met by April 6, we would engage in open confrontation. Now, we are addressing you from the regional Security Service in the Luhansk region. The building is fully under our control. We call on the entire population of the region to support us and our demands, which concern all of us—the entire Southeast. It's time to stand up for our rights and our values. Over the past day, our army has grown significantly. At this moment, we are ready to dispatch a reserve unit to the city of Donetsk if necessary. But without the general support of the people, we will not be able to change anything. Rise up, Southeast!" read a new statement issued by the militants on April 7.

The spokespersons for the group that seized the Security Service of Ukraine were Oleksii Rielke and Valery Bolotov.

Who were the leaders of the separatists?

The cover story of Valery Bolotov was based on the public organization "Union of Airborne Forces Veterans," not much was known about its activities. Such army units were never stationed in the Luhansk region. According to him, Bolotov served in the 103rd Airborne Division in Vitebsk (Belarus) and participated in the armed conflict in Nagorno-Karabakh. Apparently, at the time of the aggression against Ukraine, Bolotov was either a hired worker or the owner of several illegal coal mines in the Luhansk region. In the spring of 2014, Bolotov joined the "Luhansk Guard" and headed its branch in the city of Stakhanov, which was called the "Stakhanov Guard."

Oleksii Rielke was a more striking character. Being of German origin, this native of Stakhanov emigrated to Germany with his parents in the '90s, where he obtained citizenship and lived in Koblenz for a long time. However, he eventually returned to his homeland. Moving from Germany to the depressed mining town of the Luhansk region was a strange act from any angle. This action gave rise to various assumptions and suspicions, including the possibility that Rielke was an employee of Russian special services. In turn, the militants suspected him of working for "Western intelligence," as he remained a citizen of Germany. Perhaps that's why "the German" (as Rielke's comrades called him) did not stay long in the pro-Russian movement. In mid-April, a conflict occurred in the seized SSU building, leading to Rielke's expulsion by Bolotov's people. Soon after, "the German" was arrested in Stakhanov by Ukrainian special services and spent several months in prison until he was exchanged.

The day after the seizure of the SSU headquarters, Valentyn Nalyvaichenko, the head of the SSU, along with his deputy Andrii Levus and the Secretary of the National Security and Defense Council Andriy Parubiy arrived in Luhansk. Oleksandr Petrulevych, who had just disgracefully surrendered the building to the militants, immediately began developing a plan with them to storm the SSU in order to retake it from the invaders.

The storm was planned to take place on the night of April 7 to 8 before the militants had a chance to dig in properly. Petrulevych himself, who was inside during the seizure of the SSU and then held by the militants for several hours, saw that they were not taking serious security measures at that time. He managed to leave the building accompanied by one person, who told the guards at the entrance that they were "going out for cigarettes."

The plan was as follows: first, the SSU headquarters was to be surrounded by a double cordon of the internal troops regiment stationed in Luhansk, after which the cleanup was to be initiated by the "Alpha" special unit. According to Oleksandr Petrulevych, there were only eight "Alpha" officers in Luhansk, five of whom refused to carry out the task, citing their "moral and ethical convictions." Therefore, 120 "Alpha" officers were sent from other regions of Ukraine to Luhansk to clean out the separatists. They had participated in forceful actions against Maidan activists a month and a half before but were prepared to follow orders.

The internal troops regiment, which was supposed to secure the perimeter, was subordinate to the head of the Luhansk office of the Ministry of Internal Affairs, General Volodymyr Huslavskyi. However, at the appointed time, his fighters couldn't leave the barracks — their commander reported that the exit was blocked by a crowd of pro-Russian activists. Petrulevych later stated in court that he instructed his subordinate to verify this information, but instead of a "crowd," he saw a dozen elderly women who were indeed blocking the exit but could be dealt with without much trouble.

Without the support of the internal troops, Petrulevych didn't dare to storm the SSU.

> "Sending 'Alpha' for a storm without a blockade would have meant sending them to be killed," he recounted in court in 2017 during the criminal case against Oleksandr Yefremov.

The mission was postponed for another day: for the

night of April 8 to 9. Two additional internal troops regiments were sent to surround the quarter and the building in Luhansk. However, problems arose again due to the total disorganization of the law enforcement structures. The internal troops arrived without weapons and supplies. The situation was such that Petrulevych had to send his deputy, Oleh Zhyvotov, to the local businessman, former Party of Regions deputy Volodymyr Landyk, asking to find and provide food supplies for the soldiers. Landyk provided no assistance.

An APC was needed for the assault on the SSU building. In Luhansk at that time, there were only two such vehicles: one with the border guards and the other with the internal troops regiment (the same one that "failed" to leave in time for the assault). The command of the internal troops refused to help the SSU again, stating that their APC was "broken." After that, Petrulevych, through the SSU Anti-Terrorist Center, requested the APC from the Luhansk Border Guard unit. The head of the unit received an order to transfer the APC to the SSU but refused to execute it—he told Petrulevych that "one APC covers the entire border, and he will not give it up." As a result, the assault could not be carried out on the second night as well.

On April 9, Ukrainian special services were ready to assault the building again. However, according to Petrulevych, his people intercepted the militants' negotiations the day before, where they said that the police "would provide cover fire" in case of an assault. After this, the assault was canceled again, as suddenly, the question arose sharply about whose side the head of the regional Ministry of Internal Affairs, General Volodymyr Huslavskyi, was on in this situation.

"What storming are you talking about? We move forward, and they shoot us!" — Oleksandr Petrulevych conveyed the conversations of his fighters.

His deputy, Oleh Zhyvotov, assured that the Security Service of Ukraine intercepted conversations of the leaders of the "Army of the Southeast" — Bolotov and Rielke. "Valera, make up your mind — you're either with Huslavskyi's team or mine," Rielke supposedly said to Bolotov. Based on these interceptions, Oleh Zhyvotov, by the way, believes that initially, it was not Bolotov but "the German" who was actually in charge of the militants.

This ultimately disrupted the entire process of preparing for the assault because the head of the regional Ministry of Internal Affairs, General Huslavskyi, was part of the anti-terrorist headquarters, making it seem as if the militants had their agent in the headquarters. General Petrulevych claims that he appealed twice to the central apparatus of the Security Service of Ukraine to address the issue of General Huslavskyi's resignation — on April 7 and 9. "I wrote that if we don't replace Governor Bolotskyh and General Huslavskyi, we will lose this region," he recounted in court three years after the events. But if there were such appeals from Petrulevych, they were not heeded. Huslavskyi remained in his position until the end of April and only resigned when the situation became uncontrollable.

Around the seized SSU building, barricades began to rise quickly. In Luhansk, as in Donetsk, the police absolutely did not hinder the separatists in setting up such fortifications.

For several days trucks were freely transporting tires, boards, and other materials suitable for building barricades. The police could have blocked the access roads to the seized SSU and prevented trucks from entering, but law enforcement did not interfere with the separatists strengthening their positions.

Along those lines the law enforcement agencies in the

Donbas operated throughout the spring of 2014. In response to all questions and requests from supporters of Ukraine's territorial integrity to curb separatists and restore some order in Donetsk and Luhansk, Ministry of Internal Affairs employees usually gave one answer: the police are apolitical. Inside the MIA system, there was complete demoralization, as they were deemed "culpable" during the events on the Maidan.

Realizing that they would not receive help from the MIA, the leadership of the SSU ultimately did not dare to storm the seized Luhansk Directorate. However, Valentyn Nalyvaichenko, who headed the SSU in 2014, later began to claim that his subordinates were ready for the assault and it did not happen only because the acting President of Ukraine, Oleksandr Turchynov, ordered not to storm the building. Serhii Pashynskyi, who headed the Presidential Administration in 2014, in response, accused Nalyvaichenko of inaction.

All possible efforts to cancel the storming of the Luhansk SSU were also made by politicians from the Party of Regions. In particular, the People's Deputy from the Party of Regions, Serhii Dunaiev, a close associate of Yuriy Boyko. According to Sergiy Korsunsky, Dunaiev immediately appeared in the SSU building seized by militants and stayed there for a long time to prevent the storm.

> "Dunaiev stayed for about six days. For six days, he was there (in the SSU building. —A/N). There was a threat of a storm, so some messages were sent to Kyiv that People's Deputy Dunaiev was here to prevent the building from being stormed. We tried to make sure that Kyiv heard about these people. And it happened, negotiations began," Korsunsky said. Also, then-presidential candidates Yulia Tymoshenko, Serhiy Tihipko, Mykhailo Dobkin, and several people's deputies

from the Party of Regions, including Serhii Horokhov and Volodymyr Medianyk, tried to make statements, act as mediators, enter the building, and in some other way become part of the dialogue"

In April 2014, regional politicians probably still believed that they controlled the pro-Russian movement and hoped to implement their old plan: to scare Kyiv with the force of popular anger and then negotiate autonomy in exchange for mediating the conflict resolution.

"People are not talking about declaring a republic because they understand that there are no legal grounds for it. They are talking about the people determining which country they want to live in, how they want to pay taxes. They also want local authorities and governors to be elected locally. People do not recognize the current authorities," commented Serhii Horokhov, a member of the Party of Regions, to journalists, regarding the situation.

His words were obviously a manipulation. The people's deputy was not so much conveying the words of the separatists as attributing his own demands to them. It was clear that the legal grounds for their actions were something the militants were thinking about last. Moreover, there were several groups in the SSU building whose demands differed significantly: some demanded federalization, others demanded the creation of Novorosiia, and still others demanded the accession of the Donbas to Russia.

Like other members of the Party of Regions, Horokhov insisted that the seized SSU building should not be stormed, and the best way out of the situation was to fulfill the demands of Bolotov and his people.

"Under no circumstance should there be a storming of the SSU building. Not a drop of blood should be shed because it will be a disaster for our country. People are ready to lay down their arms if you make a compromise with them. Each side should take a step back, pull back, and come to an agreement. The current authorities need to hear the demands and sit down at the negotiating table. Because the people inside the building represent the Luhansk region," said the Member of Parliament.

On April 8, Sergiy Korsunsky entered the seized SSU building. He claims that he immediately approached Bolotov, as he knew him, and told him about his contacts with the Ukrainian authorities. Korsunsky offered Bolotov his services as a negotiator, and he agreed. Negotiations began between the separatists in the SSU and the authorities in Kyiv, and it boiled down to this: Turchynov would appoint people to key positions in the region who would satisfy both sides (Bolotov himself wanted the post of governor), while Bolotov would drop plans to hold a referendum.

The negotiations continued until April 16, but by then, the parties did not consider a key factor: the pro-Russian movement was not monolithic, and Valery Bolotov was not its sole leader. The militants who seized the building split into several factions that immediately broke into mutual conflict. The demands of the leaders varied: some were willing to engage in dialogue with the authorities, while others were more radical and considered any negotiations with the "Kyiv junta" as a betrayal.

Another leader of the separatists was adamantly against negotiations with the government— Oleksiy Mozgovoy. He had been active since the beginning of the "Russian spring" and could have led the "people's militia" of the Luhansk region himself, but the sudden emergence of Bolotov thwarted those plans. Mozgovoy reacted with jealousy and distrust to the seizure of the SSU building by the "partisans" from Stakhanov.

> "Nobody needs these negotiations. Who are we negotiating with? With traitors? With loafers? Down with the officials and the deputies who betrayed the people! Down with the oligarchy! Unite in the militia, the region will be ours," he shouted on April 15, speaking in front of the SSU building.

On April 16, the radical factions attempted to stage a "coup" in the seized SSU building and arrest Valery Bolotov, but the latter prevailed, nonetheless. On April 21, the separatists held a so-called "people's assembly" where they "officially" recognized Bolotov as the "people's governor." Oleksiy Mozgovoy and his supporters tried to break into this gathering and assert their leadership claims, but Bolotov's supporters did not allow it. Following the conflict with Bolotov, Mozgovoy and his followers left Luhansk and traveled across the region to establish their own army for combat operations against the Ukrainian armed forces.

> "This is chaos, not resistance. When negotiations are conducted with those we are fighting against, it begs the question: then who are we fighting against? How can we negotiate with the enemy we need to overthrow tomorrow?" exclaimed the leader of the "people's militia."

Later, after the start of the war, the Russian side and the separatists began to shift all responsibility for the bloodshed onto the Ukrainian government, alleging it did not want to hear from the Donbas. But in reality, the Ukrainian side tried to establish contact and negotiate with individual field commanders and leaders of the "militias." However, radical separatist commanders, like Oleksiy Mozgovoy, flatly refused negotiations and insisted on the need to wage a war of annihilation.

Negotiations regarding the appointment of Valery Bolotov as head of the regional administration were difficult. The situation was deadlocked. Appointing Bolotov and his people to key positions in the Luhansk region would have created a dangerous precedent and would have meant that Ukraine recognized its powerlessness against armed individuals who seized weapons. Would such a step have helped prevent the war? Far from certain. We cannot know how separatists would behave in such a situation. They could easily interpret such actions as a sign of the government's weakness. No one could guarantee that, having gained control over the region, paramilitary groups would agree to operate within the legal framework of Ukraine. And most importantly, if Bolotov had managed to secure himself the governor's seat through armed pressure, there would have been a great temptation to repeat this tactic in other regions.

At the end of April, the deputy current Minister of Internal Affairs, Volodymyr Yevdokymov (former head of the Luhansk branch of the Ministry) visited Luhansk and met with Valery Bolotov. During the meeting, Yevdokymov finalized with the separatist leader a number of candidates for key positions in the Luhansk region (head of the local office of the Ministry of Internal Affairs, traffic police, prosecutor), but ultimately these appointments did not take place. The situation was complicated by the fact that Bolotov did not control the radical groups, which continued to attack administrative buildings. From April 21 to April 29, in Luhansk, militants seized the prosecutor's office, the regional administration, and the state TV channel LOT. Bolotov did not give such orders—he was negotiating with Kyiv, but other commanders of the militants did not consider it necessary to consult with him. The situation in the region was even more complicated, with armed gangs emerging in every city. One after another, reports emerged of the capture of administrative buildings in Sverdlovsk, Alchevsk, and

Stakhanov. In early May, a column of cars with armed Don Cossacks from Russia openly entered the city of Antratsyt —the south of the Luhansk region came under the control of Cossack formations subordinate to the Russian ataman Mykola Kozitsyn. They did not recognize Bolotov as their leader, so the question arose about the advisability of further negotiations with his group.

Gradually, it became clear that an agreement could not be reached. Sergiy Korsunsky, who claims to have been an intermediary in these negotiations, cannot pinpoint the exact reason why this happened. Perhaps at some point, Bolotov simply snapped and gave in to the more radical groups eager to start shooting. Bolotov's negotiations with Oleg Tsaryov, a member of the Party of Regions, who at the time actively promoted the idea of an illegal referendum and the secession of Donbas from Ukraine, also played a role. Korsunsky claims that it was after meetings with Oleg Tsaryov and Valeriy Holenko that Bolotov summoned him and said he "intended to create the Luhansk People's Republic" and offered him to lead the "parliament" of the future republic. Korsunsky declined, and after that, he stopped participating in the separatist movement.

On April 26, the Bolotov supporters demanded that Kyiv "recognize Valery Bolotov as the legitimate acting governor of the Luhansk region, with the transfer to him and representatives from the region's communities of full executive authority." They gave a three-day deadline to fulfill this ultimatum. It's unlikely that the Ukrainian government would have accepted such terms, but Bolotov himself wasn't inclined to wait for three days. Already on April 27, the "Luhansk People's Republic" was proclaimed.

Despite this happening 20 days later than in Donetsk, the people of Luhansk decided to quickly make up for lost time. They scheduled the confirmation of the proclaimed

"LPR" for a "referendum" on May 11, the same date as Donetsk. Negotiations with the Ukrainian government were stopped. On April 30, Bolotov moved from the SSU premises to the building of the Luhansk Regional State Administration—to the governor's office.

NAKED EMPEROR OF THE DONBAS

Throughout the spring of 2014, one of the biggest cliffhangers of the confrontation in the Donbas revolved around when and on whose side Rinat Akhmetov would truly intervene. The position of the man who had long been considered the "master" of the Donbas could have been decisive. People expected anything and everything from Akhmetov—some believed that the oligarch would publicly support the "defiant Donbas," while others were convinced that he would create some form of a private army and ruthlessly cleanse the pro-Russian formations. However, the unexpected happened: Akhmetov either did not want or could not influence the situation. Throughout the spring, he made helpless statements, calling for some abstract peace and harmony in the Donbas, but there was no single Donbas to which the oligarch appealed at that moment. The region split into supporters and opponents of Ukraine. The latter, in turn, consisted of many groups, each of which obeyed its own commander and did not want to listen to yesterday's authorities. In the eyes of Russia's supporters, Akhmetov turned out to be as weak as Yanukovych, having lost power and no longer having the moral right to tell them what to do.

After the start of the Russian invasion of Crimea, the new Ukrainian government immediately tried to enlist the support of leaders of the largest regional financial and industrial groups in the Southeast. Ihor Kolomoiskyi was appointed governor of the Dnipropetrovsk region. In Donetsk, the position of head of the regional administration was offered to Akhmetov, but he refused to take the official position, and instead, another Donetsk oligarch, Serhiy

Taruta, took over the region. In March, while the city was repeatedly rocked by unrest and pro-Russian supporters vandalized offices and administrative buildings, Akhmetov and his associates made no attempt to take control of the situation. For the first time, the oligarch decided to intervene in the situation only in April when the separatists had already seized the Donetsk Regional State Administration and declared a "republic." On the night of April 7-8, together with Mykola Levchenko, he went to the barricades to negotiate with the occupiers and dissuade them from radical actions.

"In the evening, before Akhmetov came at night to the Donetsk Regional State Administration to talk, Mykola Levchenko and I agreed to meet with Denis Pushilin," recalls Maksym Rovinskyi. "The meeting was near the monument to Archangel Michael, not far from the administration. At that moment, it was already clear that Pushilin was "charged" by someone. He was very eager to legitimize the "DPR" in any way possible and proposed that we organize joint patrols in Donetsk with representatives of the "DPR" and the police. Pushilin began to persuade Levchenko that there were not hired "titushkas" filling the administration building, but real people, and suggested going there to talk to them. But we didn't make it. Levchenko was recognized on approach. The "DPR" representatives behaved quite aggressively towards him and tried to attack him. They were from the underbelly of society —drunk, aggressive, angry. They didn't want to listen to anything; they shouted and interrupted each other. It was impossible to communicate with them, so we didn't go any further. Pushilin himself said he couldn't guarantee our safety. After that, we left. Levchenko was annoyed by the situation but showed no intention of bringing Rinat Akhmetov to the building of the Regional

State Administration. When I started reading the news in the morning, I was surprised to see the same record of negotiations between Akhmetov and the separatists. It turned out that Kolia had taken his boss there that night. I still think it was some spontaneous decision. Probably when Levchenko realized that his authority was not enough, he decided to bring Akhmetov along. And thereby, he nullified his authority, too. Or maybe Akhmetov himself, upon learning that nobody listened to anyone in the administration, suddenly decided to go talk to the people. But either way, it became clear that day that Akhmetov no longer controlled the situation in Donetsk."

In fact, Akhmetov and Levchenko headed to the administration building because they knew the Ukrainian government was preparing a sweep. On April 7, Deputy Prime Minister Vitalii Yarema arrived in Donetsk, intending to issue orders to storm the barricades and arrest the occupiers of the Regional State Administration. Rinat Akhmetov decided to talk to the separatists to warn them about the upcoming operation and then dissuade Yarema from the assault.

While talking to the separatists, Akhmetov emotionally persuaded them to sit down for negotiations with the government and demand autonomy for Donbas, but not secession from Ukraine. Such a scenario suited Akhmetov himself, who was interested in transforming the Donbas into his own principality. The oligarch proposed to the occupiers of the administration to jointly seek changes to the Constitution, but they insisted on joining Russia.

"The issue now is about the full sovereignty of Donetsk region and accession to Russia. That's it! People are now standing for it!" representatives of the so-called "DPR" said.

The separatists assured Akhmetov that they were

ready to fight for secession from Ukraine. The oligarch pleaded for an end to bloodshed but persuaded the radicals that he shared their views, supporting most of their demands, and was willing to defend the administration alongside them against Ukrainian forces if they attempted to clear the building. Several representatives of the separatist group agreed to accompany Akhmetov to negotiate with Vitalii Yarema. During the meeting, the deputy prime minister promised them that there would be no raid of the Regional State Administration. On April 8, commenting on the situation to journalists, Yarema stated that it had been called off because the occupiers agreed to surrender the weapons previously seized and vacate the administration building. However, these promises were never fulfilled. In the end, Akhmetov simply helped the separatists buy time.

On the same day, Ukrainian forces cleared the regional administration seized by separatists in Kharkiv. There was no equivalent of Akhmetov (or Duniaev and Horokhov, like in Luhansk) in this city, and no one hindered the storming. After this clearing, there were no more mass pro-Russian rallies or attempts to seize buildings in Kharkiv. Ukraine regained full control over the region. In the Donbas, where the use of force was abandoned, attempts to find compromise and peaceful resolution of the crisis led nowhere, and the situation further deteriorated.

For some time, there was a belief in society that Akhmetov could stop the turmoil in Donetsk if he only wanted to. But Akhmetov's visit to the barricades showed that his arguments did not work. The separatists did not listen to the oligarch and refused to find a compromise.

Rinat Akhmetov, like representatives of local authorities, showed no interest in supporters of Ukraine's territorial integrity. Neither he nor his people ever attended Ukrainian rallies to support those who genuinely wanted to keep the Donbas a part of Ukraine and sought peace, not war. In terms of their worldview, Akhmetov, Levchenko, and other politicians of the "Akhmetov wing" were much closer to the separatists than to supporters of territorial unity. However, the attempts to play up to the pro-Russian formations did not help the oligarch.

Four days after the debates outside the regional administration building in Donetsk, Russian saboteurs entered the region, putting an end to all attempts at negotiation. The region quickly descended into bloody chaos.

Akhmetov realized that a war was beginning, and both sides of the fence he'd been trying to play were not set ablaze. Caught between these two fires, the wealthiest person in Ukraine, for the longest time could not believe what had happened. Until the summer, Akhmetov issued senseless and hysterical appeals addressed to everyone at once and to no one in particular, annoying everyone in the process. The culmination of this absurdity was the "Voice of Donbas" campaign, known among people as the "Honk.", On May 19, when the separatists had already conducted their illegal referendum, declared two "independent republics", and battles with artillery and armored vehicles were taking place in the north of the Donetsk region, Akhmetov urged the people of Donetsk to "honk" the horns of their cars to call for peace.

In this appeal, Akhmetov spoke out harshly against the self-proclaimed "DPR" for the first time and called on the residents of the region to resist this organization.

> "Please tell me, who in Donbas knows even one representative of this 'DPR'? What have they done for our region? What jobs have they created? Is walking around Donbas cities with rifles the defense of Donetsk residents' rights against the central government? Is looting in cities and taking peaceful civilians hostage a

fight for the happiness of our region? No! It's a fight against the residents of our region! It's a fight against the Donbas! It's the genocide of the Donbas!" red-faced Akhmetov shouted into a camera.

The trigger for such an emotional speech was the seizure by armed militants of the management of the Donetsk railway, which disrupted train traffic and caused losses to Akhmetov's enterprises.

"Today, representatives of the so-called "DPR" seized the railway. They didn't just stop the railway; they stopped the heart of the Donbas! Because without the railway, the industry of the Donbas will die. And that would mean that the Donbas will die, our hardworking region will die! Therefore, I call on all workers to come out tomorrow for a warning protest at their workplaces," the oligarch urged.

But it was too late. The conflict should have been put out at the very beginning, but instead, Akhmetov first remained silent for a long time and then tried to use the separatists for his own benefit and obstructed the clearing of the seized administration. In Mariupol, where the oligarch owned two metallurgical plants, he even allowed the directors of these enterprises to sign a memorandum with local separatist leaders. In this document, published on May 15, the CEOs of the Azovstal and Ilich Iron and Steel Works, Yurii Zinchenko and Enver Tskitishvili, together with representatives of the "DPR," demanded that the "Kyiv authorities" remove army checkpoints from Mariupol and transfer control over the city's entrances to the police and "people's militias."

Such chaotic attempts by Akhmetov and other representatives of the Party of Region to simultaneously oppose separatist groups and play along with them led to tragic consequences. For years, the Party of Regions systematically sawed off from the tree called "Ukraine" the branch called "Donbas" on which they themselves were sitting. Sooner or later, they had to fall and face the consequences.

By the end of May, Akhmetov's desperate calls to "unite" and "not let it happen" no longer made sense. The Donetsk region was already completely controlled by armed gangs who didn't care about Akhmetov or car horns. The government didn't control the region. The police didn't perform their functions. Throughout Donetsk, there were seizures, riots, and looting. Donetsk was flooded with combatants from Russia and its controlled territories of Abkhazia and South Ossetia. These people didn't know who Akhmetov was and didn't come to Donetsk to sit at any round tables.

Did Rinat Akhmetov pay the militants? Did he try to buy out the groups of the so-called "DPR" to turn them or some formations within them into his private army? In the spring of 2014, this version was quite popular. The author of these lines well remembers the incident that took place on May 25. Then, during another separatist rally in Lenin Square, one of the speakers unexpectedly called on those present to go and seize Akhmetov's residence. The idea appealed to the rally participants, and they set out on foot to storm it. Akhmetov's estate was located practically outside the city, on the territory of the botanical garden. It was about 7 kilometers from Lenin Square. But for those who dreamed of seeing the expropriation of "Donetsk Mezhyhirya," this was not a problem. Supporters of the "DPR" pulled off an impressive dash that day, but at the end of the road, activists faced disappointment. They couldn't break into the residence of the richest Donetsk resident and the neighboring office of his legendary company, "Liuks." Armed fighters of "Oplot," led by Oleksandr Zakharchenko, suddenly blocked the crowd's path near the gates. And then the nominal leader of the separatists at that time, Alexander Borodai, who came from Russia and declared himself "prime minister of the "DPR" on May 16, explained to the people that Akhmetov agreed to pay taxes to the "republic," and therefore his property couldn't be targeted for now.

Later, in 2017, the same Borodai, in one of his interviews, revealed that in May 2014, Rinat Akhmetov paid money to the field commander Oleksandr Khodakovsky, who led the armed formation "Vostok."

"Khodakovsky was on Akhmetov's funding. At one point, he tried to bring me a suitcase with $0.5 million from Rinat Akhmetov in front of witnesses. I returned this suitcase to Khodakovsky, and he allegedly spent it on financing the 'Vostok' battalion. I admit I saw him as a temporary ally. I understood that Khodakovsky was playing his game along with Rinat Akhmetov," Borodai revealed.

In the same interview, Borodai claimed that one of his tasks in Donetsk was to "neutralize Akhmetov's influence" in the "DPR" and emphasized that Rinat Akhmetov was the actual master of the "people's republic" in the spring of 2014.

In reality, Akhmetov never had full control over the so-called "DPR" because, in the spring of 2014, this organization was not yet a single structure with a clear hierarchy. In each city, their own warlords ruled, who hardly coordinated their actions with each other. It can be argued that Akhmetov had no influence over Strelkov's group, which, in April 2014, took control of the northern Donetsk region. Nor did the oligarch's influence extend to Ihor Bezler's formation in Horlivka. However, the "DPR government" formed after the illegal referendum on May 11 consisted almost entirely of people who had previously worked for the city authorities and were associated with the Party of Regions. Akhmetov's connection with the separatist leaders in Mariupol was even more evident, where the "DPR" was led by the Kuzmenko brothers, Denys and Dmytro.

The Kuzmenko brothers had a criminal past but did not hide their connections with law enforcement and local government representatives. Pre-war photographs of them standing alongside the mayor of Yenakiieve, Valerii Oliinyk, and the high-ranking Mariupol police officer Mykhailo Uzun are easily found on the internet. Before Mariupol was cleared of illegal armed groups, the Kuzmenko brothers communicated well with the city's mayor, Yurii Khotlubei, police leadership, and directors of Akhmetov's metallurgical plants, meeting with them at the same table and signing memorandums of joint actions.

Pavlo Gubarev also spoke about Rinat Akhmetov's collaboration with pro-Russian activists. In an interview he gave to a "Rossiiskaia Gazeta" on May 12, 2014, after being released in an exchange, Gubarev said:

> "In these conditions, leaders of the so-called 'people's militia' began to emerge in all cities. And the ruling party, our eastern oligarchs, resorted to convenient methods of bribery. There were probably no threats discussed, rather bribery and scheming—that's how they started working with the activists of the 'People's Militia.' It turned out that two-thirds of the activists were already on Akhmetov's payroll. A very small group of people remained faithful to the idea but still took money. Everyone took money!"

Later, Gubarev, like Borodai, also mentioned Akhmetov's cooperation with the armed formation of the field commander of the "DPR", Oleksandr Khodakovsky.

> "The unit led by Khodakovsky, and he himself acknowledged this (although he later deleted the video), was created by Rinat Akhmetov as a security

detail. Besides holding certain frontlines, Khodakovsky and 'Vostok' also provided security for Akhmetov's enterprises," Gubarev recounted in an interview with Russian writer Maksym Kalashnikov in December, 2020.

Obviously, the plans of the Donetsk clans did not include the secession of the Donbas from Ukraine. Everything indicates that both Akhmetov, Bobkov, and other politicians who toyed with separatist groups simply wanted to use armed formations to strengthen their positions in negotiations with the new government. The Party of Regions dreamed of bargaining for maximum autonomy for themselves and securing for the Donbas the status of a "state within a state," which it essentially was from the early 1990s. However, these plans were shattered on April 12, 2014, when a new force emerged in the Donetsk region, over which the Donetsk oligarchs no longer had any control.

Early that morning, the town of Slovyansk, located in the northern part of the Donetsk region, was seized by a small group of Russian saboteurs led by an FSB employee, Igor Girkin, who called himself Igor Strelkov.

TRIGGER OF WAR

In mid-March, the first slow and somber convoys of military vehicles began to appear on the roads of the Donbas. The Ukrainian army was mobilizing forces to the eastern borders in response to the threat of military invasion from Russia. The sight of outdated, rusty tanks and artillery tractors, made back in the days of the USSR, raised doubts about the condition of the armed forces and their ability to engage in combat operations. The country was drained by corruption and ineffective management, and the state of the army reflected the overall state of Ukraine's economy.

The appearance of Ukrainian military equipment angered supporters of Russia. In Luhansk and Donetsk, many still hoped that Putin would annex the Donbas along the lines of the Crimean scenario and that Ukraine would not resist. But the arrival of the military changed everything. Ukraine was preparing to defend its territory, and for the separatists, this was undoubtedly bad news. Their leaders urged the population to block the movement of military columns. Checkpoints began to appear on the roads of the Donbas. Mobile groups of separatists were keeping watch at railway stations to monitor the movement of trains with Ukrainian equipment. Pro-Russian group leaders claimed that Ukraine was planning to use the army "against the people," although the events in Crimea provided a clear rationale for why troops were being sent to the east.

On March 15, a train with Ukrainian equipment was blocked at the Vilkhova station, near Luhansk. Pro-Russian supporters blocked the rails and barricaded the railway tracks with scrap metal. Their actions were led by Rodion Miroshnyk, a regional council deputy from the Party of Regions. In the Donetsk region on the same day, pro-Russian supporters with tricolor flags blocked the road along the path of a military convoy near Volnovakha. The crowd shouted at the soldiers, "Go home, why do you need this?" After some time, the military convoy turned around and went back. It was clear that the Ukrainian Armed Forces soldiers were not eager to engage in combat and didn't quite understand what was happening around them.

The anticipation of ominous events hung in the air, yet direct clashes and bloodshed did not initially occur. Until the arrival of Russian saboteurs in the region, a fragile peace was maintained. The turning point came with the armed incursion into Slovyansk by a group commanded by Igor Girkin (Strelkov). As Girkin later admitted in his interviews, he and his men came to Donbas with a specific purpose—to start a war.

> "I was the one that pulled the trigger of war. If our unit hadn't crossed the border, everything would have ended like it did in Kharkiv, like in Odesa. There would have been several dozen killed, burned, arrested. And that would have been the end of it. But the momentum of the war, which continues to this day, was set in motion by our unit," Igor Girkin boasted in an interview with the Russian nationalist newspaper "Zavtra."

Local pro-Russian supporters in Donetsk, including Pavlo Gubarev, confirmed Girkin's decisive role in unleashing the war.

> "Strelkov was the first to arrive, and nothing stopped him. It is precisely without him that the cause would have faltered in Donetsk and Luhansk. It would have faltered just like it did in Odesa and Kharkiv. He is the one who drew an uprising from a simple, unarmed, toothless street protest. It is Strelkov who saved this protest from being simply stifled and drowned in blood," Gubarev recounted in an interview with Russian writer

and blogger Maksym Kalashnikov in December 2020.

Girkin explained why he specifically chose Slovyansk. According to him, there was the most powerful local separatist organization in the region. Indeed, even before the appearance of Russian saboteurs in the city, armed individuals led by Vyacheslav Ponomariov, the future "people's mayor" of Slovyansk, were already in control. By the end of March, members of Ponomariov's group, dressed in camouflage and bulletproof vests, began to take shifts at the traffic police post together with the police and got into a conflict with the activists of the "Road Control" group. When the activists asked the police why unknown armed individuals, including Ponomariov, were at the post with them, the militants attacked the members of "Road Control" and started beating them with chains and clubs.

Ponomariov, in his interview given to the Russian website "Antifascist" in April 2016, described the formation of his group as follows:

> "February 21, 2014, could be called the day of organizing the people's brigade of Slovyansk. That evening, at 7 pm, in Lenin Park near the Monument to the Liberator, seventy concerned residents of the city gathered. On the same day, after discussing the situation in Kyiv, we decided to work on creating self-defense units. Since a large portion of the police force (about a hundred people) had been deployed to Kyiv, the city became practically defenseless. It was decided to organize patrols of the city after dark, as well as to provide security for rallies and protests. The city was divided into twelve sectors, and units were formed based on territorial divisions: squads, platoons, and companies. I formed separate groups of Cossacks, former military personnel, and hunters. Parallel ideological work was carried out, and I appointed a deputy political officer. The head of the local branch

of the Communist Party of Ukraine, Anatolii Khmelovyi, and Communist Party activists were engaged in work with the population."

In the same interview, Ponomariov talked about his contacts with the police, which agreed to cooperate with his formation even before the start of the anti-Ukrainian unrest in Donetsk.

"On February 23, I had a conversation with the Deputy Chief of the Ministry of Internal Affairs, Bielianin. Achieving a principled agreement regarding maintaining law and order in the city as a result of the conversation, we began to work together. I allocated our guys to reinforce the checkpoints of the traffic police. By agreement, we took full control of certain areas of the city," he recounted.

Also, according to Ponomariov, he managed to negotiate with the traffic police officers to let through to Slovyansk a convoy of fighters led by Igor Girkin (Strelkov) without hindrance:

"On April 11, I had a Skype conversation with Kateryna Gubareva. She said that an assistance group was coming to me in Slovyansk. Trusted people with whom I was in touch called, and we agreed on the time and place of the meeting. Since I had good personal relations with the traffic police officers along the Rostov-Kharkiv highway, I instructed them so the transport heading to Slovyansk would not be stopped or checked. I met the vehicles in Debaltseve. That's how I met the commander of the group, Strelkov Igor Ivanovych."

One more reason Girkin chose Slovyansk was its favorable geographic location. It was situated at the intersection of important roads and served as the "northern gate" to the Donbas region. After capturing Slovyansk, the entire region fell under Strelkov's control. Additionally, there were urban clusters beyond the city where they could hide in case of Ukrainian forces offense.

Pavlo Gubarev's book "The Torch of Novorosiia" describes the incursion of Girkin's group into Ukrainian territory. Armed militants easily traveled from Crimea through the Rostov region and crossed the state border into Ukraine, which suggests that the Russian side provided them with a "green corridor." The Ukrainian border was poorly guarded at that time, allowing the Russian militants to pass unimpeded.

Girkin's intention was to ignite conflict and initiate military actions that local paramilitary formations hesitated to undertake. And then to consolidate and lead disparate units. At the time of the Russian diversionary unit's incursion, the situation in the region was highly charged, yet there was no one willing to light the fuse. Thus, the fire of war in Donbas had to be imported from Russia, and retired FSB agent Igor Girkin became the Prometheus willing to bring it.

This plan wasn't Strelkov's invention. In the mid-1960s, Russian white emigrant Yevhenii Mesner, who fled Russia after the "Reds" victory, coined the term "miatiezhevoina" ("insurgency,") meaning a hybrid of war and coup, or rather a war disguised as a coup. Mesner dedicated several articles and books to it, detailing how such wars are conducted and why they can be more effective than traditional ones.

> "A new form of armed conflict has emerged, which we can call 'insurgency,' in which warriors are not only soldiers, or not so much soldiers, as popular movements," wrote Mesner. "The warfare of insurgents, saboteurs, terrorists, propagandists will have enormous dimensions in the future."

In 2014, no one in Ukraine used Mesner's outdated term, but instead, the phrase "hybrid warfare" came into use, a different word but not that different in meaning. Russia effectively entered into a war with Ukraine but officially did not participate in it. Instead of regular units of the Russian army, at the initial stage of the war, paramilitary groups of Cossacks and Russian nationalists entered Ukraine, which the Russian side allowed to pass through the border unhindered. The Kremlin sent to Ukraine something akin to private military companies (PMCs). Such formations were not stipulated by Russian law, but this did not prevent various Cossack groups and similar organizations from existing on the territory of the Russian Federation. Some of them openly called themselves PMCs. For instance, there was the PMC "Yenot C.O.R.P.," which had its own website, openly posted about its participation in combat in eastern Ukraine but it was formally registered only as a public organization.

Igor Strelkov himself never referred to his unit in such a way, but de facto, his formation was little different from the well-known Russian PMC "Wagner," which also exists unofficially. The difference lies only in the names of the curators of these formations. While the sponsorship of "Wagner" is attributed to the Russian oligarch Yevgeny Prigozhin, Strelkov, and Borodai did not hide their connection with another Russian billionaire—Konstantin Malofeev. For a long time, Kremlin spokesmen explained Borodai and Strelkov's appearance in Donetsk as Malofeev's own initiative, but only very naive people could believe this version. Russia provided wide support to the militants, sending weapons, equipment, and ammunition to the Donbas, which would have been impossible if Strelkov acted against the will of the Russian government. Konstantin Malofeev himself would probably get in trouble if his actions went against the Kremlin's plans.

The capture of Slovyansk was drastically different from all other seizures of administrative buildings that had occurred in Donbas before. If previously such seizures happened spontaneously and resembled more of a riot, in Slovyansk, the city council and the police department were seized in a coordinated and precise manner. Armed individuals appeared at all entrances to the city and quickly set up their checkpoints. The Slovyansk police and those in nearby major cities in the Donetsk region offered no resistance to the invaders, although there were few saboteurs - only a few dozen people.

Throughout March, the police justified their inaction by the nature of the disturbances. They claimed that activists were storming administrative buildings in crowds, with unarmed women and pensioners at the forefront, making it impossible to use force against them, considering the events on Maidan. However, in Slovyansk, the sabotage of law enforcement became evident because now the administrative buildings were occupied not by "peaceful activists" but by heavily armed militants in military uniforms, and no one attempted to stop them. The author of these lines personally arrived in Slovyansk on April 12, shortly after the appearance of saboteurs in the city, and witnessed with his own eyes how two militants stopped the police "PAZik" at the entrance to the city from Kramatorsk and ordered the law enforcement officers to turn back. Despite the fact that the bus was carrying Ministry of Internal Affairs personnel in full gear, they followed the instructions of the "green man" without any hesitation.

The attempt by Ukrainian special forces troops the next day to enter Slovyansk and gather intelligence encountered armed resistance. Saboteurs ruthlessly opened fire and killed Captain of the SSU Hennadii Bilichenko. Several Ukrainian law enforcement officers were wounded.

Bilichenko's death became the formal pretext for the start of an anti-terrorist operation (ATO) against militants in Slovyansk.

However, the armed clashes did not start immediately. The first serious battle involving the Ukrainian military on the outskirts of Slovyansk occurred only on May 2. The troops were not capable of quick and decisive action. The army, after years of neglect, was in a poor state and was not ready for combat. A country ravaged by corruption could not rapidly restore its military strength. Confusion reigned in the highest offices. The Ukrainian authorities feared a full-scale Russian invasion and, therefore, tried to act cautiously. Military operations escalated only at the end of May.

"As they realized that Russia would not react, the shelling became stronger, the actions of armored vehicles and aircraft more massive. By early June, they were finally convinced that Russia would not intervene directly, so they went all out," recalled Girkin in his interview.

In the next few days after the capture of Slovyansk, a wave of seizures of administrative buildings and police departments swept across the entire region. Soon, flags of the so-called "DPR" and RF were flying over all city and district councils. Footage from Horlivka circulated all over Ukraine, showing police officers obediently lining up in formation and following the commands of a man in camouflage who identified himself as a "Russian army lieutenant colonel." The ease with which the police agreed to submit to someone who appeared out of nowhere and didn't even show them any documents was striking. It was obvious that the law enforcement officers didn't even attempt to resist, and the Ukrainian State in the Donbas was surrendering positions to the "little green men" as easily as in Crimea.

Soon, it became clear that the "lieutenant colonel of the Russian army," who had the Horlivka policemen stand at attention, was actually a resident of Horlivka named Igor Bezler. Before the war, Bezler worked at a municipal enterprise and did not play a prominent role in the city. Therefore, those who remembered Bezler from those times were struck by the change in him. In an instant, he transformed from an unremarkable middle-aged citizen into a brazen and dangerous bandit, whose cruelty was rumored throughout the region. Bezler was indeed a military man. Later, it turned out that, like Girkin, in February–March 2014, he was in Crimea, where he assisted the Russians in annexing the peninsula, then he returned to Horlivka, where he organized a group of militants and took control of the city.

Girkin and Bezler were already acquainted by the time of their arrival in the Donbas. They actually met in Crimea, as Girkin later recounted. "People's mayor" of Slovyansk and the head of the local "militia" Vyacheslav Ponomariov, admitted in his interview with a well-known Russian war correspondent, Semen Pehov, in April 2021 that in March 2014, he also traveled to Crimea to coordinate his actions with the Russians. These circumstances indicate that the actions of armed groups in the Donbas in the spring of 2014 were not spontaneous and disjointed. The units of field commanders were coordinated with Russia, which used the same people for the Crimean and Donbas campaigns but did not acknowledge its involvement in the events in the Donbas.

In the face of complete government and police inaction against the separatists, only a few desperate citizens who wanted to preserve a unified Ukraine attempted to resist. In Horlivka, such a brave individual turned out to be the local council deputy Volodymyr Rybak. On April 17, when separatists raised the flag of the self-proclaimed "DPR" over the city council building, Rybak tried to tear it down and restore the Ukrainian flag in its place. However, the pro-Russian crowd prevented him from doing so. Rybak was seized and put into a car by several militants of Bezler, who took the deputy to the insurgent-held Slovyansk. No one saw Rybak alive again. A few days later, his body, showing signs of torture, was found in a river on the outskirts of Slovyansk. Along with it, the body of a student, Yurii Popravka, who had been tortured to death, was also found. Popravka had volunteered to fight against the militants but was immediately captured and executed by Strelkov's militants.

The cruelty with which the Russian saboteurs acted left no doubt that their goal was indeed warfare. Igor Girkin, staging acts of violence, could not have been unaware of the reaction his actions would provoke. With several wars behind him, he knew exactly how they would typically start.

The local authorities of Slovyansk, as well as the leadership of the surrounding areas, unhesitatingly went into service with the Russian armed group. Deputies and mayors had a choice—to stay and work for the separatists or leave the captured cities. However, not everyone chose to leave. Most members of the Slovyansk city council decided to collaborate with the occupiers. Besides the Communists, who joined Ponomariov's group and began preparing an anti-Ukrainian uprising in the city even before Girkin's appearance, the Party of Regions faction also agreed to serve the militants. On April 30, at the demand of the militants, the city councilors from the Party of Regions forced the resignation of the city mayor, Nelia Shtepa, and appointed Vyacheslav Ponomariov as the "people's mayor" in her place. Among those who voted for this appointment was the future mayor of Slovyansk, Vadym Liakh, who was a city council deputy at the time. After the city was cleared of armed groups, Liakh had no legal problems, unlike Nelia Shtepa, against whom a criminal case was opened, and who spent several years in detention accused of cooperating with terrorists.

Repelling attacks of Ukrainian forces, the militants

began preparing for a "referendum" scheduled for May 11, as appointed by a "temporary government of the "DPR" sitting in the captured Regional State Administration. Initially, nobody believed that the separatists would have enough power to pull off this spectacle. However, after armed groups took over a large part of the region, it became clear that they were gradually approaching their goal. Ukraine could not thwart their plans. Regaining control of the region could only be achieved through military means, but the exhausted state lacked the resources for it. Military commandants of the militants became the real authorities in the cities of the Donbas. The demoralized police surrendered without a fight, began to carry out orders of the militants, and patrol the streets together with the representatives of the "volunteer squads." The Security Service of Ukraine maintained amicable neutrality. Deputies and officials were left with only a decorative function, preparing polling stations for the "expression of the will of the people," which was supposed to be the culmination of the "Russian spring".

ENLIGHTENING SOCIOLOGY

In April 2014, when the events had already escalated, the Kyiv International Institute of Sociology (KIIS) conducted a study of public opinion in the eastern regions of Ukraine. The research results indicated chaos in the minds of citizens and a significant increase in anti-Ukrainian sentiments, but supporters of Ukraine in the Donbas were in the majority. The situation was objectively difficult but far from hopeless.

According to the KIIS survey, about 70% of Donbas residents considered the government of Arseniy Yatsenyuk and Acting President Oleksandr Turchynov illegitimate, while 60% considered Viktor Yanukovych illegitimate as well. 65% viewed the Maidan as an armed coup organized by the opposition with Western support, while 45% believed that Yanukovych should have dispersed the Maidan by force, although 35% were against such a scenario. 43% believed that Yanukovych and the Party of Regions were personally responsible for the killings on the Maidan, while 48% blamed the opposition. At the same time, 55% believed that the police had no right to use weapons against protesters. Paradoxically, 60% of residents of the Luhansk and Donetsk regions considered the "Right Sector" a "myth" and a "fringe organization with no real weight and should be disarmed," yet approximately the same number of people believed that the "Right Sector" influenced the government. These statements obviously contradicted each other, and the only way to explain this confusion in people's minds was through the influence of propaganda.

Moreover, there were no aggressive anti-Ukrainian sentiments in the region. The seizure of administrative buildings was unquestionably supported by only 10-15% of those surveyed, with another 10–15% being somewhat supportive of the process. However, 72% of residents in the Donetsk region and 59% in the Luhansk region viewed the seizures negatively. Nearly half believed that the seizure of administrative buildings could not be justified in any way, and approximately one-third justified these actions only because people in other Ukrainian regions had previously acted similarly. A quarter considered this method the last resort to "make themselves heard by the central government."

What were people afraid of?

Most of the respondents were most afraid of the collapse of the Ukrainian economy (43%), followed by the severance of economic ties with Russia (36%) and the high level of banditry (50% in the Donetsk region, 30% in Luhansk). Next were the risks of unpaid salaries and pensions, nationalism and radicalism, and the threat of civil war (all around 27-29%, with the latter being over 40% in the Donetsk region). It is worth noting that membership in NATO, the shutdown of Russian TV channels, the sole national language, and the potential visa system with Russia did not greatly concern the population—the survey indicated about 7-10% of citizens included these points in their list of concerns.

What were they expecting from the new government?

The rating of expectations was quite typical: support for industrial enterprises (35-40%), disarmament of illegal armed formations (approximately 35-45%), restoration of relations with Russia (almost 30%), balanced cultural policy (approximately 25-35%), rejection of nationalist and radical rhetoric. At the same time, federalization as a means of preserving the unity of the state was considered by slightly more than 20% (42% considered this method of organizing the functioning of the state optimal), while another 20% sought "public dialogue between Kyiv and the South-East."

Sociologists asked direct questions about the separation of the eastern regions from Ukraine and joining Russia. This idea was confidently and with some reservations supported by 30% of the people, while the majority—over 50%—wanted to continue living in Ukraine. Almost every fourth person was ready to take to the streets for joining Russia, and approximately 10% would support sending in Russian troops. At that time, about a third of the people felt themselves in a state of war with Russia, and more than 55% believed that there was no war, with roughly the same amount expecting specifically a "civil war."

Nobody rushed to grab weapons. 55% were willing to do so for self-defense and the defense of their loved ones, almost 30% were not prepared to fight under any circumstances. Only 6% were willing to personally fight against the "junta." Less than 20% of local residents expected military assistance from Russia, and almost 55% were against such assistance.

"In general, the sentiments turned out to be not so radical and militant. The main thing that local residents want is material security and less extremism. Protest sentiments in the region are certainly present, although it cannot be said that they are overwhelming. In their majority, people do not intend to take up arms and do not support radical methods of struggle. In order to alleviate social tension, the new authorities need, first of all, to convince the people of the east that they are safe and that their basic life interests will not be violated, and they themselves will be heard," wrote the Luhansk online publication "Vostochnyi Variant" in April 2014.

The sociological survey was conducted in April, precisely during the seizure of the SSU building in Luhansk and the appearance of Igor Girkin's groups in Slovyansk. By the end of April, when the militants managed to disconnect Ukrainian channels in the cities under their control, Russian propaganda had flooded the entire information space. The main channels for obtaining information for many became Russian social networks like "Odnoklassniki" and "VKontakte," as well as Russian television channels. The events of May 2 in Odesa, preparations for the "referendum," and a powerful anti-Ukrainian information campaign also significantly influenced public sentiments.

The survey by KIIS is likely the most objective study of the sentiments in the region at that time (at least, we don't have data from more authoritative sources). And its results showed that radical pro-Russian sentiments in the region were not dominant. Even considering a certain margin of error due to many being afraid to honestly answer about their desire to secede from Ukraine, there could be no talk of any total advantage for separatists. Later, even representatives of the separatists admitted this in their interviews, accusing residents of Donbas of passivity, insufficient love for Russia, and unwillingness to support the "militia."

Such sentiments meant that each side in the struggle for the Donbas had someone to rely on, and control of the region belonged to whoever could seize the initiative. As we already know, it was the pro-Russian side that succeeded, with the decisive actions of militants who came to fight from Russia and the treacherous position of local elites being the guarantee of their success. The Ukrainian State, on the contrary, acted too slowly and indecisively, and this resulted in fatal consequences for those citizens who stood for the Ukrainian Donbas.

"REFERENDUM"

When the occupiers of the Donetsk Regional Administration announced their intention on April 7 to hold a separatist referendum in the region and separate from Ukraine, it looked like a lame prank. The situation in the Donbas then still significantly differed from the situation in Crimea. There were no Russian troops in the Donetsk region, and the separatists seemed like just a bunch of misfits, whose strength was only enough to control the regional administration building. However, within just a few days, the situation changed dramatically. Armed groups appeared in major cities, which began seizing administrative buildings, tearing down Ukrainian flags from them, and hoisting black-blue-red tricolors in their place. The flag of the "Intermovement of Donbas," invented by Dmytro Kornilov in the early '90s, became a symbol of anti-Ukrainian rebellion and a war omen.

The appearance of armed individuals caused euphoria among supporters of joining Russia. The separatist leaders assured that after the referendum on May 11, Russia would definitely have to deploy its troops and annex Donbas just as it did with Crimea. No one even thought about what to do if Moscow suddenly did not want to take the eastern Ukrainian regions for itself.

Later, in one of his interviews, Denis Pushilin revealed that all the hopes of Donetsk separatists for the Crimean scenario were self-deception because the anti-Ukrainian uprising in Donetsk was not supported by the regional council deputies.

"We, of course, wanted and, perhaps, pictured that there would be the same scenario as in Crimea. But it was deception. Maybe self-deception... We all remember well that the referendum in Crimea was conducted by the acting authorities. These were the ones elected under Ukrainian laws. This is what we asked our regional council for, but since the deputies dispersed, we had to take everything upon ourselves... No matter what we say, but we proclaimed ourselves", confessed Pushilin in an interview on one of the Donetsk TV channels in 2016.

However, it would be naive to believe that Russia did not annex the Donbas in 2014 for this reason alone. The Crimean "referendum," which took place under the barrels of Russian military rifles, was just as far from legitimacy as the declaration of "republics" in Luhansk and Donetsk. The reasons why Russia did not annex the Donbas in 2014 were different. Russia simply did not need this region. But despite this, separatist leaders promised the people of the Donbas a "promised land" and called for burning bridges with Ukraine.

Nominally, the organization of the referendum in Donbas was handled by the so-called "central election commissions" (CEC) of the "DPR" and "LPR." But in reality, the process was not so much controlled by separatists as it was by representatives of the local authorities. For example, in Donetsk, the "CEC" of the self-proclaimed "DPR" was led by Roman Liahin, who had previously worked in the youth organization of the Party of Regions, "Young Regions." At that time, there were simply no personnel or structures within the "militias" capable of organizing such a large-scale event, especially in the Luhansk region. Sergiy Korsunsky emphasized in his interview that Bolotov and his associates were simply unable to organize a referendum at the regional level, so officials and the nomenklatura took charge of organizing it.

"You understand that the 'referendum' took place on May 11, and Bolotov was in the seized SSU building until April 29, so he couldn't have been involved in organizing the 'referendum' conducted in just ten days. Personally, my assumption is that the incumbent authorities were behind all of this. On May 5, there was a meeting of mayors of cities in the Luhansk region. At this congress, they adopted a resolution on holding the 'referendum.' Bolotov and Tsaryov chaired the meeting. But they couldn't have organized it all in just five days," Korsunsky reasoned. (*Further details about this meeting will be discussed later.*) In the second half of April, a kind of dual power was established throughout the Donbas. The cities had both legitimate local authorities and centers of the 'DPR' and 'LPR,' whose representatives imposed their will on officials. Employees of the Ministry of Internal Affairs and the Security Service nominally remained subordinate to Kyiv and did not declare their allegiance to the separatists openly, but in fact, they did not hinder the militants and cooperated with the leaders of armed groups. In these conditions, deputies and officials did everything to help the separatists conduct the 'referendum' and create the desired image."

Assistance was provided to separatists even in those cities where there were no large armed groups of the so-called "DPR". For example, in Dzerzhynsk (now Toretsk), city authorities sided with the militants from the very beginning, participated in separatist rallies, and urged people to resist the "Kyiv junta." Supporters of the self-proclaimed "DPR" in this city didn't even need to seize the city council. The mayor of the city, Volodymyr Slieptsov, provided two offices to members of the "DPR" and allocated necessary office equipment.

The results of the "expression of will" in the Donetsk region were predetermined even before the voting day. In reality, no one counted the votes because the "referendum" from the beginning didn't even remotely resemble a legitimate process. Ballots were printed on a regular printer, and voting could be done without a passport. However, the anti-Ukrainian part of the population came to the polling stations. In many places, long queues of people willing to vote formed early in the morning. People were convinced that they were voting to join Russia, although there was not a single word about the neighboring country on the ballots. There was only one question: whether citizens supported the "act of state independence of the "DPR." According to the separatists, 90% of those who voted answered this question positively.

Voting took place amid intense fighting. On May 2 in Slovyansk, serious clashes occurred between members of Strelkov's group and Ukrainian security forces, who attempted to storm the city. Both sides suffered losses. Russian saboteurs managed to shoot down two Ukrainian helicopters. These events played into the hands of the separatists and helped mobilize their supporters for the "referendum."

Even more mobilizing was the tragedy in Odesa, where dozens of pro-Russian supporters died as a result of street clashes and the fire at the Trade Unions Building, which occurred during the clashes. Although the conflict on the streets of Odesa was initiated by pro-Russian activists, who were the first to open fire with firearms and kill two participants of the pro-Ukrainian movement, the circumstances in Donetsk were not investigated. The instinct of "our people are being attacked" kicked in.

Local propaganda also worked tirelessly. Supporters of secession from Ukraine convinced their fellow countrymen that "Ukrainian punishers" were planning to commit genocide against the people of the Donbas, and that the "Kyiv junta" was building concentration camps for Russian-speaking people.

"Construction of a concentration camp is nearing completion under the village of Zhdanivka in the Donetsk region, intended for all dissenters against the current government. Those who are not killed will be imprisoned for up to 15 years (under the new law)," read the leaflets that separatists were posting on the streets of cities in Luhansk region.

They made it look like an unfinished temporary detention center for illegal immigrants was a concentration camp. Despite the blatant absurdity of such stories, even such clumsy propaganda worked and bore fruit.

In Luhansk, as we already know, the decision to hold a referendum was made after some hesitation. Active preparation for it began only after negotiations with the Ukrainian government regarding the appointment of Valery Bolotov as governor of the Luhansk region reached a deadlock. On May 5, Bolotov, along with People's Deputy from the Party of Regions Oleg Tsaryov, gathered in Luhansk a "people's council" of mayors from the region's cities. During the meeting, which was also attended by deputies of the regional council, the first deputy mayor of Luhansk, Manolis Pilavov, and Verkhovna Rada People's Deputies from the region Volodymyr Struk and Serhii Horokhov, it was announced the "appointment" of Valery Bolotov as the "governor" of Luhansk region and the "subordination" of all law enforcement agencies to him. This solidified Bolotov's role as the "official" leader of Luhansk separatists. It was also announced at this meeting that the referendum on the creation of the "Luhansk People's Republic" would take place on May 11, simultaneously with a similar procedure in the Donetsk region. The ballot, just like in Donetsk, contained only one question: "Do you support the act of state independence of the "Luhansk People's Republic?" There were two options for answers: yes or no.

"This does not mean that you are going against Ukraine," lied the present People's Deputy Oleg Tsaryov, "it means that you are giving yourselves—the governor and the council— the opportunity in the future to make decisions to form a federative Ukraine and offer all regions to join. You know that the Donetsk region referendum will proceed with the same decision. After this, you can appeal to all regions of Ukraine and ask them to follow your example... I am more than confident that the entire southeast will support your decision, maybe even the central, maybe even the western Ukraine. This path gives you the opportunity to take all the powers into your hands and then hand them over to Kyiv or any other capital— whichever it may be. But it's your decision. After you vote in the referendum, you will become a negotiating party, and it will no longer be an internal Ukrainian conflict; it will be a conflict between two sides, where you will be represented."

"If for any reason someone is not ready to participate in this historic process, declare it now. We will find other people ready to take on the responsibility," Valery Bolotov addressed the mayors and deputies.

None of those present spoke up to protest. The Luhansk Regional Council immediately supported the "initiative of the residents of the Luhansk region to hold a referendum on the status of the Luhansk region," although it contradicted existing legislation.

Organizing voting in the Luhansk region was not successful for the separatists everywhere. For instance, in cities and rural areas north of Luhansk oblast, which were under Ukrainian control until 2022, there was little activity regarding referendums in 2014. In Starobilsk, Svatove, and Markivka, the messages from separatists were met either passively or even aggressively; it all depended on the stance of local officials and community leaders. In some of these settlements, pro-Russian groups managed to arrive, attack local leaders, and set up their flags on administrative buildings. But after the departure of the "capture unit," yellow-blue flags were raised again. There was no support among the locals for the idea of separation from Ukraine. To resist the separatists, minimal resistance from the local activists and officials was enough, as the invaders lacked the human resources to physically control such vast territories. As a result, the "referendum" took place only on the territories of the Donbas, in areas where heavy industry was concentrated.

The involvement of local authorities in organizing the "referendum" became a decisive factor. The real force that provided the separatists with the needed image was the workers of executive committees, mayors, and heads of city and district councils. There is no doubt that the disorganized, hastily formed groups of so-called "militia" in the spring of 2014 could not have independently ensured anything remotely resembling a vote. The assistance of officials not only made the "referendum" possible but also, to some extent, legitimized the actions of paramilitary groups. The populace received a signal that the "referendum" was not just the affair of self-proclaimed individuals from the streets but also of entirely legitimate employees of local administrations.

Why, then, were mayors and local council deputies so willing to help the separatists and did not attempt to sabotage the scenario they proposed? The decisive role here was played by the position of the leaders of oligarchic clans who controlled the Donbas and could give unofficial instructions to officials.

Many believed that the key decision on political and administrative support for the referendum was made by the most influential politician in Luhansk, Oleksandr Yefremov. In 2016, Viktor Tykhonov, his former associate, hinted at Yefremov's involvement in the events of the "Russian spring":

> "I don't know about Donetsk, but in Luhansk, as it seemed to me, nothing was happening. Then I realized that the former head of the regional administration, Yefremov, along with a certain group of people, tried to show that we could also do something," he recounted in an interview with the Russian publication "Politnavigator."

Moreover, Tykhonov himself also had a significant influence on the local political scene, particularly on the head of the regional council Valeriy Holenko, but at the very least, he did nothing to bring the deputies to their senses, and at most, morally supported the pro-Russian direction.

On May 12, in the square near the regional administration building, Valery Bolotov and Oleg Tsaryov declared the "independence of the "LPR" based on the "results of the referendum." Tsaryov immediately proposed that the "Luhansk People's Republic" unite with the "Donetsk People's Republic" by signing a corresponding agreement and also stated that the main tasks of the "young republic" were to stop the war and form its own government. His words directly contradicted his actions. Unconstitutional calls for the country's collapse clearly did not contribute to the cessation of military actions; on the contrary, they only provoked them. However, Tsaryov soon lost any authority and control over the situation in the Donbas, becoming persona non grata in the "republics."

Despite the complete loss of legitimacy and the transition of power into the hands of militants, the Luhansk Regional Council issued a statement in which it continued to push its narrative, calling for federalization and insisting that the Ukrainian government was to blame for everything.

"On May 11, a popular referendum took place in the Luhansk region, during which the residents of the region clearly expressed their will and demonstrated that they do not want to live in Ukraine as it is today. The absolute majority of people voted for the right to determine their own way of life. This right can be granted to them by Ukraine transitioning to a federal state structure. Therefore, we demand that the current central government hear the will of the people and immediately, in an emergency session, make changes to the Constitution to ensure the process of federalization. In the current situation, this is the only option and the last chance to preserve Ukraine. Otherwise, the responsibility for the collapse of the state will fall entirely on the central government. Another fundamental decision that must be made without delay is the legislative consolidation of the national status of the Russian language. In the current situation, it is extremely important to ensure the safety of people who are under threat due to the fact that the authorities unleashed fratricidal war, deploying military units against dissenters and arming radicals. We insist that the anti-terrorist operation, which essentially is a forceful suppression of protests, must be immediately terminated. At the same time, residents of the eastern regions participating in protests against the current central government must be legislatively guaranteed amnesty," stated the document.

On May 21, 2014, Oleksandr Yefremov, along with his protégé - Member of Parliament Serhii Horokhov, participated in a roundtable discussion at the Russian State Duma, openly siding with illegal armed groups. During his speech, Yefremov completely ignored the fact of Russian military presence in Ukraine.

"Events took such a turn that the central channels of Ukrainian TV started showing footage where people in camouflage, armed with rifles, would come to various institutions, drag the leaders of these institutions by their ties, kneel them down in squares, handcuff them, and this frightened people. And they began to ask themselves: if the authorities cannot bring order in this direction today, then we need to do something ourselves. This triggered a certain response in Crimea. And then, following Crimea, a certain reaction in eastern Ukraine, particularly in the Donetsk and Luhansk regions. When you realize that nobody can protect you and your family, then men who have courage and conscience eventually make decisions for themselves to defend their territory and their families. Then, the Ukrainian government, undoubtedly not without some advice, made the decision that these people should not be talked to but rather declared separatists, declared people who commit terrorist acts, and directed armed forces against them. This is happening today to a greater extent in the Donetsk region, in Slovyansk," said Yefremov.

The Luhansk politician didn't say a word about the fact that the "Crimea reaction" was actually a "Moscow reaction," and that the "little green men" without insignia, who seized the peninsula in February 2014, were actually Russian soldiers. He didn't mention that the Ukrainian armed forces were directed to Slovyansk after the city was captured by Igor Girkin's group of Russian saboteurs. He "forgot" to mention the atrocities committed by the "Donbas defenders" against peaceful residents. At the time of his speech, it was already known about the brutal murder of Volodymyr Rybak, a deputy of the Horlivka City Council, in Slovyansk, about the murdered family from Antratsyt, whom the "militants" shot on the highway near the Dovzhanskyi border checkpoint right in their cars on the night of May

9 (they didn't stop at the illegal checkpoint), as well as a number of other high-profile crimes. Yefremov's associate, Serhii Horokhov, expressed even more radical views. Unlike Yefremov, who talked about extinguishing the conflict through the federalization of Ukraine, Horokhov stated that federalization would no longer help and called on Russia to intervene directly in the Ukrainian situation.

> "Perhaps yesterday we could have talked about the federal structure of the state, but I fear that ship has sailed. Today, the majority of residents of Luhansk and Donetsk have already shown, by 80%, that they do not recognize the authority in Kyiv. They don't want to live as before, and they want their opinions to be taken into account. And at the end of my speech, I want to convey to you the words of the people of Luhansk to the fraternal Russian people. They appeal to you with a request to move from political statements to concrete actions," he said.

Horokhov did not specify just what actions he had in mind. However, in that situation, it was obvious that it was about the deployment of Russian troops in the Donbas and the annexation of the region by the Russian Federation. His speech was a direct call for this. It is worth noting that the Donetsk authorities did not dare to make such a call.

Similar statements by politicians did not help resolve the conflict but only inflamed passions.

On May 21, military actions began in the Luhansk region. In the morning, Ukrainian troops headed towards Lysychansk through the bridge near Rubizhne. However, the road was blocked by a group of local residents, after which pro-Russian formations led by Oleksiy Mozgovoy ambushed and fired at the military. Having lost men and equipment, the soldiers were forced to retreat. The spilled blood further intensified the crisis and deepened the hatred.

The funerals of the fallen soldiers of Mozgovoy turned into large spontaneous rallies. Commenting on what happened, Mozgovoy in his address promised to reach Odesa and Kyiv.

The Luhansk Regional Council, meanwhile, lived in its own invented world. On May 23, deputies, who had already lost all influence, expressed no confidence in the acting head of the Regional State Administration, Iryna Verihina, who had no impact whatsoever and threatened to leave the Party of Regions if Oleksandr Yefremov was removed from his position as head of the Party of Regions group in parliament. In the Luhansk region, there was a war on the streets; people were being kidnapped and killed, but still, the fate of the "honorary citizen of Luhansk region," Oleksandr Yefremov, concerned the deputies the most. However, nobody paid attention to them anymore. The Luhansk Regional Council lasted a few months longer than Donetsk's but ended its activities just as ingloriously.

On June 2, early in the morning, militants began storming the office of the border guard detachment located on the outskirts of a large residential area in Luhansk, broke into apartments in high-rise buildings, and started shooting at the border guards from windows. That same day, Ukrainian aviation unsuccessfully struck the building of the Luhansk Regional State Administration. Apparently, the target was to destroy Valery Bolotov in the governor's office on the second floor, but the shell flew through the park and hit the facade, killing eight people. On June 14, during landing at Luhansk airport, a plane was shot down with a MANPADS, killing 49 Ukrainian soldiers. The game of "miners who simply do not recognize the "Kyiv junta" and have the right to protest" was finally over; it became evident that professionals were already fighting against Ukraine in Luhansk.

In the Donetsk region, the situation at this time was

somewhat different from that in Luhansk. Shortly after the "referendum," separatists also formed a "government" of the self-proclaimed republic there, but unlike in Luhansk, it was not led by a local leader but by a newcomer and previously unknown Moscow political technologist, Alexander Borodai. Such an appointment left no doubt that the Russian side was directly involved in the events in eastern Ukraine and was managing the processes of creating the "republics."

Later, in an interview, one of the organizers of the separatist "referendum" in Donetsk, Oleksii Aleksandrov, who clashed with Borodai, talked about how the latter managed to take over the leadership of the separatists.

> "Disaster came in the form of Borodai. Of course, he was just a minor functionary, but everything went downhill with his arrival. It started when, during the heat of the referendum, he took the head of the CEC, Liahin, hostage and tried to blame us for sabotage and working for Kyiv. The guy wanted to take credit for our work, which was almost completed at that time. [...] Activists stormed the CEC building, rescued Liahin, and kicked out the troublemakers. Unfortunately, not for long. Soon, Borodai reappeared with credentials from 'respected individuals' from Moscow. Then there were authoritative calls with requests-orders to accept and appoint him. He loudly proclaimed that 'a special operation of Russian special services is underway in the Donbas, everyone should beware, he is responsible for the deployment of Russian special forces units to Donbas,' and so on," Aleksandrov recounted.

Among other "ministers" were both well-known leaders of the separatists (Andrei Purgin, Oleksandr Khryakov, Borys Lytvynov, Roman Liahin) and individuals associated with the Party of Regions but who had not previously participated in the unrest: the head of the apparatus of the Donetsk city organization of the Party of Regions Oleksii Hranovskyi, the chief editor of the "Municipal Newspaper" Olena Blokha, the business partner of deputy Yukhym Zvyahilsky, Oleksandr Kaliuskyi, and his manager Valerii Rassadnikov.

According to the press secretary of Mayor Lukyanchenko, Maksym Rovinskyi, the appearance of these people in the the "government" of the so-called Donetsk People's Republic was not accidental.

"Hranovskyi and Blokha were delegated to the first composition of the 'DPR' government by Bohachov. They were his people. At the same time, he himself was afraid to join the government and stayed in the shadows. In fact, he simply set up these people because no one knew how the whole story would end," Rovinskyi explained.

The hope of maintaining their own influence and control over the process was held by Donetsk regional leaders until early July—until the day when Igor Girkin's formations entered Donetsk after retreating from Slovyansk. Up until that time, the city remained relatively calm, the city council operated, and even the police nominally reported to Kyiv. Mayor Oleksandr Lukyanchenko left the city after a brief conversation with Girkin, who proposed to the mayor to blow up several multi-story buildings in the Petrovskyi district to block the entrances to Donetsk with debris and stop the possible advance of Ukrainian troops. In case of refusal to cooperate, Girkin threatened to put Lukyanchenko in the basement. *(A threat to be detained and tortured at a whim. Stemming from basement as a readily accessible and convenient holding location. —T. Ed.)*

However, at that moment, it was hardly possible to talk about any control at all. After the "referendum," the Donbas plunged into anarchy. Gunfights raged in the streets, weapons circulated freely, and there were daily reports of abductions and killings. Armed groups in different cities struggled to find common ground and often clashed with each other. In an intercepted phone conversation that took place in July and was made public by the SSU, Borodai described the situation in Donetsk as "seven-commandership." The situation in the Luhansk region was even more complicated. The territory there was divided among people loyal to Bolotov, the gang of Mozgovoy, and Cossack formations. Entire convoys of weapons entered Ukraine from Russia at night.

"The Donbas clans," which had ruled the region for decades without opposition, lost everything within weeks. The Party of Regions had long sown the wind of separatism and anti-Ukrainian sentiment in the Donbas, and in the end, they reaped the storm that scattered them like rubbish.

RUSSIAN FACTOR

For over years of conflict in eastern Ukraine, the world has not come to a unified opinion on how to interpret these events. The war in the Donbas exhibited characteristics of both an international and a civil conflict. Therefore, depending on one's political stance, each person chooses the interpretation that they feel most comfortable with. Supporters of Russia deny Moscow's direct involvement in Ukrainian events. Supporters of Ukraine label the war as "hybrid" and consider Russia the aggressor.

The purpose of this book is not to dwell on legal terms but to call things by their names. It is quite obvious that without the involvement of Russian saboteurs, without the powerful informational influence of the annexation of Crimea, without the Kremlin's overt propaganda and threats to send troops into Ukraine, the conflict in the Donbas would not have been ignited. Everything was moving towards the point where local leaders of the Party of Regions could negotiate political and financial bonuses for themselves and then settle down until the next elections, as had happened before. However, the Russian side made every effort to incite shooting in the Donbas. When the shooting did not start for a long time, Russia brought militants to Slovyansk and did everything to escalate the war into a stage of exhausting, protracted conflict.

Long before the war began, Russia systematically "nurtured" the elites of the southern and eastern regions of Ukraine, trying to tie Ukraine to itself through these elites. The Crimean and Donbas clans were the most cooperative. During political crises, they traditionally appealed to Russia, and in 2014, they openly began working towards the country's collapse.

The Donetsk political elite never concealed its ties with the Russian Federation but insisted that they were purely business-oriented. As early as 1996, an organization called "Zemliatstvo donbasivtsiv" ("Donbass fraternity") was established in Moscow, which was involved in establishing formal and informal connections between the Donetsk leadership and Russian authorities and business circles. The organization included not only Moscow politicians and businessmen with Donetsk roots but also active Ukrainian officials and deputies. Its members, including the most influential representatives of the "Donetsk group"—Rinat Akhmetov, Borys Kolesnikov, Tetiana Bakhtieieva, Valentyn Landyk, Volodymyr Rybak—remained members even after the start of the conflict. With the onset of hostilities, the organization openly sided with the illegal armed formations of the "LPR" and "DPR." However, Ukrainian politicians who were members of the organization did not express disagreement with this position and did not comment on it. There was also the "Luhansk Zemliatstvo" (Luhansk fraternity) in Moscow, which included all the most prominent representatives of the "Luhansk clan," including Oleksandr Yefremov and Viktor Tykhonov.

After the Orange Revolution, the contacts of Donbas politicians with Russian politicians and political scientists took on the character of a kind of trolling of Kyiv. Holding conferences and round tables with representatives of Russia, the regional leaders discussed pressing, scandalous issues that divided Ukrainian society, including the possible future federalization. Naturally, discussing such fundamental matters with representatives of another state without fail provoked tension within Ukraine. However, it was precisely this kind of "hype" that the Party of Regions counted on.

For example, Mykola Levchenko not only organized a propaganda exhibition in Donetsk in 2008, justifying

Russian military aggression in Georgia, but also boasted friendly relations with the leader of the Liberal Democratic Party of Russia (LDPR) Vladimir Zhyrynovskyi, known for his anti-Ukrainian views. In 2006, LDPR State Duma deputy Oleksii Mitrofanov even came to Donetsk for Levchenko's birthday, which he celebrated at the "Chicago" nightclub.

However, the most frequent Russian visitor to Ukraine in the 2000s was State Duma deputy Konstantin Zatulin, who headed the "Institute for CIS countries" in Russia. Zatulin regularly visited Donbas, Crimea, and Odesa, and each of his visits to Ukraine was accompanied by anti-Ukrainian statements and ended in scandal. For example, on March 1, 2008, at the second congress in Sievierodonetsk, where Zatulin was invited by the Luhansk regional representatives, the State Duma deputy declared that Sievierodonetsk and Luhansk are historically Russian lands and that he feels them as part of his homeland. During the period from 2005 to 2010, Zatulin was declared persona non grata twice and banned from entering the country.

Such actions were not only due to the fact that Russians disliked Yushchenko and saw him as a threat. After Yanukovych came to power and Ukraine again made a geopolitical turn towards the Russian Federation, Russian politicians did not stop making scandalous statements. It seemed that the Russians deliberately tried to provoke tension in Ukraine, and the regional elite of the Donbas played along with them in this.

In March 2010, Zatulin, together with another State Duma deputy, Sergey Markov, and Russian Ambassador Mykhail Zurabov, came to Donetsk for the conference "Russian–Ukrainian Relations in New Political Environment." There, the Russian guests welcomed the appointment of the new-old Donetsk governor Anatoliy Blyznyuk and, as usual, talked about federalization. At this meeting, Zatulin once again stated that the eastern regions feed Ukraine and, therefore, their opinion in Ukraine should take precedence.

"Western regions need to understand: whoever pays the piper calls the tune. The cultural demands of those who foot the bill for music in Ukraine - the eastern regions - must be met. People living here should stop being considered 'bad Ukrainians' on central channels because they are much more patriotic, contributing to the country's wealth and prosperity," he said.

Just two months later, in May 2010, Zatulin visited Luhansk, where the local "nobility" unveiled a monument to the victims of the UPA. There, the Russian politician once again took the opportunity to contribute to the division of Ukrainian society and stated that "the west and east of Ukraine cannot be united at the expense of betraying the memory of Soviet soldiers." The opening of such a controversial monument by representatives of the Luhansk political elite together with a Russian deputy was clearly a provocation that could in no way contribute to the building of civil harmony. Moreover, at that time, there was no political necessity for such a move—the presidential elections had already ended, and the Party of Regions had won them.

In addition to Zatulin's provocations and those of his colleagues, networks of cultural and pseudo-cultural organizations were actively built in Donbas, and even paramilitary Cossack organizations were under the control of the Russian Don Cossacks Army.

Pro-Russian politicians in Ukraine, of course, denied all accusations that they were working in the interests of another country, emphasizing that they took such a position solely out of heartfelt conviction. They claimed it was for Ukraine's benefit. Regionalists who supported separatists and left Ukraine after the start of the war began to speak more openly about cooperation with Moscow. For example, in his interview in 2016, Oleksandr Bobkov revealed that since the mid-2000s, he had been actively cooperating with various Russian structures and even received an award for this from the Russian president.

"Since 2006, after the establishment of the Interregional Union of Middle Business Representatives, I often interacted with civil organizations from Europe, Israel, Brazil, and especially the Russian Federation. In Ukraine, the public organization 'Ukrainian-Russian Dialogue' was created, where I served as vice president, and the 'Academy of Russian Studies' in Kyiv, which involved numerous contacts, scientific conferences, business forums, and missions, exchange of cultural values, promotion of Russian history and culture in Ukraine. During Viktor Yushchenko's presidency, there was an attempt to rewrite Ukrainian history. Our organization published a book 'Essays on the History of Ukraine,' for which President Yushchenko labeled us as traitors to Ukraine. The only reason we did not suffer or face repression for publishing the book was Yushchenko's low rating. I do not hide that for my active work in improving relations with Russia; I was honored by the President of the Russian Federation with an award. My position regarding Russia has always been that it is a fraternal country to the Donbas, and we are good neighbors, fraternal peoples," explained the Donetsk politician.

The Russian Order of Friendship was also awarded to one of the main speakers on the topic of federalization, Viktor Tykhonov. Currently, Oleksandr Bobkov resides in Russia, while Viktor Tykhonov is in annexed Crimea. *(Tykhonov died in Crimea in 2020 – T. Ed.)*

In November 2017, in an interview with the

Russian television channel "Tsargrad," Alexander Borodai openly admitted that Russia had been buying up Ukrainian politicians, but it did not yield the results that the Kremlin had hoped for.

"Colossal organizational efforts and enormous sums of money were spent to keep Ukraine in the vector, in the zone of influence of the 'Russian world' and the Russian idea. This did not happen because everyone to whom we gave money, everyone we organized, told us at the end of the day: 'I forgive myself all that I owe!'" stated Borodai.

He did not mention specific names, but his confession is of great importance even if it's phrased like this. A representative of the Russian side confirmed for the first time what was previously only suspected in Ukraine—at least some pro-Russian politicians were bought, while others defended Russian interests for personal gain. It is important that this statement was made not by a random political analyst or journalist but by someone close to Vladislav Surkov, who has long been considered in Russia as the curator of the Ukrainian direction. Therefore, Borodai knew well what he was talking about.

However, if before 2014, Russia's intervention in Ukrainian internal affairs was limited to peaceful means, then after the revolutionary events, the Kremlin shifted to military intervention. Russian troops appeared in Crimea, after which all questions about whether Moscow had expansionist plans regarding Ukraine disappeared by themselves. The entire country froze in anticipation of a Russian blitzkrieg, but in the southern and eastern regions of Ukraine, Russia chose a different tactic and attempted to incite anti-Ukrainian uprisings through local activists and pro-Russian politicians. The recordings of negotiations by the advisor to the President of Russia, Sergey Glazyev, who attempted to implement this plan in the spring of 2014, provide the best insight into how this was happening. Glazyev urged pro-Russian activists over the phone to take people to the streets and appeal to Russia for help. In the audio recording published by the General Prosecutor's Office of Ukraine in 2016, Glazyev's key phrase is recorded, which best reflects the tactics of the Russians in Ukraine. "We only use force to support the people, nothing more. And if there are no people, then what support can there be?" Glazyev persuaded one of his Ukrainian interlocutors.

The essence of this phrase accurately reflects the logic of the so-called "Russian spring." For the Kremlin to act in Ukraine, it needed cover. It considered the possibility of deploying troops only in those regions where there was support, where the "fifth column" composed of Ukrainian citizens could be used as a shield.

Russian militant Alexander Zhuchkovskyi, who arrived in the seized Slovyansk in the spring of 2014 from St. Petersburg and joined Strelkov's group, confirms that Glazyev did indeed call pro-Russian activists from different regions of Ukraine in the spring of 2014 and promised them support from the Russian Federation.

> "I remember how Glazyev in the spring of 2014 was calling the leaders of the rebellious regions and saying that Russia wouldn't abandon them, that Putin had the right to deploy troops... Glazyev was probably encouraged in the Kremlin at that time, too—like, well done, keep working, we'll support you. So, he, with all his patriotic zeal, rushed to work and made promises. But they misled him, and along with him— all of Novorosiia," Zhuchkovskyi wrote on his VKontakte page in August 2018.

Did Glazyev really get "misled," as the Russian militant writes about it? It's unlikely that this expression is appropriate here. Most probably, the Kremlin decided not to get involved in "Novorosiia" because the "rebellious regions" turned out to be not so rebellious after all. In Zaporizhzhia, Mykolaiv, Kherson, and Dnipropetrovsk, there weren't many pro-Russian activists. In Odesa and Kharkiv, more people took to the streets, but their leaders were unable to organize protests properly and everything quickly fizzled out. No matter how hard Glazyev tried, no matter how much he urged people to take to the streets, massive anti-Ukrainian protests were successfully provoked only in two eastern regions. And there, as Glazyev promised, armed people from Russia eventually appeared. Therefore, the words about "Novorosiia being misled" seem more like an attempt to portray wishful thinking as reality because there was no one to be "misled." As Glazyev himself said from the very beginning, "If there are no people, then what support can there be?"

Probably, initially, the Russians counted on the civil conflict in Ukraine to start spontaneously, without external assistance. However, when it became clear that Ukrainians, despite all differences, did not want to kill each other, it was necessary to send the participants of the annexation of Crimea—Igor Girkin and Igor Bezler—to Donbas, with the task of "triggering the war."

In Zhuchkovskyi's book "85 Days of Slovyansk," which was released in the summer of 2018, there is a fragment that describes the invasion of Igor Girkin-Strelkov's group into Ukraine.

> "On the night of April 12, 52 Strelkov's people appeared in the Rostov region, left all their documents there, marched on foot for up to 15 kilometers, and crossed the border with Ukraine at a predetermined point. From there, they reached a location where Donetsk activists met them with transportation. During the operation preparation, Strelkov requested to deliver an army truck

GAZ-66. The activists couldn't get this vehicle but found a five-ton truck from the Ukrainian company 'Nova Poshta' along with the driver of this company, who initially didn't even realize the historical events he was participating in.

At the border, Strelkov, in the presence of a trembling driver, without ceremony, asked the meet-up group: "Driver is our guy or we will need to get rid of him?" They replied that he was their guy, and 'getting rid of him' was unnecessary. This incident stunned the Donetsk activists, who psychologically were not yet prepared for decisive actions."

This short excerpt actually fully explains what happened in 2014 in Donbas. A group of thugs from the territory of the Russian Federation invaded Ukraine, and they, unlike the locals, were ready without hesitation "to get rid of" even random people, not to mention soldiers or law enforcement officers.

An even more characteristic description of Strelkov's saboteurs is found in **Pavlo** Gubarev's book "The Torch of Novorosiia":

"Do you know what distinguished the Strelkov's guys from the locals? There was a scent of war and some kind of irrevocable determination about them. They came in and, actually, understood that they were going to fight and shed blood."

There were no reasons to "fight and shed blood" in April 2014. At that moment, the political confrontation could still have been resolved peacefully. However, the Russians who came to Ukraine with "irrevocable determination to shed blood" acted at their own discretion. And after blood was shed, it became clear that the bridges were burned, and the whirlwind of violence had started spinning on its own, as is usually the case in all conflicts of this kind.

In the aforementioned book by Zhuchkovskyi, the idea is repeatedly expressed that there were extremely few people in the Donetsk region willing to fight, and local separatist leaders were unable to initiate combat operations and resist Ukrainian troops. For example, one of Pavlo Gubarev's closest associates, Serhii Tsyplakov, expressed this idea in a conversation with Zhuchkovskyi. According to him, the locals were unable to organize either mass peaceful protests or armed uprisings. The people of the Donbas did not follow the separatists and, for the most part, did not support them.

"In March-April 2014, a rather stalemate situation emerged. We couldn't achieve much with non-violent protest, and we didn't have the strength for armed rebellion," admitted Tsyplakov.

He also confirmed that before the invasion of Donbas by Strelkov's group, there were only about two hundred people in the "militia." Undoubtedly, this number of people was not enough to fight the Ukrainian army. In fact, local pro-Russian activists in Donbas agreed only to help Strelkov's group cross the border and reach Slovyansk on a "Nova Poshta" truck. Of course, this indicates that there really was no civil war in Donbas in the spring of 2014. Only the intervention of Russians led to full-scale hostilities.

However, besides the direct involvement of Russian saboteurs, one cannot overlook the colossal mobilization effect exerted on Russia's supporters by the annexation of Crimea and the propagandistic reports on Russian television. Pro-Russian citizens took up arms and joined the ranks of the illegal formations of the "DPR" and "LPR" with a firm belief that Russia would not stop at Crimea and would send troops to the Donbas immediately. Separatists believed that the Russian army stood behind them, ready to send to Ukraine dark-green-clad men. They counted on Russia to intervene, to stand up for them, and not to leave them alone against the Ukrainian Armed Forces. The "Republics" were not seriously considered by anyone, nor did anyone believe that they could survive for long in any form. Propaganda convinced the people of the Donbas that the "DPR" and "LPR" were just an interim stage.

In the spring of 2014, before the eyes of the residents of Donbas, there was the example of Crimea, where everything seemed to follow the same script — first, mass protests, then the formation of the so-called "self-defense units of Crimea," and then an illegal referendum. Crimea remained an unrecognized state for only a day—from March 17 to March 18, after which it was officially "accepted into the Russian Federation." Crimean parliamentarians then explained that adopting a declaration of independence was necessary "for the legal formalization of Crimea's accession to Russia." Therefore, in the Donbas, they expected that the Russian government would act in a similar way to Donetsk and Luhansk.

The author of these lines met with Viktor Tykhonov at the end of March 2014. At the time, Tykhonov was a member of parliament from the Party of Regions and one of the most influential figures in the Luhansk region. The annexation of Crimea had already occurred, the Donbas was shaking weekly from anti-Ukrainian actions, and he was expecting that Russian troops would soon come to the Donbas. "You don't understand what's happening. The same thing will happen with the Donbas," Tykhonov assured with some weird, almost euphoric delight. It was strange to see a 65-year-old man not understanding that war would destroy all his assets—both financial and political.

When it became clear that the Kremlin had no intention of recognizing the "DPR" and "LPR" and "reuniting" with them, it was already too late. Cities were burning. Armored vehicles rumbled through the streets, and authority definitively passed to field commanders and their Russian handlers, who coordinated the actions of the militants and provided them with weapons and ammunition. If at the very beginning of the "Russian spring," Glazyev desperately needed locals in the city squares, by the summer of 2014, nobody cared about what people had to say.

As cynical as it may sound, during this period, residents of the Donbas were more useful to Russia dead than alive. In order for the fire of war to flare up, they had to suffer vividly, die dramatically, and evoke sympathy from the Russian public.

Russian television extensively and in detail portrayed death. Propaganda attributed shocking atrocities to Ukrainian soldiers, depicted a camp for illegal migrants, built even before the war in the city of Zhdanivka in the Donetsk region, as a "concentration camp for Russian-speaking people," portrayed supporters of Ukrainian unity as cruel fiends and Nazis. Almost every news broadcast told viewers about new victims of "punishers." These stories about "lynched boys" and "concentration camps for Russian speakers" pushed especially trusting and vulnerable citizens of Ukraine, Russia, and other former Soviet republics to join pro-Russian paramilitary groups and "take revenge" on Ukrainian soldiers for war crimes that never actually occurred.

From the beginning of the conflict, separatists still hoped that Russia would eventually decide to openly send troops and annex Donbas. However, the more time passed, the more evident it became that Russia would not take this step. For the pro-Russian movement, this meant betrayal —since Russia effectively incited people to rebel, implying through its propagandists and leaders of the "Russian Spring" that the Donbas could follow the path of Crimea. But after the war had already begun and all paths to peaceful resolution were cut off, it suddenly became clear that "no one promised anything to the Donbas." The hopes of irredentists for joining Russia did not materialize. And the saddest part is there was no one to present claims to on this matter. After all, the Russian leadership never directly declared claims to Donetsk and Luhansk. And all sorts of field commanders, second-rate politicians, and "people's governors" could promise anything they wanted—after all, they were just ordinary impostors, not authorized by official Moscow.

In the heat of the conflict, it became clear that Russia simply wanted continuous carnage in the east of Ukraine, so it provided the "separatists" with weapons and resources just enough to prevent the Ukrainian side from achieving victory and to ensure that the war did not end with the complete elimination of rebellious separatist entities. The Russian tactic boiled down to regularly stoking the fire of carnage with new ammunition and weapons while sending mercenaries to the front lines and never acknowledging Kremiln's involvement. As early as 2015, the now killed leader of the Luhansk separatists, Valery Bolotov (who at that time had fled from the Donbas and was already living in Moscow), openly stated that the militants themselves shelled residential areas of Luhansk with mortars and blamed the Ukrainian army to incite stronger hatred of Ukraine. And this method proved to be effective.

Later, the true intent of the Russian leadership became apparent even to pro-Russian militants. Many prominent participants of the events in 2014 were disappointed, but they could no longer change the situation. Moreover, for many fighters of paramilitary pro-Russian groups, the idea that the Russians deceived and betrayed them became unbearable. So, they continue to convince themselves, to this day, that there was no betrayal and that reunification with Russia will still happen in the near future—they just need to believe and endure. Any attempts to prove otherwise are dismissed as "enemy tricks." Meanwhile, each new day of such endurance results in new casualties on the front lines, the futility of which becomes increasingly evident.

Even direct statements from the Russian leadership that Donbas belongs to Ukraine have not destroyed the hopes of irredentists. No one wants to admit that years of war, numerous deaths, and destruction have been in vain, and that once a powerful industrial region has become a bargaining chip in Vladimir Putin's geopolitical games and those of his entourage.

Why did Russia need a war in the Donbas at all if, having regained part of its territory, it did not rush to annex it? The best answer to this question was given by the aforementioned member of the Russian State Duma and founder of the "Institute of CIS Countries" Konstantyn Zatulin. In an interview with the Russian publication "Federal News Agency," published on September 5, 2018, Zatulin stated:

> "We understand that after we removed Crimea from the internal Ukrainian context, removing Donetsk and Luhansk means depriving our allies of that part of pro-Russian sentiment among Russians and Ukrainians that remains on the other side of Ukraine. In this case, we proceeded from the idea that Donetsk and Luhansk need to be reintegrated into the common political field with Ukraine, but on fair terms. That is, without reprisals, without settling scores, with a special status—as elements of a federation or confederation. And the return of Donetsk and Luhansk in this status will be the catalyst for a chain reaction of federalization of Ukraine. And a federal Ukraine is what the heart needs to calm

down."

Russian public figure and writer Nikolai Starikov expressed this idea even more succinctly. He called the Donbas "the ball and chain on Ukraine's leg," necessary to keep Ukraine within the orbit of Russian influence.

It is obvious that the depressed mining territories, unlike the Crimean Peninsula, did not hold great value for Russia—it has plenty of its own territories just like that. However, returning them to Ukraine on its own terms, in exchange for federalization, abandonment of European integration, and NATO membership, fully agrees with the logic of the Kremlin. According to this plan, the areas of the Donetsk and Luhansk regions under Russia's control should receive a special status in Ukraine and become something akin to a blocking stake, allowing Russia to keep Ukraine on a short leash. This will also make into a counterbalance for those regions of Ukraine that are patriotic and support further integration with the European Union.

Do the supporters of the self-proclaimed "LPR" and "DPR" agree that the Donbas should remain part of Ukraine for the sake of the Kremlin's interests? Hardly. Such an outcome would render all the dramatic events and heavy losses of previous years meaningless. Moreover, the role of being a "ball and chain on Ukraine's leg," the brakes on European integration prepared for the region in Moscow, is simply demeaning. Regardless of how the Donbas drama ends, it can already be confidently stated today that the opinion of Donbas residents will be considered last in resolving this conflict. No matter how hard the Russian side tried to get Ukrainian recognition of the so-called "people's republics," it led to nothing; neither Ukraine nor Russia recognized the newly formed entities. The official Kremlin regularly emphasizes that there are no alternatives to the Minsk agreements, which state that there are no "people's republics" in the Donbas, only separate districts of the Donetsk and Luhansk regions, which sooner or later must return to Ukraine's jurisdiction.

.

EPILOGUE

For over years, the war in the Donbas has failed to yield any meaningful resolution. The "Russian spring" has ended, giving way to a "Russian limbo." The conflict has long entered a protracted stage, and the Donbas has joined the somber list of global hotspots where life always revolves around war. History shows that such violent hotspots can smolder for decades.

Following the onset of active hostilities, the unrecognized republics with make-believe independence have turned into criminal ghettos. Amidst concrete factories, mine headframes, and Soviet-era five-story apartment buildings in industrial towns, passions boiled over. Armed groups, having seized weapons, began fighting not only with Ukraine but also among themselves for territorial control. Only the intervention of Russian curators brought some semblance of order to the territories under separatist control. In this struggle, one after another, field commanders who became famous in early 2014 perished. They were ruthlessly eliminated: shot, blown up in elevators and restaurants, burned on deserted highways connecting embattled cities, tortured, and hung in basements and prison cells where their former allies imprisoned them.

As it was clear from the very beginning, the economy of the Donbas could not function properly in an unrecognized state, and it declined. The myth of the region "feeding the whole of Ukraine" played a cruel joke on the residents of the Donbas. Believing the tales of politicians, supporters of the separatists were convinced that after separating from Ukraine, the region would only benefit and be able to sustain itself through its own resources. However, reality was vastly different from election campaign leaflets.

The outdated industry of the Donbas required significant subsidies and investments, industrial cooperatives, and markets. Annually, the coal industry alone received up to $2 billion from the Ukrainian national budget, otherwise it could not operate properly. Additionally, industrial cities traditionally had a high percentage of retirees because workers in hazardous industries such as metallurgy, chemicals, and coal enterprises qualified for early retirement. A well-known case is when the field commander of the self-proclaimed "LPR", Pavlo Dremov, admitted with surprise that he didn't realize the number of pensioners in Stakhanov (his gang controlled the city until 2015). According to him, in a city with a population of 77,000 residents, there were as many as 31,000 retirees, and the city budget had no money to cover their pensions. *(Pension system in Ukraine is based largely on solidarity and subsidies. The Pension Fund of Ukraine uses compulsory contributions from current workers to pay current retirees. —T. Ed.)*

None of the major goals declared by the leaders of the anti-Ukrainian uprising in the spring of 2014 were realized during the years of conflict. Initially, it became clear that Russia had no intention of recognizing or annexing the hastily declared "people's republics" proclaimed by the militants, then the so-called "Novorosiia project" was quietly phased out. Russia didn't even consider it necessary to unite into one entity the detached districts of the Donetsk and Luhansk regions. To this day, they exist as two separate quasi-states, divided by a useless border.

Instead of the promised improvement in the standard of living after "breaking away from impoverished Ukraine," the Donbas fell into an economic and demographic pit. Tens of thousands of people lost their jobs, hundreds of thousands left their homes and moved to Russia or to territories under Ukrainian control. Those who remained soon discovered that in the "people's republics," people had far fewer rights, freedoms, and opportunities than in the "anti-people" and "fascist" Ukraine. The unrecognized entities, obtained at the cost of such sacrifices and losses, turned out to be even less suitable for life than the Ukrainian state, which was so heavily criticized for its low standard of living, corruption, and poor laws.

Who is to blame for the fact that the Donbas became the arena of hostilities and the fate of the region unfolded in such a tragic way? There is no consensus on this question. Some blame Ukraine, some blame Russia, and some primarily hold responsible residents of the Donbas, as a large percentage of them betrayed their country and fell for the attractive promises of irredentist-separatists. However, judging impartially, it must be acknowledged that each side bears some responsibility. The difference lies only in the form of this responsibility. Russia's responsibility is that of an aggressor who, through its agents, ignited a military conflict on the territory of a neighboring state. At the same time, Ukraine's responsibility can be characterized as negligence, failure to take necessary self-defense measures, unwillingness to soberly assess the situation, and take steps to rectify it. The "hybrid war" in the form conducted by the Russian Federation became possible solely due to the weakness of the Ukrainian state. A large number of internal problems and contradictions, the presence of pro-Russian elites in eastern Ukraine that emerged in the 1990s with the tacit approval of Kyiv, reluctance to hold the organizers of the Sievierodonetsk Congress in 2004 accountable—all these factors allowed Russia to ignite the war and camouflage its military intervention as a civil conflict.

Throughout its years of independence, Ukraine has failed to assess the risks of separatism in the Donbas region and pull this depressed region out of a chronic crisis. Not fully understanding the problems of these territories, state leaders could not devise a plan for dealing with them, nor did they pay attention to the issue of creating and supporting pro-Ukrainian elites in the Donbas. The region was left to the mercy of local criminal groups and "red directors," who quickly assessed the situation and learned to exploit the embittered sentiments of its poor residents.

There were no powerful nationalist or pro-European political forces in the Donbas. Those with political ambitions had two paths: either to the fringe or to earn a living with the Party of Regions. Over the course of 10 years, from 2004 to 2014, few activists in the Donbas saw fighting against the Party of Regions as worthwhile. They believed that most leaders of the pro-Western orientation wouldn't bother with the Donbas, lacked even a basic understanding of the context, and became disillusioned. Those who had enough political weight and could influence the situation in the Donbas in March 2014 also remained silent because they were confident that no one would dare touch Akhmetov and that Yefremov would be able to negotiate successfully, just like in 2004. A Jewish proverb says: a hole in the fence is an invitation to thieves. And the Ukrainian fence before 2014 was simply riddled with holes. Corruption, the dominance of oligarchic clans, outdated laws and institutions, and an inefficient economy all together had a cumulative effect, leading to the political crisis of 2013–2014, followed by Russian intervention and military actions in eastern Ukraine. Weakened by endless elite quarrels, the corrupt and impoverished state became easy prey and could not defend the inviolability of its borders. And while in Crimea, Ukraine yielded to the pressure of the regular Russian army, in the Donbas in the spring of 2014, the state was losing even to the fragmented, poorly organized separatist groups and small sabotage units of Russians.

Press Secretary of the Mayor of Donetsk, Maksym Rovinskyi, characterized the situation that arose in the spring of 2014 in the capital of the Donbas as follows:

> "It was only the weakness of the Ukrainian state in the Donbas that allowed what ultimately happened. It wasn't the strength of those who did it; it was our weakness. The absence of any resistance led to the initiative shifting to the opposite side. No coordinated actions were taken by pro-Russian formations. On their side, there were many disparate groups that struggled to work together and were at odds with each other. Yet they managed to prevail because we were even less organized and motivated."

These words are largely consistent with reality. In the spring of 2014, the Ukrainian state indeed demonstrated complete helplessness in the Donbas and made no effort to assert itself within its existing borders.

It cannot be said that the anti-Ukrainian rebellion in the Donbas was a completely unforeseen event. Few believed that the situation would escalate to such an extent, but pro-Russian organizations and politicians never really hid their intentions. Civil war was threatened to Ukraine in newspapers and brochures of small fringe organizations from the early '90s until 2014. Menacing prophecies were also scattered in the political advertisements of the Party of Regions and in the works of local writers. After the start of the war in 2014, these articles from old brochures and advertising leaflets began to be presented as examples of the "foresight" of Donbas politicians and publicists. But in reality, the promises of civil war in the propaganda were always more akin to threats than to predictions.

> "All that we predicted in our leaflet turned out to be a frightening truth: the collapse of the economy, civil war, interethnic hostility, and the resurgence of Bandera's legacy—all these have become realities of today. Once again, it confirms that we were right," said Volodymyr

Kornilov in 2015, talking about the first leaflets of the "Intermovement of Donbas."

But can we really call the promise of one side to take up arms if the other side doesn't comply a "prediction"? Hardly. It's called by a completely different word—blackmail. A person who takes up arms is not a prophet but a combatant. It is essential to understand this distinction clearly.

The central government in Kyiv should have promptly noticed alarming trends and taken necessary measures to prevent the realization of these intentions, but it didn't. It failed to do so because it itself failed to become a genuine Ukrainian elite. Being individuals born and mentally shaped in the USSR, the first presidents of Ukraine, by sheer momentum, continued to build the Ukrainian SSR—slightly modernized but still colonial and dependent on Russia and oriented towards Moscow. President Kuchma, often called the architect of the Ukrainian state in its current form, was a typical "red director." Forces nostalgic for the USSR were closer to his worldview than Ukrainian nationalist democrats advocating for breaking away from Moscow's sphere of influence. And corrupt Russian politicians and oligarchs were more understandable than European leaders. Attempts to break away from the Soviet discourse only began in 2005 under President Yushchenko—fourteen years after Ukraine officially gained independence.

These fourteen years were a lost time, and this loss led to further catastrophe. During this period, local politico-feudal clans emerged, strengthened, and legalized themselves in the east of the country, cultivating separatist and irredentist sentiments among local residents. Viktor Yushchenko had a chance to turn this situation around; however, he couldn't eliminate corruption and criminality and opted to negotiate with the Donbas oligarchic clans in 2005–2006 rather than confront them.

However, while events of the past are more or less clear to us, the future of Donbas is shrouded in a bloody fog. After years of war, we still don't have answers to the questions we had in 2014—whether Ukraine will regain control over the occupied territories, whether the region will recover from the consequences of the conflict and rise from the ashes of war, whether Ukrainian citizens on both sides of the ceasefire line will reach an agreement, and how Ukraine's relations with Russia will be built after all that has happened in recent years.

It is evident that thousands of lost lives cannot be recovered. And it is unlikely that the Donbas, maimed and devastated by war, will be able to play the same role in the economic and political life of the country in the future as it did before 2014, even if Russia returns it to Ukraine. The past cannot be undone, but lessons can be learned from it to avoid repeating the tragedy in the future.

Can we say today that Ukrainian society and the Ukrainian government have learned lessons from the events in Donbas? No. Present-day Ukraine suffers from the same vices as it did 10–15 years ago, and it is seen with the naked eye. The system created by Leonid Kuchma has not disappeared anywhere. We, as before, live in a country that was built according to his interests and desires. Its resources are still mainly owned by the same oligarchs, its regions still resemble feudal estates, and instead of laws, informal agreements and the rule of force continue to prevail. Life in economically devastated industrial cities in eastern Ukraine (and not only there) is permeated with despair and hopelessness. Representatives of the old regional elites, who made every effort to provoke anti-Ukrainian uprisings in the spring of 2014, still control the region and slowly grind down the remnants of the Soviet industry.

The districts of the Donetsk and Luhansk regions,

freed from illegal armed formations, have returned today to the state they were in before the war. The economic situation is unstable, the prospects of the industrial centers in the region are bleak, and anti-Ukrainian stereotypes still prevail in Donbas society. In this fertile ground for any negativity, the bacteria of separatism easily multiply, lying dormant during periods of relative stability but inevitably making themselves known during the next crisis. Similar risks persist not only in the Donbas but also in Kharkiv, Odesa, and other regions of the country where there are forces ready to bet on separatism and dream of securing official status as federation subjects for their feudal estates.

It's not too late to change the situation. While the return of Donetsk and Luhansk at this stage is not entirely within our control and may never happen at all, restoring order in the territories under the state's control today is achievable. Creating new regional elites, supporting and developing new sectors of the economy capable of replacing outdated plants and mines, assisting small businesses—these are measures that can help reformat the regions of eastern Ukraine, breathe new life into depressed industrial cities, provide opportunities for self-fulfillment for their residents, and make their lives in Ukraine more appealing.

However, this is a completely different story and a topic for a separate inquiry.

TABLE OF CONTENT

PROLOGUE

TURNING POINT

PART ONE

PIONEERS FROM THE '90S

DONETSK TRICOLOR

STRIKE IN DONETSK AND THE 1994 REFERENDUM

NEW "LUHANSK CLAN"

PART TWO

ALLIANCE OF KUCHMA WITH THE DONETSK FACTION

RENAISSANCE OF THE KOMSOMOL

TWILIGHT ZONE OF THE ECONOMIC CRISIS

LUHANSK MAIDAN

PART THREE

"RISE UP, UKRAINE"

PRIME MINISTER FROM THE PENITENTIARY

COLD SHOWER FOR YUSHCHENKO

THE BURNING YEAR 2004

SIEVIERODONETSK CRISIS

PART FOUR

YUSHCHENKO'S LOST CHANCE
BLACKMAIL WITH FEDERALIZATION

BORN BY THE MAIDAN.

SEPARATIST MOVEMENTS IN THE DONBAS IN THE MID-2000s

PART FIVE
UNSUCCESSFUL MULTI-VECTOR POLICY OF YANUKOVYCH

MEDVEDCHUK AND OTHERS

LAND OF SHALE GAS
SHATTERED HOPES

AGONY

THUNDER IN THE EAST

PART SIX
BLOODY SPRING IN DONETSK
WHERE DID PAVLO GUBAREV COME FROM, AND HOW DID HE BECOME THE "PEOPLE'S GOVERNOR"

CONFRONTATION IN LUHANSK

CHAOS AND VIOLENCE

GODFATHER OF THE "DPR"

SECRETS OF THE LUHANSK SSU
NAKED EMPEROR OF THE DONBAS
TRIGGER OF WAR
ENLIGHTENING SOCIOLOGY
"REFERENDUM"

RUSSIAN FACTOR

EPILOGUE

ABOUT THE AUTHOR

Denys Kazanskyi

Denys Kazanskyi has been a journalist since 2011; prior to 2014, he resided and worked in Donetsk. He is an investigative journalist, TV presenter, and video blogger with an audience of more than 1 million subscribers in Ukraine.

Denys Kazanskyi is also the author of Black Fever, which was published in 2015 and delves into the topic of illegal coal mining in the Donbas region.

ABOUT THE AUTHOR

Maryna Vorotyntseva

Maryna Vorotyntseva has been a journalist since 2003. Prior to 2014, she was the co-founder and chief editor of the newspaper and online publication Vostochny Variant, based in Luhansk.

After her journalism work, Vorotyntseva has been a PR, communications, and marketing consultant. She has held leadership positions in communication departments within public institutions and private companies, collaborating closely with various politicians. Vorotyntseva has extensive experience managing media projects during electoral campaigns and crafting and implementing marketing strategies for businesses.

Denys Kazanskyi, Maryna Vorotyntseva
How Ukraine Lost Donbas

Ukrainian edition:
Editor: Maryna Vorotyntseva
Corrector: Olena Kravchenko.
Layout: Oleksandr Sivets.
Published in 2020.

Translation from Ukrainian to English - Anastasiya Fehir, editor – Marichka Androshchuk, chief editor and curator Marta Hosovska.
Published in 2024.

Cover design: Kateryna Solomatina, Tetiana Nechay

Please visit our website: https://lostdonbass.com.ua
Second edition revised and expanded.

Publishing House: LLC "Chorna HoranPublishing House"
Address: 03113, Ukraine, Kyiv, Dehtiarivska St., 43/1, office 24. Certificate DK №7601 dated 16.07.2020

Phone number: +38067 887 66 49
Rights and questions: chornagorabook@gmail.com

Made in United States
North Haven, CT
25 August 2025

72115987R00196